Impassioned Jurisprudence

Aperçus: *Histories Texts Cultures*

a Bucknell series

Series Editor: Greg Clingham

Aperçu (apersü). 1882. [Fr.] *A summary exposition, a conspectus.*

Relations among historiography, culture, and textual representation are presently complex and rich in possibilities. Aperçus is a series of books exploring the connections between these crucial terms. Revisionist in intention, Aperçus seeks to open up new possibilities for humanistic knowledge and study, and thus to deepen and extend our understanding of what history, culture, and texts have been and are, as these terms are made to bear on each other by new thinking and writing.

Titles in the Series

Critical Pasts: Writing Criticism, Writing History
ed. Philip Smallwood

History and Nation
ed. Julia Rudolph

Europe Observed: Multiple Gazes in Early Modern Encounters
ed. Kumkum Chatterjee and Clement Hawes

Beyond Douglass: New Perspectives on Early African American Literature
ed. Michael J. Drexler and Ed White.

The Patient
ed. Kimberly Myers and Harold Schweizer

Masculinity, Senses, Spirit
ed. Katherine M. Faull

Freedom of Speech: The History of an Idea
ed. Elizabeth Powers

Scotland As Science Fiction
ed. Caroline McCracken-Flesher

Encountering China: Early Modern European Responses
ed. Rachana Sachdev and Qingju Li

Sade's Sensibilities
ed. Kate Parker and Norbert Sclippa

Storytelling in Science and Literature
ed. Margery Arent Safir

Impassioned Jurisprudence: Law, Literature, and Emotion, 1760–1848
ed. Nancy E. Johnson

Impassioned Jurisprudence

Law, Literature, and Emotion, 1760–1848

Edited by
Nancy E. Johnson

Lewisburg: Bucknell University Press

Published by Bucknell University Press
Co-published with The Rowman & Littlefield Publishing Group, Inc.
4501 Forbes Boulevard, Suite 200, Lanham, Maryland 20706
www.rlpgbooks.com

Unit A, Whitacre Mews, 26-34 Stannary Street, London SE11 4AB

British Library Cataloguing in Publication Information Available

Library of Congress Cataloging-in-Publication Data

Impassioned jurisprudence : law, literature, and emotion, 1760-1848 / edited by Nancy E. Johnson.
pages cm. — (Aperçus : histories texts cultures)
Includes bibliographical references and index.
ISBN 978-1-61148-675-9 (cloth : alk. paper) — ISBN 978-1-61148-677-3 (pbk. : alk. paper) — ISBN 978-1-61148-676-6 (electronic) 1. Law—England—History. 2. Law and literature. I. Johnson, Nancy E., 1956- editor.

KD606.I48 2015
349.4209'034—dc23 2015005920

Contents

Acknowledgments

I WOULD LIKE TO THANK THE PRESIDENT AND THE PROVOST at the State University of New York at New Paltz for the sabbatical leave that enabled me to finish this collection of essays. I wish to thank, as well, Bob DeMaria, Gordon Turnbull, Tara Goshal Wallace, Michael Bundock, and Kate Chisholm for their assistance in conceptualizing the volume and for advice on everything from titles to timelines; Greg Clingham and Pamelia Dailey at Bucknell University Press for their clear and helpful guidance; Susan Walker at the Lewis Walpole Library for her aid with the cover image; and the contributors who worked so cooperatively and professionally.

Nancy E. Johnson

Introduction

IN THIS VOLUME OF COLLECTED ESSAYS, SCHOLARS OF THE interdisciplinary field of law and literature write about the role of emotion in English law and legal theory in the late eighteenth and early nineteenth centuries. Examining both legal and literary texts, the authors here consider the emotion that infuses the law and find that feeling, sentiment, and passion are integral to juridical thought as well as legislation. Despite the law's claims to reason, emotion is a pervasive force. Emotion variously challenges and stabilizes the law; it is vital to the education of the law and to explaining the evolution of legal developments; it elucidates the effects of gender and economics; it shapes young lawyers and public views of the law; it raises questions of constitutionality, and it influences perceptions of kingship. As the law developed through the seventeenth and eighteenth centuries (a span of time that saw the English Civil War, the Glorious Revolution, and the American and the French Revolutions), reason was invoked to ensure fairness and equity—a much-needed assurance as "the citizenry" began to coalesce into a force that demanded its rights. Yet, as the scholars in this collection will argue, an investigation of the rational discourse of the law reveals at its core the processes of emotion, and a study of literature that engages with the law exposes the potency of emotion in the practice and understanding of the law.

The historical period covered in these essays, 1760–1848, marks a maturation of juridical thought that emerged out of seventeenth- and early eighteenth-century jurisprudence. Of increasing concern are the rights of persons and the protection of property, a reconsideration of the role of Parliament and the monarchy in governing the nation, and a need to articulate and explain the law to a broadening readership. The two texts that bookend this collection of essays, Sir William Blackstone's *Commentaries on the Laws of England* (1765–1769) and Lord Macaulay's *The History of England* (1848, 1855, and 1861), are indicators of a major shift of legal discourse into the public domain. In the four-volume *Commentaries,* as Simon Stern observes in his essay, Blackstone seeks to articulate the rationale and organizational codes and values of English common law. *Commentaries* originated as lectures, and while the lucid and systematic synthesis of the common law was initially prepared for students, it also readied the *Commentaries* for publication and public consumption. By 1848, when Macaulay published the first two volumes of his *History,* the public was well prepared for the historical explanations of law that Macaulay offered. As Ian Ward notes in his essay, Macaulay's widely popular *History* was a staple of the Victorian household, and it had a decidedly public purpose: to calm the nation. From 1760 to 1848, as the public became more engaged with legal thought and legislation, we see a movement from a reliance on logic to the employment of emotion to instruct the public and stabilize the nation.

The celebration of the law as a site of reason has a long history in English jurisprudence. "Reason is the life of the law" and "[t]he law . . . is perfection of reason," wrote Sir Edward Coke in *Commentary upon Littleton* (1628), the first of his four-volume *Institutes of the Lawes of England.*[1] Sir Matthew Hale likewise saw in reason the ability to bring order to chaos and allow the highest of general principles to reign over individual prejudice, although law was required to administer reason in a just manner. "[T]o avoid that greate uncertainty in the application of reason by particular persons to particular Instances, . . ." noted Hale in "Reflections . . . on Mr. Hobbes His Dialogue of the Lawe" (1682), "the wiser Sort of the world have in all ages agreed upon Some certaine Laws and rules and methods of administration of Cōmon Justice."[2] In a state of nature, John Locke observed, reason is in itself a law—a law that "teaches" humanity "that being all equal and independent, no one ought to harm another in his Life, Health, Liberty or Possessions."[3] Moreover, the value of the law increased dramatically when contractarians such as Locke began to envisage the law displacing inherited authority as the origin of political power. According to Locke, the law had the potential to provide cohesion and discipline in the social contract, protect individual liberty and property, and regulate and punish "only for the public good."[4] The law was a bearer of liberty, and with such a central place and prominent role in the social contract, it was imperative that the law be perceived as rational because therein resides fairness and equity as opposed to partiality and intolerance. Such high ideals were not to be impaired by emotion; otherwise, citizens of a social contract were destined for the kind of dissipated existence, driven by unrestrained competition and aggression, that is imagined by Hobbes in *Leviathan* (1651).

Still, as early jurists continued to place their faith in reason and considered it the most reliable method of inquiry and equity, we begin to see jurists investigating and accounting for human passions in the paradigms they constructed for societies shaped and governed by law. In *Two Books of the Elements of Universal Jurisprudence* (1660), Samuel von Pufendorf, a German philosopher whose work had a significant influence on English jurists, argues that natural law requires us to control emotions and bring them under the command of reason because, like "drunkenness" and "irregular sex relations," they impair our judgment and "frequently carry us off to those things which are harmful for ourselves and others." While this precept "flows" from natural law, according to Pufendorf, emotions and appetite have long been governed by a separate force of regulation, "natural instinct." Nature, "being doubtful of reason's dictate alone," provided natural instinct to support reason's dictate. Reason may teach us self-preservation, but natural instinct gives us a "love" of life.[5] Reason, in and of itself, also eludes the scientific approach that Pufendorf applies to natural law. Of the two foundational principles of universal jurisprudence, "the rational . . . and the experimental," only the latter "is perceived from the comparison and perception of particulars uniformly corresponding to one another." The former, the principle of rationality, "flows from reason itself, without the perception of particulars, or without undertaking an examination, merely from the bare intuition of the mind."[6] The certainty of the experimental principle is proven by observation, and rationality by axiom. Therefore, the rationality that is thought to be the pride of humanity, that is meant to guide the law, direct legislation, and structure the legal trial, is reliant on a primitive natural instinct and an unobservable intuition. Reason does not enjoy a solitary reign.[7]

By the time we get to the mid-eighteenth century, with the publication of David Hume's *A Treatise of Human Nature* (1739–1740), we see a more extensive study of human passions in concepts of justice. In Book III, "Of Morals," where he investigates the operations of justice, Hume opens with an observation about the drawbacks of rational argument. "There is an inconvenience," Hume writes, "which attunes all abstruse reasoning, that it may silence, without convincing an antagonist, and requires the same intense study to make us sensible of its force, that was at first requisite for its invention."[8] If we consider this observation in regard to a legal trial—a site where antagonists vie for supremacy of argument and try to persuade a judge and jury by reasoning as effectively as possible—we see the limited value of rationality, especially that which is obtuse. Hume suggests that complicated arguments—while logically sound—will not have the desired effect on an audience. As he continues, Hume constructs an imaginary scene, replete with figurative language, that does more than serve as the pathos of a persuasive argument; it explains the process of arriving at a judgment. "When we leave our closet," Hume argues, "and engage in the common affairs of life, its [abstruse reasoning's] conclusions seem to vanish, like the phantoms of the night on the appearance of the morning; and 'tis difficult for us to retain even that conviction, which we had attain'd with difficulty" (507). Reason, the foundational operation of the law—and most often represented as clear, steady light—can be as fleeting and ephemeral as a "phantom of the night."

When considering the role of law in the social contract, Hume also accounts for emotion and points to the necessity and desire for a system of law to protect property and govern the passions. "By this means"—that is, by the establishment of law—"every one knows what he may safely possess; and the passions are restrain'd in their partial and contradictory motions" (541). However, Hume makes clear that "such a restraint"—that is, the law—is not "contrary to these passions" because "if so, it cou'd never be enter'd into, nor maintain'd"; law is contrary only to the "heedless and impetuous movement" of the passions, not to its more measured operations. Central to Hume's argument is the relation between morals and passions. Passions are influenced by morals (541), and when "[m]orals excite passions, and produce or prevent actions," Hume argues, "[r]eason is utterly impotent" (509).

Hence, from Pufendorf to Hume, the celebration of reason in the law is tempered by an acknowledgment that human passions are at work in the processes of the law. This was the tradition that informed Blackstone, Macaulay, and other jurists and legal historians. This was also the tradition with which literature engaged when novelists, poets, and diarists investigated the sovereignty of reason and the agency of emotion. Literary texts were the locus of extensive debate over moral philosophy and jurisprudence. In literature, the forces of human emotion as they determine the law and as they were affected by the law, could be unmasked, satirized, and studied. Alexander Pope, in his Horatian satire *The Rape of the Lock* (1714), reminds us that human appetite trumps judgment when "The hungry Judges soon the Sentence sign, / And Wretches hang that Jury-men may Dine" (Canto III, lines 21–22). The Earl of Rochester in "A Satyr against Reason and Mankind" (1679) exposes the rational man deluded by "Reason, which fifty times for one does err; / Reason, an *Ignis fatuus* in the Mind" (11–12). Abandoning "Light of Nature" and "Sense," reason takes us into "Error's Fenny Bogs and Thorny Brakes," and finally into "Doubt's boundless Sea" where we drown in skepticism (13–14). Similar to Pufendorf's scheme in which he finds a place for human desires, Rochester defines right reason as that which "distinguishes by Sense, / And gives us Rules of good and ill from thence; / That bounds Desires with a reforming Will, / To keep 'em more in vigor, not to Kill" (100–104).

William Wordsworth exposes passion at the root of law in "Section X, 'Rob Roy's Grave'" of *Memorials of a Tour in Scotland* (1803). Law is created to control passions and guide our thoughts and actions. However, in the voice of Rob Roy, we are offered an alternative to the false control of the law; while the law puzzles and blinds, the heart tells us "what to do."

> We have a passion—make a law,
> Too false to guide us or control!
> And for the law itself we fight
> In bitterness of soul.
> And, puzzled, blinded thus, we lose
> Distinctions that are plain and few:
> These find I graven on my heart:
> *That* tells me what to do. (X. 25–32)

Daniel Defoe's heroines in *Moll Flanders* (1722) and *Roxana* (1724) turn to the underworld of crime and don disguises because they lack the protection of marriage laws. Both passion and the law betray them, and money—an available currency that yields them power, unlike legal subjectivity—becomes their salvation. Mary Wollstonecraft in her posthumously published novel *The Wrongs of Woman: or, Maria* (1798) tells a tale about the legal "wrongs" (as opposed to "rights") that target women and are embedded in the law. She transforms the trope of English law as a gothic castle to show us the horrors that women face as they confront the law when denied legal subjecthood. While her protagonists are emotionally scarred and overwhelmed by their legal sufferings, we see that the law itself is driven and manipulated by passion—passion in the hands of men who enjoy legal agency.

During the time when juridical texts like Blackstone's *Commentaries* were moving legal thought into the public domain, literature also participated in educating the public about the law. The novel, in particular, became a site of inquiry into assumptions about foundational juridical principles and consequences of legislation and custom. Two of the literary texts analyzed in this volume, Frances Burney's *The Wanderer; or Female Difficulties* (1814) and Sir Walter Scott's *Ivanhoe* (1820), serve as examples of literature's engagement with legal thought and history. Like Blackstone's *Commentaries* and Macaulay's *History*, they frame the role of literature in constituting evidence that legal discourse and legal issues are now firmly set in the public domain and in contributing to the public's understanding of the law—its rationale, its function, and its integration of emotion. Burney's philosophical novel and Scott's historical novel, as Melissa Ganz and Erin Sheley argue respectively in their essays, are important documents for a study of the law because they reveal its biases and limited protection. In each case, it is the law's treatment of women that undermines its claims to equity and fairness—its claims to logic and reason.

In both legal and literary discourse, then, we find authors exploring the relationship between the law as a rational discourse and the role of emotion in juridical thought, legislation, and the workings of justice in a civil legal system. In the essays that follow, scholars of law and literature investigate how the passions have been integrated into the law and legal thought by examining juridical texts, the life-writing of a barrister, novels that articulate the particular dilemmas of women, and constitutional turmoil that precipitates a reexamination of the rights of Britons thrown into flux with the Regency Crisis and then reaffirmed in the constitutional settlement of 1688–1690. Each author finds that human emotions have a powerful impact on the law—its enactment, its function, and its modification in the social contract.

Two of the essays in this collection look at legal texts that account for the role of the passions in what is deemed to be a rational discourse. Simon Stern examines Blackstone's treatment of emotion and the law in what is perhaps the most influential legal text of the eighteenth century, *Commentaries on the Laws of England*. Stern finds that Blackstone engages the emotions to reaffirm the rationality, order, and coherence of the law. He reminds us that Blackstone's *Commentaries* began as pedagogical lectures and that one of Blackstone's goals was to encourage young lawyers to develop an affective relationship with the law. In turn, Blackstone endows the law with agency, including its own desires and preferences; the aspiration of rationality is itself a "legal passion," an "emotional impulse." When writing about criminal law, Blackstone turns emotion into an object to elucidate the types of passions that should be considered when judging the actions of a criminal. Distinguishing between impulsive, ungovernable actions and those that are more deliberative, Blackstone again examines the function of passion in relation to reason to determine the moral responsibility of the criminal. In closing, Stern moves to the topic of property and returns to the figure of the reader of *Commentaries*—the student of the law—to explain Blackstone's evocation of emotion when writing about the right of property.

The second essay on legal thought is "Narrative and Sentiment in Adam Smith's *Lectures on Jurisprudence*." This essay is a study of Smith's use of stories to account for sentiment in the law. Like Blackstone's *Commentaries*, Smith's juridical theory was posited in lectures to students, although what remains are reports of those lectures rather than Smith's original text. Nonetheless, the reports provide a consistent view of the value of narrative, first as a pedagogical device, second as an integral part of the law, and third as fluid and consumable property. We find sentiment, defined by Smith as "motivation," "passion," "feeling," and "natural human disposition," throughout the law, but especially in laws governing inheritance, marriage, and slavery. We use narrative, and at times the impartial spectator, to discern the correct sentiment in determining what is just when emotion plays an influential role in the legislation and the interpretation of lawfulness. Because of its useful function—to account for sentiment in the law—narrative becomes a valuable form of property. The value of narrative is also enhanced by its fluidity. The facts of historical narrative, for example, can be used by multiple authors; they are part of the public domain; they are used and then returned. This vision of narrative and the law, according to Smith, is the most suitable for jurisprudence in the age of commerce.

Another configuration of law and literature is the lawyer/author whose language moves into the crossroads of both disciplines. J. T. Scanlan's essay brings us into the world of James Boswell, an eighteenth-century barrister who is also an accomplished biographer. According to Scanlan, Boswell's training and practice in the law is what prepared him to write the *Life of Samuel Johnson* (1791), an enduring biography of engaging detail, insight, and entertainment. While Boswell comes of age as a lawyer, he does so as well as a writer. This figure of the lawyer/author was a familiar one in eighteenth-century Edinburgh—the milieu of Boswell's legal career—where the law was central to civic and intellectual interests and legal work was akin to literary work. Boswell's instruction in law's reasoning and his own love of life dovetail in the *London Journal* (1762–1763). For example, when Boswell writes of his passionate intrigues, he sometimes does so as an "eloquent barrister"; he uses the diction and rhetoric of the law to enhance his romantic persuasiveness. The law, Scanlan argues, transformed Boswell's writing and provided him with an eloquent vehicle for his passionate embrace of life—his life, Johnson's life, as well as the lives of others.

While juridical texts betray the forces of emotion, even as they espouse the rationality of the law, literature is better placed to reveal the multivalent complexities of emotion as the law affects women. Excluded largely from legal discourse, women tended to express their concerns in narrative. In her essay on Frances Burney's novel *The Wanderer; or, Female Difficulties*, Melissa J. Ganz analyzes Burney's representation of marriage laws through a narrative comparison of French and English legislation, culture, and practice. Ganz suggests that in *The Wanderer* Burney is responding to the rendering of marriage as a civil contract by the National Assembly in France and comparing this legislation to that of Great Britain, in particular Lord Hardwicke's Marriage Act of 1753. Marriage could be entered into more easily in France than in England, where the Marriage Act required the posting of banns or the purchase of an ecclesiastical license, the presence of witnesses, and a public ceremony. Both policies, however, were controversial—the latter undergoing attempts to revise and repeal the legislation, particularly in 1812 and 1813, the years just before the publication of *The Wanderer*. Ganz argues that the novel offers a critique of both the French and British laws governing marriage because they undermine women's agency and they generate emotional violence. While Burney endorses England's model of marriage over that of France, she envisages marriage as an affective agreement between two equal agents and she recommends reform to the patriarchal principles that structure English marriage laws.

Erin Sheley turns to two female characters in two of Sir Walter Scott's texts, Constance de Beverly in Scott's epic poem *Marmion* (1808) and Rebecca of York in Scott's novel *Ivanhoe*, to consider how the figure of the condemned woman tells a story of legal identity, and how her sentimentalized body becomes a touchstone in legal discourse. Both characters undergo legal trials in which they are fixed, objectified, and transformed into historical objects. In their "aestheticized stillness," they become cultural significations of the contradiction inherent in the burning of women for the purpose of protecting their delicacy and privacy. Simultaneously, they become representations of the need for legal evolution and laws that respond to changes over time—an assertion made by Hale in "Considerations Touching the Amendment or Alteration of Lawes" (1665) and Blackstone in *Commentaries*. In both instances, the female body is situated in two historical moments and thus two legal systems in the English tradition with diverse assumptions about the law. The female body is used to navigate through penal discourses, legal contradictions, and juridical evolutions to arrive at an assurance of the legitimacy of the British constitution and the sustainability of British law if it responds to change.

The passions operate not only on the level of personal crises of legal identity or in the development of a young lawyer and writer, but also in the framework, the very edifice, of British government and the social contract in the eighteenth and nineteenth centuries. Essays by Peter de Bolla and Ian Ward examine the significance of emotion on the level of kingship and the constitution. Peter de Bolla observes that at the core of the Regency Crisis of 1788–1789, a crisis that threatened the delicate tripartite balance of government, was sentiment. Drawing on diaries such as those of Robert Fulke Greville and Lady Harcourt, as well as Parliamentary Reports, de Bolla casts into relief the emotional complexity of responses to the king's madness and the struggle to clarify the source of liberty and legal rights when that source—the king—is impaired physically and mentally. Eighteenth-century law denied legal rights to the insane; hence, what happens when the origin of that law, the king, descends into madness? What are the juridical consequences of the violence done to the king? How does a nation handle the emotions that attach to the torture enacted on the body of the king? These are some of the questions that de Bolla addresses in his essay as he underscores the critical issues debated in the Regency Crisis, and as he concludes that sentiment played a vital role in allowing the king, despite his "absence," to remain whole.

Ian Ward's essay revisits the constitutional settlement of 1688–1690 through the narrative of Lord Macaulay's *History of England*. While written in the Burkean tradition, Ward argues, Macaulay's *History* diverges from the sublime emotion of Edmund Burke's *Reflections on the Revolution in France* (1790), instead offering Victorian England a sense of calm reassurance and dignity. Eschewing historical analysis, Macaulay addressed the imagination of readers, engaging their emotions as much as their minds. Ward notes resonances between the turmoil of 1688 and the social unrest of 1848, not least in Macaulay's desire to stimulate some kind of emotional resistance to further prospective revolution.

Accordingly, Macaulay preferred a consciously dramatic style of history in order to stimulate the pathos of his audience. It was not a matter of stimulating excitement, but providing reassurance. The revolution of 1688 precluded the need for another.

In sum, the essays in this collection seek to re-historicize theoretical questions of the interdisciplinary field of law and literature by focusing on a pivotal time in the development of juridical thought and practice. The seventeenth century saw major changes to conceptualizations about the law, including a growing secularization of the law and an attempt to clarify universal and individual rights. Coke and Hale establish many of the precedents for Locke and the other contractarians who locate political authority in the law and thereby begin a long process of endowing a citizenry with protective rights. In the 1760s juridical thought and practice move securely into the public sphere with the publication of Blackstone's *Commentaries*. Literature brings the law, as envisaged by contractarians, to the public considerably earlier in the eighteenth century with the novels of Defoe in the 1720s and Richardson and Fielding in the 1740s and 1750s.[9] But it is in the 1760s that law and literature set up a dialogue in the public domain, in a setting that is ripe for a discussion of law and emotion thanks to the intensifying interest in sentiment and sensibility in literature.

Examining the intersections of law and literature in the late eighteenth and early nineteenth centuries contributes to the vast body of work in this field by elucidating early acknowledgments of contingency and contradiction in the very jurisprudence that represented the law as a site of reason and truth. The critical legal studies movement, in conjunction with the poststructuralism that dominated literary theory at the time, challenged hermeneutical suppositions about the law. When theorists such as James Boyd White declared the activities of the law to be rhetorical and Robert Cover asserted that narrative is the mechanism that locates and gives meaning to legal institutions,[10] while Paul de Man and Jacques Derrida destabilized the meaning of language, rhetoric, and narrative,[11] scholars of law and literature grappled with hermeneutical indeterminacy and contested the law's ability to elicit truth.[12]

Studying emotion in what Ian Ward calls the "twin projects" of law and literature—law as literature and law in literature—authors of the essays in this collection find common ground in the two disciplines.[13] Scanlan's investigation into James Boswell and his career as both a lawyer and a biographer, drawing attention to the emotion behind his rhetoric in both forms of writing, calls to mind White's assertion of the law as language and rhetoric, set in both a "culture" and a "community."[14] An analysis of Adam Smith's use of narrative sentiment in his *Lectures on Jurisprudence* provides evidence of the pervasive presence of storytelling in legal transactions, as proposed by Peter Brooks and Paul Gewirtz in their volume of essays, *Law's Stories*.[15] The violence of the law as suggested by Robert Cover in his essay "Violence and the Word" is corroborated by the story of George III, his madness, and the torture of treatment as told to us by Peter de Bolla.[16] Resistance to the idea that the law is rhetorical and comprised of narrative—such as arguments made by Richard Posner[17]—is often based on the same premise of rationality, as is resistance to acknowledging the power of emotion in the law. But a review of early juridical texts, such as those from the late eighteenth and early nineteenth century—and literature from the same period of time—defy such opposition. In addition, more recent work on law and literature has begun to explore the agency of emotion. Martha C. Nussbaum's book *Political Emotions: Why Love Matters for Justice* is just the latest in her extended work on the power of emotions.[18] *Subversion and Sympathy: Gender, Law and the British Novel*, coedited by Nussbaum and Alison L. LaCroix, is another collection of essays that inquires into the representations of intrigue, violence, punishment, and the various complexities of human existence as it is protected by, and as it confronts, the law.[19]

The inquiries into emotion and the law in this volume also make an important contribution to the field of sensibility studies that locates a burgeoning interest in emotion in eighteenth-century literature, as well as medical and other social discourses.[20] Jean H. Hagstrum explains that it is in the so-called age of reason that we see "love," in its various forms of affective and sexual desire, kinship, and philanthropy, begin to elicit a concerted attention.[21] Janet Todd observes the rise of sentimental fiction in the 1740s and 1750s and the more sophisticated fiction of sensibility from 1760 forward.[22] According to Todd, sentimental literature, often featuring stock characters and conventional tragedies, is meant to arouse pathos and bring readers to tears. Literature of sensibility, which usually boasts of more complex characters, plots, and moral questions, challenges the reader's mind as much as her emotions and requires what Ann Van Sant refers to as "moral and aesthetic responsiveness."[23] Robert Brissenden finds a common thread in literature of sentiment to be a form of "virtue in distress," which prompts sympathy, compassion, and benevolence.[24] Barbara Benedict draws our attention to the concerns with potential excess in what G. J. Barker Benfield terms "the cult of sensibility," and regards most literature of sentiment to be conservative, trapping emotion "within social limits."[25]

Hannah More's poem *Sensibility: An Epistle to the Honourable Mrs. Boscawen* (1782) provides us with an indication of how "sensibility," by the latter part of the eighteenth century, tries to account for the passions and their relation to reason.[26] More admits of her personified "Sensibility" that "Thy subtle essence still eludes the chains / Of definition, and defeats her pains" (lines 235–36), but in the lines that follow, she provides us with its distinctive features. Sensibility, More suggests, is marked by a quick and unprompted compassion.

> Sweet SENSIBILITY! thou keen delight!
> Unprompted moral! Sullen sense of light!
> Perception exquisite! fair virtue's seed!
> Thou quick precursor of the lib'ral deed!
> Thou hasty conscience! reason's blushing morn!
> Instinctive kindness e'er reflection's born!
> Prompt sense of equity! to thee belongs
> The swift redress of unexamin'd wrongs:
> Eager to serve the cause perhaps untried,
> But always apt to choose the suff'ring side; (237–46)

Sensibility is celebrated here, but also in this passage, we see that sensibility is the "blushing morn" to reason, responses to suffering are "hasty," and the cause is "untried." In the lines that immediately precede this oft-quoted passage, More addresses the law directly, disclosing a tension between the sympathy of sensibility and the law.

> Yet while we claim the sympathy divine,
> Which makes, O man, the woes of others thine;
> While her fair triumphs swell the modish page,
> She drives the sterner virtues from the stage;

> While FEELING boasts her ever-tearful eye,
> Fair truth, firm faith, and manly justice fly;
> Justice, prime good! From whose prolific law,
> All worth, all virtue, their strong essence draw. (219–26)

While sympathy and compassion (identified as female) have their place in addressing inequities, "Justice" and its "prolific law" (identified as masculine) are superior; the latter are the mainstays of truth, faith, and "prime good." More also signals a danger that feelings—whose "fair triumphs" are "modish" and thus fleeting—might eclipse the law and its "sterner virtues." That More in 1782 feels the need to issue a warning about the undue influence of sympathy in the cult of sensibility, over and above justice and the law, which she distinguishes from sympathy, points to a growing dominance of the passions. More will be prescient about the rise of passion as it operates in the French Revolution, but she will use sensibility and drawn on the reader's sympathies in her abolitionist poem, *The Slave Trade; A Poem* (1787/1988). While she condemns "fierce Faction's tool" and "mad Misrule," which both reject "Reason's reign" (lines 23–25), More asks readers to empathize with the Africans sold into slavery by reminding them that the slaves are made up of the same passions as the British citizenry: "For they have keen affections, soft desires, / Love strong as death, and active patriot fires" (69–70).[27] In the interest of justice, More draws directly on readers' sympathies when she forces them to picture a ravaged nation and a suffering mother and child.

> Whene'er to Afric's shores I turn my eyes,
> Horrors of deepest, deadliest guilt arise;
> I see, by more than Fancy's mirror shown,
> The burning village, and the blazing town:
> See the dire victim torn from social life,
> See the sacred infant, hear the shrieking wife!
> She, wretch forlorn! is dragged by hostile hands,
> To distant tyrants sold, in distant lands!
> Transmitted miseries, and successive chains,
> The sole sad heritage her child obtains! (95–104)

As Hannah More moved between distrusting emotions and not only acknowledging their role in justice but also employing them to bring about justice, so did Blackstone, Smith, Macaulay, and other jurists and legal historians, as well as other literary authors like Burney, Boswell, and Scott. Arguably, the literary investigations of sentiment and sensibility of the mid-eighteenth century allowed the law to explore more candidly how the passions function within legal thought and practice. Both movements concerned themselves increasingly with the readership—the public, the citizenry—and its understanding of law and emotion.[28] Embedded in the legal and literary texts of the period are early concerns about, and challenges to, the very assumptions on which the relationship between the citizenry and the law are based; we find, as well, some of the same debates that engage the law and literature movement over language, interpretation, and the role of human emotion. Legal and literary authors of the eighteenth and early nineteenth centuries inquired into the effect of ever-present human passion that seemed to undermine the belief that reason would be the great liberator and equalizer. Law and literature scholars of the twenty-first century, in the essays that follow, provide a window into the dynamics of human emotion that persist in legal and literary thought, that determine our concepts of individual liberty and protection of life and property, that make the law palatable in a social community or drive a citizenry to rebel—or, in the end, to provide them with the comfort and reassurance they need to be content.

Notes

1. Quoted in Allen D. Boyer, *Sir Edward Coke and the Elizabethan Age* (Stanford, CA: Stanford University Press, 2011), 84.

2. Sir Matthew Hale, "Reflections by the Lrd. Cheife Justice Hale on Mr. Hobbes His Dialogue of the Lawe" in *A History of English Law* by Sir William Holdsworth, vol. 5 (London: Methuen & Co., 1945), 503.

3. John Locke, *Two Treatises of Government*, ed. Peter Laslett (Cambridge: Cambridge University Press, 1988), 271.

4. See Locke, 268. "*Political Power*, . . ." Locke writes, "I take to be *a Right* of making Laws with Penalties of Death, and consequently all less Penalties, for the Regulating and Preserving of Property, and of employing the force of the Community, in the Execution of such Laws, and in the defense of the Common-wealth from Foreign Injury, and all this only for the Publick Good."

5. Samuel Pufendorf, *Two Books of the Elements of Universal Jurisprudence*, ed. Thomas Behme (Indianapolis, IN: Liberty Fund, 2009), 332–34.

6. Pufendorf, *Two Books*, 283–84.

7. Hale also notes that reason meets with difficulty in the discipline of the law: "Of all Kind of Subjects where about ye reasoning Facultie is conversant, there is none of So greate a difficulty

for the Faculty of reason to guide it Selfe and come to any Steddiness as that of Laws" ("Reflections," 502).

8. David Hume, *A Treatise of Human Nature*, ed. Ernest G. Mossner (New York: Penguin Classics, 1984), 507.

9. All three of Daniel Defoe's novels, *Robinson Crusoe*, *Moll Flanders*, and *Roxana* represent legal thought; however, *Moll Flanders* most directly references the law. See Melissa J. Ganz, "*Moll Flanders* and English Marriage Law," *Eighteenth-Century Fiction* 17:2 (2005): 157–82. Samuel Richardson's *Clarissa* takes on questions of the law, inheritance, and sexuality. See Thomas O. Beebee, "Doing Clarissa's Will: Samuel Richardson's Legal Genres," *International Journal of Law and Semiotics* 2:5 (1989): 159–82; Ann K. Wagner, "Sexual Assault in the Shadow of the Law: Character and Proof in Samuel Richardson's *Clarissa*," *Law and Literature* 25:2 (2013): 311–26. Henry Fielding, a magistrate as well as a novelist, invokes the law in *Tom Jones* and *Amelia*. See Allen D. Boyer, "Justice Fielding, the Novel, and the Law," *Yale Journal of Law and the Humanities* 4:1.8 (1992): 187–207; John Bender, *Imagining the Penitentiary: Fiction and the Architecture of Mind in Eighteenth-Century England* (Chicago: The University of Chicago Press), 1987.

10. James Boyd White, *Heracles' Bow: Essays on the Rhetoric and Poetics of the Law* (Madison: University of Wisconsin Press, 1985), 33; Robert Cover, "Nomos and Narrative" in *Narrative, Violence, and the Law: The Essays of Robert Cover*, ed. Martha Minow, Michael Ryan, and Austin Sarat (Ann Arbor: University of Michigan Press, 1992), 95–96.

11. See for example, Paul de Man, *Allegories of Reading: Figural Language in Rousseau, Nietzsche, Rilke, and Proust* (New Haven, CT: Yale University Press, 1979); Jacques Derrida, *Of Grammatology* (Baltimore: Johns Hopkins University Press, 1998).

12. For further discussion of hermeneutics and the law and literature movement, see Ian Ward, "Law and Literature: A Continuing Debate," in *Law and Literature: Possibilities and Perspectives* (Cambridge: Cambridge University Press, 1995), 3–27.

13. Ward, *Law and Literature*, 6.

14. White, *Heracles' Bow*, xi.

15. Peter Brooks and Paul Gewirtz, eds., *Law's Stories: Narrative and Rhetoric in the Law* (New Haven, CT: Yale University Press, 1996).

16. Robert Cover, "Violence and the Word," in *Narrative, Violence, and the Law: The Essays of Robert Cover*, ed. Martha Minow, Michael Ryan, and Austin Sarat (Ann Arbor: University of Michigan Press, 1992), 203–38.

17. Richard Posner, *Law and Literature: A Misunderstood Relation*, 3rd ed. (Cambridge, MA: Harvard University Press, 1988).

18. Martha C. Nussbaum, *Political Emotions: Why Love Matters for Justice* (Cambridge, MA: Harvard University Press, 2013).

19. Martha C. Nussbaum and Alison L. LaCroix, eds., *Subversion and Sympathy: Gender, Law and the British Novel* (New York: Oxford University Press, 2013).

20. For a precise discussion of sentiment and sensibility in medical and theological discourse, see Ann Jessie Van Sant, *Eighteenth-Century Sensibility and the Novel: The Senses in Social Context* (Cambridge: Cambridge University Press, 1993).

21. Jean H. Hagstrum, *Sex and Sensibility: Ideal and Erotic Love from Milton to Mozart* (Chicago: The University of Chicago Press, 1980). Hagstrum provides a taxonomy of "sentiment" from the 1740s, when

sentiment is ascribed to thought and judgment, to the 1760s, when sentiment refers to "refined, tender emotions with an erotic coloration" (7). Quoting from the OED, he notes that by the early nineteenth century, sentimental came to mean "'[c]apacity for refined emotion; delicate sensitiveness of taste; also readiness to feel compassion for suffering, and to be moved by the pathetic in literature or art'" (9).

22. Janet Todd, *Sensibility: An Introduction* (London: Methuen, 1986), 1–9.

23. Van Sant, *Eighteenth-Century Sensibility*, 4. Van Sant distinguishes between the two concepts, "sentiment" and "sensibility," by identifying sentiment with the workings of the mind and sensibility with the body.

24. Robert Brissenden, *Virtue in Distress: Studies in the Novel of Sentiment from Richardson to Sade* (New York: Barnes & Noble, 1974), 29–31.

25. Barbara Benedict, *Framing Feeling: Sentiment and Style in English Prose Fiction 1745–1800* (New York: AMS Press, 1994), 1–2, 11–12, 19. Benedict also argues that literary sentimentalism led to fears of excess in sympathy because sympathy, which is usually associated with women, could lead to a "'feminized' culture" (9). See also G. J. Barker-Benfield, *The Culture of Sensibility: Sex and Society in Eighteenth-Century Britain* (Chicago: The University of Chicago Press, 1992).

26. *The Poetical Works of Hannah More* (London: Scott, Webster & Geary, 1836), 395–404. Mrs. Boscawen was Frances Evelyn Glanville (1719–1805), a bluestocking hostess. In 1742, she had married Edward Boscawen (1711–1761), Admiral of the Blue (1758).

27. *The Poetical Works of Hannah More*, 405–14.

28. For more on readership and sensibility, see John Mullan, *Sentiment and Sociability: The Language of Feeling in the Eighteenth Century* (Oxford: Oxford University Press, 1988).

Simon Stern

Blackstone's Legal Actors: The Passions of a Rational Jurist

THE SUCCESS OF BLACKSTONE'S *COMMENTARIES* IS USUALLY attributed to the ambition of his project: to give a synthetic and integrated overview of the common law, whose intricacy had, up to that time, been seen as a definitive feature of legal thought and method.[1] Others had proclaimed that reason was the touchstone of the law, but Blackstone sought to make good on this assertion by providing an organized and methodical account that showed how the doctrines and procedures of common-law courts could be justified and could be revealed as consistent across the various domains in which the courts operated. Blackstone's effort, however strained, to display the law's coherence, helps to explain why the *Commentaries* were taken up by so many generations of avid readers, but the book's success also owes something to Blackstone's method of showcasing this coherence and soliciting the reader's enthusiasm for it.[2] Daniel Boorstin, in discussing the aesthetic conception that informs Blackstone's search for coherence and order, rightly presents these neoclassical virtues as the objects of Blackstone's contemplation,[3] but that description implies that feeling enters into the world of the *Commentaries* only in the passive sense that the law's orderly structure becomes a source of pleasure to the person who discerns it. Blackstone does not simply methodize the law; he also personifies the law as an active force that produces consistency, and he similarly casts the reader as someone who partakes of the same sensibility and appreciates the same virtues. Blackstone places both the law and the law student in an affective relation to the rationalizing aims promoted in the *Commentaries*. By positing, within the text, a reader who attaches to the law in this fashion, Blackstone encourages his reader to take it for granted that this sense of attachment is part and parcel of the study of law.

In enlisting the emotions in the service of rationality, Blackstone seems to anticipate Ronald de Sousa's view that reason and emotion are not simply complementary—that is, distinct parts of a whole—but can in some instances be interrelated aspects of the same enterprise. De Sousa writes, "Despite a common prejudice, reason and emotion are not natural antagonists. On the contrary, . . . when the calculi of reason have become sufficiently sophisticated, they would be powerless in their own terms, except for the contribution of emotion."[4] The emotions play various roles in the *Commentaries*, including that of reason's antagonist, but the affective orientation of Blackstone's pedagogy also promotes a view of emotional rationality—not so much the wisdom of trusting in one's gut feelings, but rather the emotive appeal that summons the legal mind and flows from its operations.

While in some respects Blackstone's treatment of passion typifies an Enlightenment commitment to the elevation of thought over emotion, in other respects his account is remarkably prescient. Law, in Blackstone's account, is itself identified with certain desires and preferences—traits that Blackstone urges the student to identify with as well. Blackstone seems to recognize that, as Susan Bandes and Jeremy Blumenthal put it, "emotion and cognition interact," and that by acknowledging the role of emotion "as an essential component of social and institutional dynamics," we gain a better understanding of "the conditions that lead to legal change."[5] Perhaps the *Commentaries* might have achieved the same success even if Blackstone's approach had been blandly programmatic and expository, but in appealing to an audience that is conceived as sharing the same values that the law strives for, Blackstone ingeniously conjures up a reader who is already on the path to becoming a consummate lawyer, already an enthusiast of the same goals that the law seeks, in its personified form within the text, so that the law's desires and the reader's aims seem to merge.

In what follows, I begin by examining Blackstone's figuration of the law and its passions, and the pattern in which he attributes the same dispositions to the reader. Next, I turn to Blackstone's treatment of emotion in the criminal law, which describes the violent impulses of passionate actors—now presented as objects rather than subjects of legal thought—whose feelings are distinguished from the emotions that inform the law's operations and that animate the law's human exponent. Finally, I consider the place of emotion in Blackstone's often-quoted paean to the imaginative power of the property right—a tribute that also positions the property owner and his "affections" as the objects of legal thought, while nevertheless allowing them some claim to the emotional rationality that has already been conferred on the reader. When this passage is considered in relation to Blackstone's other accounts of legal passion, the property owner emerges as a figure whose feelings might themselves be the product of a Blackstonian legal education.

Law's Rational Emotions

Law is often an actor in Blackstone's account: it entertains ideas; it pays regard to human frailty; it makes suppositions, presumptions, and implications; it takes notice of some things and ignores others; and it even displays certain penchants and inclinations.[6] Just as these personifications endow the law with an agency that helps to account for legal development, they also imply that the alterations can be attributed to a source that makes adjustments and expresses preferences as part of a centralized, integrating process.[7] The "series of minute contrivances" that characterize the process of legal change are admirable not only because of their gradual movement, which avoids "any great legislative revolution in the old established forms,"[8] but also because they can be assumed to emanate from the same constant impulses over time. They may occasionally leave irregular fragments in their wake, but the underlying drive toward symmetry can be trusted to tidy them up later.[9]

Blackstone's most salient observations along these lines occur when he speaks of the law's own desire for coherence and consistency. For example, with respect to advowsons for which the patron has the right to designate the appointee (an advowson donative), Blackstone notes that if the patron should choose, even on a single occasion, to waive that right, and to allow the bishop to name the officeholder, "the law, which loves uniformity, will interpret it to be done with an intention of giving it up for ever; and will thereupon reduce it to the standard of other ecclesiastical livings."[10] In writing about the forfeiture of goods and chattels, as a result of a criminal conviction, Blackstone again refers to the law's love of uniformity to explain why such a forfeiture must follow "in every one of the higher kinds of offence"—namely, in cases of "high treason[,] . . . petit treason, felonies of all sorts[,] . . . [and] self-murder."[11] In cases of such serious crimes, all of the defendant's property—both chattels and real property—would be subject to forfeiture if the defendant was attainted after being convicted. Yet as Blackstone observes, "goods and chattels are forfeited by *conviction*," whereas "[l]ands are forfeited upon *attainder*, and not before."[12] As it turns out, activating the forfeiture at these different points in the legal proceedings has the potential to

create an inconsistency: "[I]n many . . . cases where goods are forfeited, there never is any attainder," because attainder may apply only if the defendant is sentenced to death or proclaimed an outlaw. In such a case, the chattels would be forfeit, but not the land. Nevertheless, Blackstone justifies the process in the name of consistency, explaining that if the defendant should receive a sentence of death or outlawry, it would be inconsistent for the land to be forfeit, while leaving the goods and chattels as assets of the defendant's estate. It follows, Blackstone concludes, that if the property of the defendant is to be forfeit, that must occur "upon conviction, or not at all; and, being necessarily upon conviction in those [cases involving a possible sentence of death or outlawry], it is so ordered in all other cases, for the law loves uniformity."[13]

One need not review these doctrines in detail to see that the love of uniformity is neither a necessary nor a sufficient justification for the results that Blackstone describes. English common law in the eighteenth century tolerated many exceptions and inconsistencies. The case of the donor's waiver for an advowson could easily have been accommodated as a temporary, rather than a permanent, departure from the prior practice. Alternatively, the treatment of waiver as a permanent condition could easily be explained on the ground that any waiver of a right to control the transfer of property will eliminate that right for once and all, because it simplifies the legal conditions governing the property and eliminates a possible source of uncertainty. This rationale—the elimination of uncertainty—offers an equally plausible explanation that was readily available in Blackstone's era,[14] and it often applies even when uniformity would not be the result. Where the enforcement of a right is widespread, so that the way to create uniformity would be to treat a waiver as a one-time aberration, it might nevertheless seem preferable to give permanent effect to the waiver, so that third parties do not perceive the right as winking in and out of existence. As for the forfeiture of chattels upon conviction of a felony, not only might this result in inconsistency, as already noted, but the policy could in any case be easily explained simply as a penalty that the sovereign is entitled to impose on those convicted of serious crimes.[15] Indeed, that explanation would have the virtue of explaining why the lesser forfeiture (of chattels, but not of land) is always appropriate—namely, because the sovereign, exhibiting grace and restraint, chooses always to exact the lower penalty, and reserves the higher one only for cases in which the nature of the offense itself demands it. In both instances uniformity may be achieved by diminishing a party's rights, but one could imagine an equally pervasive uniformity achieved by a law that cherishes rights and demands very strong justifications to overcome any presumption in favor of depriving persons of property claims.

These examples do not show that the love of uniformity is an inaccurate explanation; rather, they show that it applies so easily, where it can be offered, that it does not explain very much. The notable feature in both instances, and in many others that appear in the *Commentaries*, is Blackstone's readiness to reach for uniformity as a rationale. His enthusiasm for it is part and parcel of his conception of the common law generally, and of the ideal student of the common law. Throughout the *Commentaries*, Blackstone extolls the common law for its harmony, consistency, symmetry, and proportionality.[16] And in extolling these virtues, he often makes a point of identifying the reader as someone who is capable of appreciating them—someone who would seek out those virtues himself.[17]

A crucial feature of this legal passion, and one that accords perfectly with its aim, is its abiding nature. To be sure, Blackstone does equate certain emotions with "occasional, intense, unpredictable moods that interfere with a steady state of rationality,"[18] as we will see in his treatment of criminal law. In his characterization of the law's own inclinations, however, Blackstone shows no reluctance to present its rationality as itself a kind of passion. He highlights what Bandes and Blumenthal call "the affective component[s] of law" and indeed he makes these components essential to law's functioning. The love of uniformity constantly drives the law's operations, and one of the distinctive features of Blackstone's pedagogy involves his efforts to instill the same desire in the student. Numerous passages in the *Commentaries* might be understood as glosses on Bandes's and Blumenthal's observation about our capacity to redirect our emotional energies: "Not only can emotions be managed, they can be educated."[19] The *Commentaries* are so thoroughly suffused with references to law's emotional impulses that even the reader who does not consciously register this effect might nevertheless feel its impact. As Bandes and Blumethal observe, "[T]his educative capacity exists . . . even for intuitive, unconscious emotions."[20]

One of the passages that most fully captures these features appears early in the second volume of the *Commentaries*. Blackstone explains that a full understanding of property law requires frequent resort to historical examples, even if the practice might appear irrelevant to the study of contemporary law:

> [T]hough, in the course of our observations in this and many other parts of the present book, we may have occasion to search pretty highly into the antiquities of our English jurisprudence, yet surely no industrious student will imagine his time mis-employed, when he is led to consider that the obsolete doctrines of our laws are frequently the foundation, upon which what remains is erected; and that it is impracticable to comprehend many rules of the modern law, in a scholarlike scientifical manner, without having recourse to the antient. Nor will these researches be altogether void of rational entertainment as well as use: as in viewing the majestic ruins of Rome or Athens, of Balbec or Palmyra, it administers both pleasure and instruction to compare them with the draughts of the same edifices, in their pristine proportion and splendor.[21]

The study of obsolete law is useful but also yields rational entertainment, just as the traveler who gazes on majestic ruins derives both instruction and pleasure from the opportunity. The informative and entertaining aspects of the experience, it seems, arise from the same source. The ancient ruins, beheld in their present state of decay, would be a fascinating object of contemplation even if they had no modern counterparts, but because they are the precursors of contemporary efforts, the original symmetry of these antiquities, insofar as the observer can recognize it, is also satisfying and offers a template for the correct proportions of modern structures. (This point seems to have registered on at least one of Blackstone's readers, Peter du Ponceau, who in the early nineteenth century would translate the architectural simile into a sculptural one, recommending "gradual and almost insensible" alterations with "the delicate chisel, and not the rough axe," because "our system of laws" resembles "one of those ancient statues of Phidias or Praxiteles, which have been in part mutilated or defaced by the hand of time."[22]) Finally, the contrast between the object's current state and its former grandeur is itself an instructive reminder of the fate of all human projects.

Blackstone's architectural metaphor, encompassing the foundations on which modern law is erected, anticipates his much better-known comparison of the common law to a refurbished gothic castle. What emerges more clearly from this elaboration of the analogy is the way in which the student shares the same traits that distinguish the law—or more precisely, the way in which Blackstone's pedagogy serves at once to identify a set of paradigmatically legal virtues and to strive, while identifying those virtues, to inculcate them in the student as well, and hence to create students who are equal to the law's configurations. The scholar-like scientific approach to law equips students with the ability to find rational entertainment in their studies, and also to use the same talents in their travels abroad, to antique lands.

The pupil who approaches the study of law in this spirit will share Blackstone's fondness for the common law and his hostility toward the legislators who have ventured to rearrange it. The pristine proportions of the law's original structure, Blackstone explains, have been altered not simply through the passage of time, but more insidiously through the ill-advised efforts of various parliaments that have faddishly introduced new regulations that do not comport with the common law:

> The common law of England has fared like other venerable edifices of antiquity, which rash and unexperienced workmen have ventured to new-dress and refine, with all the rage of modern improvement. Hence frequently its symmetry has been destroyed, its proportions distorted, and its majestic simplicity exchanged for specious embellishments and fantastic novelties.[23]

Again, the primordial virtues inherent in the common law—the symmetry and simplicity of a balanced, integrated, coherent system—do not need to be defended or justified, because they are so obviously the proper basis of a legal aesthetic. In conveying his impatience and disgust implicitly, Blackstone models the attitude of the legally informed gentleman whom the student should aspire to become.

At the outset of the *Commentaries*, in the introductory chapter to the
8 first volume, Blackstone outlines the benefits that will redound to the legal system when it is studied in the scientific manner he recommends:

> The advantages that might result to the science of the law itself, . . . perhaps would be very considerable. The leisure and abilities of the learned . . . might either suggest expedients, or execute those dictated by wiser heads, for improving its method, retrenching its superfluities, and reconciling the little contrarieties, which the practice of many centuries will necessarily create in any human system: a task, which those who are deeply employed in business, and the more active scenes of the profession, can hardly condescend to engage in.[24]

Here, the project of smoothing out the inconsistencies, readjusting the parts to make them more symmetrical, is expressly the aim of this comprehensive overview. By implication, the pupil who undertakes this course of study will not only come to admire the system as it exists, but will come away with the skill and the desire to reform the system where it has gone astray. In fact, Blackstone suggests relatively little by way of reform in the *Commentaries*, and the proposals he does offer relate primarily (though not exclusively) to legislation rather than reform of the common law.[25] Yet even if the project of reconciliation and retrenchment receives less attention than Blackstone seems to promise at the outset, his description of the task lends a dignity and sense of purpose to an enterprise that might otherwise seem essentially practical and even self-interested.[26]

Blackstone's achievement, then, consists as much in his image of the lawyer as in his image of the law. In delineating a rational and orderly structure for the law, Blackstone also imagines its ideal observer, consumer, and exponent: someone similarly inclined to preserve the law's carefully crafted proportions and to restore them where they have been disturbed. Arguably Coke's *Institutes*, or Hale's *Analysis of the Law*, could similarly be examined in terms of a postulated reader who is adequate to the subject, but in Blackstone's case this figure seems to be imagined more consciously and is endowed with very different attributes from those that a reading of Coke or Hale might yield—doubtless a result of the *Commentaries'* origin as lectures to students. Indeed, the attributes of Blackstone's lawyer are different from the ones that characterize most lawyers in eighteenth-century fiction and drama. Portrayals of lawyers and judges in nineteenth-century literature and in legal treatises, however, include a wider variety of personalities, including many more examples of the sort of urbane, equable, and calmly judicious figure whom Blackstone contemplates. The *Commentaries* are often credited as inaugurating a new tradition of legal treatise-writing among Anglo-American lawyers, but in seeking to rationalize the law, Blackstone also helped to imagine its expositor as a paradigm of rationality, a figure for whom the law's drive toward uniformity and consistency is itself a source of affection.

Criminal Passions

In contrast to the alignment between rationality and emotion that underwrites the *Commentaries'* pedagogical efforts, Blackstone associates emotion with the suspension of rational thought when he turns to the criminal law. The fourth volume of the *Commentaries*, which takes up this subject, presents emotional actors as objects of the law's concern rather than as adjutants of the law's operations. Thus his account alternates between what Dan Kahan and Martha Nussbaum have called "the mechanistic and the evaluative conceptions of emotion," corresponding respectively to a view of "emotions as forces that do not contain or respond to thought" and a view holding that "emotions express cognitive appraisals" and can be "shape[d] . . . through moral education."[27] However, Blackstone does not assume that a person overcome by an emotional force should necessarily be treated "tenderly" by the law. At first blush, it might appear that he relies on the evaluative conception when focusing on the educative process by which his reader is brought to share the law's penchants, and that he uses the mechanistic conception when considering the kinds of emotional responses that justify mitigation of a criminal defendant's liability. That distinction, however, would reflect a more deeply psychological view of the emotions and their responsiveness to manipulation than the *Commentaries* affords. Indeed, as many scholars have observed, when discussing the issue of intention in criminal law—a subject that offers wide scope for psychological inquiry—Blackstone remains content with an external account that assesses intention on the basis of the defendant's actions.[28] While he draws on both the mechanistic and the evaluative views of emotion,

he does not consistently relate these views to the implications associated with them today. To be sure, in some instances Blackstone suggests that when violence results from mechanistic emotions, the actor's punishment should be mitigated, but he does not suggest that as a general matter, the law should be less severe in those cases.

At the beginning of his discussion of criminal law, Blackstone blends the mechanistic and evaluative conceptions in what amounts to a plea for leniency and an exhortation to study the subject carefully:

> The infirmities of the best among us, the vices and ungovernable passions of others, the instability of all human affairs, and the numberless unforeseen events, which the compass of a day may bring forth, will teach us (upon a moment's reflection) that to know with precision what the laws of our country have forbidden, and the deplorable consequences to which a wilful disobedience may expose us, is a matter of universal concern.[29]

"Ungovernable" passions are, of course, incapable of being deterred by the actor's awareness of the attendant punishment, whereas the crime of the "wilfully" disobedient actor consists in part in his stubborn persistence in the face of a prohibition that he should have heeded. The whole passage carries the sense that crimes occur because of random chance, as much as because of any habitual disposition.[30] At the same time, however, Blackstone also suggests that we can avoid the deplorable consequences that fortune might tempt us to provoke, by learning "precis[ely]" what is prohibited. The effect is to place criminal behavior in an uncertain territory which, by virtue of being located halfway between the ungovernable and the educable, is always capable of being associated with either one.

To be sure, in some instances Blackstone makes a point of arguing for leniency because of crimes committed under the sway of strong emotions. Thus, for example, he observes that "the violence of passion . . . may sometimes alleviate a crime; as theft, in case of hunger, is far more worthy of compassion, than when committed through avarice, or to supply one in luxurious excesses."[31] A classic context for this point involves the distinction between manslaughter and murder. In recapitulating the distinction, Blackstone offers no observations about the allowance made for unreflective anger, but presents the doctrine as if its rationale were self-explanatory: "[M]anslaughter arises from the sudden heat of the passions, murder from the wickedness of the heart."[32] Therefore, he continues,

> if upon a sudden quarrel two persons fight, and one of them kills the other, this is manslaughter: and so it is, if they upon such an occasion go out and fight in a field; for this is one continued act of passion: and the law pays that regard to human frailty, as not to put a hasty and a deliberate act upon the same footing with regard to guilt. So also if a man be greatly provoked, as by pulling his nose, or other great indignity, and immediately kills the aggressor, . . . it is manslaughter. But in this, and in every other case of homicide upon provocation, if there be a sufficient cooling-time for passion to subside and reason to interpose, and the person so provoked afterwards kills the other, this is deliberate revenge and not heat of blood, and accordingly amounts to murder.[33]

In explaining why the person actuated by provocation incurs a lesser penalty, Blackstone contrasts passion and reason, equating the hasty act with the passionate one. The implication is not so much that a stricter penalty would have no deterrent effect, but rather that the passionate actor simply lacks the kind of deliberate intent that would justify treating him as a murderer. In short, law pays "regard to human frailty" when passion blocks the formation of intent, and this effect seems to be measurable entirely in temporal terms.

According to this view, someone acting under the sway of an ongoing passion is not entitled to the same consideration, and therefore even a "continued act of passion" must be relatively brief. This explains why Blackstone can acknowledge that the love of gambling may be completely overwhelming, and yet he does not conclude that the impassioned gambler deserves any clemency:

> [G]aming in high life . . . [is] a passion to which every valuable consideration is made a sacrifice . . . When men are thus intoxicated with so frantic a spirit, laws will be of little avail: because the same false sense of honour, that prompts a man to sacrifice himself, will deter him from appealing to the magistrate. Yet it is proper that laws should be, and be known publicly, that gentlemen may learn what penalties they wilfully incur.[34]

12 That the gambler is frantic and intoxicated does not, apparently, mean that he cannot act with deliberation, as the final sentence makes clear. As this passage shows, the question is not whether the law can have a deterrent effect; after all, Blackstone readily acknowledges that "laws will be of little avail." Rather, the question is whether the actor is in thrall to a brief and reactive passion, or one that, simply because of its duration, can be assumed to allow for deliberation. In the one case, passion simply prevents the formation of rational thought; in the other, passion and reason seem to coexist, at least to the point where the actor deserves no solicitude for allowing passion to gain the upper hand. The contrast between homicide and gambling underscores Blackstone's lack of interest in a more densely psychological account of criminal behavior. In effect, he turns to an objective standard—temporal duration—to resolve a problem that later commentators would strive to understand in much more individualized terms.

In arguing for the reform of criminal law, Blackstone similarly associates passion with haste, and in that context, again, he opposes it to rationality. He suggests that the asymmetries and disproportionalities that have ruined the criminal law—in particular, the overuse of capital punishment—can be put down to careless legislatures:

> The enacting of penalties, to which a whole nation shall be subject, ought not to be left as a matter of indifference to the passions or interests of a few, who upon temporary motives may prefer or support such a bill; but be calmly and maturely considered by persons, who know what provisions the law has already made to remedy the mischief complained of, who can from experience foresee the probable consequences of those which are now proposed, and who will judge without passion or prejudice how adequate they are to the evil.[35]

For the same reason, Blackstone notes that when members of the House of Commons charge a governmental official with criminal abuse of his power, he cannot be tried "before the ordinary tribunals, which would naturally be swayed by the authority of so powerful an accuser." Rather, "this branch of the legislature, which represents the people, must bring its charge before the other branch, which consists of the nobility, who have neither the same interests, nor the same passions as popular assemblies."[36]

If the law student can be regarded as temperamentally eligible to sit in the House of Lords (even if not necessarily qualified by birth to do so), the criminal actor—at least the one whose crime is motivated by passion—acts with the same rashness as the popular assembly. The field of criminal law provides Blackstone with an alternative sphere for explaining the relation between emotion and reason, and it allows him, by implication, to set off even more strongly the virtues of rational passions that characterize the law and its exponent—the passions of the calm, steady, contemplative, and thorough scholar.[37]

Property and Affect

These reflections on the objects of the lawyer's attention and the rational feelings that actuate the spirit of legal inquiry, in turn, may offer a means of reconsidering one of Blackstone's most famous pronouncements about the feelings that the law inspires. At the beginning of the second volume, when introducing the subject of property and describing its attractions, Blackstone writes,

> There is nothing which so generally strikes the imagination, and engages the affections of mankind, as the right of property; or that sole and despotic dominion which one man claims and exercises over the external things of

> the world, in total exclusion of the right of any other individual in the universe.[38]

Given that much of the volume is dedicated to enumerating the many doctrines that undercut this dream of exclusive control, commentators have wondered whether this opening sketch should be taken literally or ironically.[39] The vision of a landlord securely presiding over his little fiefdom soon gives way to an extended discussion of the tenure system, itself based on the premise that all land is held of the king.

In the context of Blackstone's other reflections on the passions that law exhibits and accounts for, his reflections on the affective powers of the property right are notable for the assurance with which they are ascribed to "mankind" in general. The "affections" that Blackstone contemplates here do not flow from the law itself (as with the love of uniformity, noted earlier), nor are they objects of the law's solicitude (as with some of the figures in criminal law); rather, these affections are inspired by a set of beliefs about the structure and endowments that the law facilitates. Cast in the generalizing cadences that mark the first sentence of Austen's *Pride and Prejudice*, this description, like Austen's, evidently applies to a very specific group: in this case, the same audience to whom Blackstone has recommended the study of law at the beginning of the first volume.[40] There, he observes that if nothing else, "the understanding of a few leading principles, relating to estates and conveyancing, may form some check and guard upon a gentleman's inferior agents, and preserve him at least from very gross and notorious imposition."[41] In short, Blackstone describes the affections that might be shared by the student who has been educated—who is being educated—by the *Commentaries*. We might take this passage as an index of the student's own development, as a marker of the distance between the fond but somewhat naïve desires of the legally uninformed gentleman and the sober understanding of the one who emerges at the end of this course of instruction. On that view, the vision of "sole and despotic dominion" is not ironic so much as heuristic, a convenient starting point that will lead to a fuller and more complex picture, but nevertheless an appealing starting point insofar as it accounts for the subject's allure.

Indeed, Blackstone does not seem to regard the absolutist vision as simply mistaken, given that he also refers to it—without any talk of imagination or affection—in the first volume. After discussing personal security and personal liberty, he explains that "[t]he third absolute right, inherent in every Englishman, is that of property: which consists in the free use, enjoyment, and disposal, of all his acquisitions, without any control or diminution, save only by the laws of the land."[42] The final qualifier, of course, accounts for most of the second volume, and reminds us again of the work still to be achieved before the student can arrive at a full understanding of this right and its attendant powers. As with the better-known passage, however, this one seems to celebrate the sense of control it envisions, and to suggest that the property owner's longing for exclusive control represents a legitimate aspiration. Blackstone ultimately qualifies this "absolute" right, but he presents the landowner's vision of sole dominion as one of the abiding, rational passions of the law, not one of the temporary, irrational passions that the law charitably accommodates as a concession to human frailty.

Thus if the fondly imagined right of control betokens an exaggerated sense of untrammeled power, that attitude turns out to serve as an auspicious premise for the landowner's legal education. Just as the law itself, according to the metaphor of the modernized castle, continues to preserve a due sense of proportion as it keeps making small adjustments, the landowner begins with a sense of unified dominion and order (which he administers), and is gradually led to understand the ways in which he must cede control, insofar as "the laws of the land" require it. Indeed, if his home is his castle, then he is the custodian of the very edifice that embodies the law in Blackstone's account. Seemingly a member of the same audience to whom the *Commentaries* are addressed, this gentleman harbors the same passions that Blackstone associates with the law. The landlord's imagined dominion does not simply present a foil for the view of property law that Blackstone will proceed to elaborate, but it also identifies the landlord himself as an example of the figure whose legal education forms the subject of the *Commentaries*.

Notes

For comments on earlier drafts, thanks to Susan Bandes, Wilf Prest, and Kathryn Temple.

1. References throughout are to William Blackstone, *Commentaries on the Laws of England*, 4 vols. (Oxford: Clarendon Press, 1765–1769).

2. According to Edward Gibbon, Blackstone sometimes exhibited the wrong kind of emotional attachment in his efforts to demonstrate the underlying coherence of the law. Gibbon observed that in addressing the law's defects, Blackstone showed "the becoming tenderness of a pious son who would wish to conceal the infirmities of his parent." British Museum Add. MSS 34,881, f. 216v; quoted in Sir William Holdsworth, *A History of English Law* (London: Methuen, 1938), XII: 728.

3. Daniel J. Boorstin, *The Mysterious Science of the Law: An Essay on Blackstone's Commentaries* (Chicago: The University of Chicago Press, 1941, 1996), 91–99.

4. Ronald de Sousa, *The Rationality of Emotion* (Cambridge, MA: MIT Press, 1987), xv.

5. Susan A. Bandes and Jeremy A. Blumenthal, "Emotion and the Law," *Annual Review of Law and Social Science* 8 (2012): 162.

6. Consider, for example, the following examples from the *Commentaries*: "Such indulgence does the law shew to the frailty of human nature" (1:438); "such public oppressions as tend to dissolve the constitution . . . are cases which the law will not, out of decency, suppose; being incapable of distrusting those, whom it has invested with any part of the supreme power" (1:237); "the law will take notice [of property in land] and not of [property covered by water]" (2:18); "exceptions to general rules, and common right, are ever looked upon by the law in an unfavourable view" (2:24); "the law will not suppose it possible" for a parson to agree to take a smaller modus than he is entitled to (2:30); "the law presumes that he, who buys an office, will by bribery, extortion, or other unlawful means, make his purchase good, to the manifest detriment of the public" (2:36–37); "the law, in favour of infants, is always jealous of guardians" (2:89); "the law . . . is always ready to catch at any thing in favour of liberty" (2:94); "we may judge of the favourable disposition, that the law . . . hath always shewn to [copyholders]" (2:98); "the law prefers . . . simple and ordinary remedies" (3:233).

7. Michael Meehan, in describing the *Commentaries* as a "biography," similarly hints at the significance of personification in Blackstone's account. Meehan writes that "Blackstone's *Commentaries* is presented as a form of legal biography, a tale of the 'inner' struggling to re-manifest itself outwardly." Michael Meehan, "An Anatomy of Australian Law or 'The Human Element in Legal Argument,'" in J. Neville Turner and Pamela Williams, eds., *The Happy Couple: Law and Literature* (Sydney: Federation Press, 1994), 384. This habit of personification was one of the features that Bentham fixed on, in his attack of Blackstone's conservatism: "[S]ome . . . look upon it as a kind of presumption and ingratitude, and rebellion, and cruelty, . . . to suffer any one so much as to imagine, that an old-established law could in any respect be a fit object of condemnation. Whether it has been a kind of *personification* that has been the cause of this, as if the Law were a living Creature . . . I shall not here enquire." Jeremy Bentham, *A Fragment on Government; Being an Examination of What Is Delivered, on the Subject of Government in General in the Introduction to Sir William Blackstone's Commentaries* (London: T. Payne and E. Brooke, 1776), xiii.

8. Blackstone, *Commentaries*, 3:268.

9. Blackstone's account of incremental legal change has, of course, been discussed extensively. See, e.g., David Lieberman, *The Province of Legislation Determined: Legal Theory in Eighteenth-Century Britain* (Cambridge: Cambridge University Press, 1989), 56–67; Kunal M. Parker, *Common Law, History, and Democracy in America, 1790–1900: Legal Thought before Modernism* (Cambridge: Cambridge University Press, 2011), 63–64; Eleanor F. Shevlin, "'Imaginary Productions' and 'Minute Contrivances': Law, Fiction, and Property in Eighteenth-Century England," *Studies in Eighteenth Century Culture* 28 (1999): 131–54; Wolfram Schmidgen, *Eighteenth-Century Fiction and the Law of Property* (Cambridge: Cambridge University Press, 2002), 165–66; Dieter Polloczek, *Literature and Legal Discourse: Equity and Ethics from Sterne to Conrad* (Cambridge: Cambridge University Press, 1999), 107–8.

10. Blackstone, *Commentaries*, 2:24.

11. Ibid., 4:379–80.

12. Ibid., 4:380 (emphasis in original).

13. Ibid.

14. See, for example, Noy v. Ellis, (1676) 2 Chan. Cas. 220, 221; 22 Eng. Rep. 918, 919 ("it was needful that the Point should be settled; and no Matter what the Law is, so it be certain"); Butler v. Duncomb, (1718), 1 P.W. 448, 452; 24 Eng. Rep. 466, 467 ("where Things are settled, and rendered certain, it will not be so material how, as long as they are so, and . . . all People know how to act"); Walton v. Tryon, (1753) Dick. 244, 245; 21 Eng. Rep. 262 ("Certainty is the mother of repose, and therefore the law aims at certainty").

15. Andrew Amos, in his mid-nineteenth-century treatise on Hale, pointed to another inconsistency created by this policy, noting that whereas in this passage, Blackstone justifies forfeiture before the defendant receives a final sentence, elsewhere he delivers a "eulogy on the practice of waiting for an attainder upon escheats," because (as Blackstone puts it), there always remains "a possibility of the innocence of a convicted prisoner; something may be offered in arrest of judgment, . . . and thereupon the conviction may be quashed." Amos concludes, "It must be admitted that it required an ingenious and inveterate optimist to extol the policy of the law, both in waiting for judgment, and in not waiting for it." Andrew Amos, *Ruins of Time: Exemplified in Sir Matthew Hale's History of the Pleas of the Crown* (London: Stevens and Norton, 1856), 54–55.

16. Again, numerous commentators have discussed this tendency; see, for example, Boorstin, 91–99; Wilfrid Prest, "Blackstone as Architect: Constructing the *Commentaries*," *Yale Journal of Law and the Humanities* 15 (2003): 103–33; for a recent discussion, see Matthew Mauger, "'Observe how parts with parts unite / In one harmonious rule of right': William Blackstone's Verses on the Laws of England," *Law and Humanities* 6 (2012): 179–96.

17. The student and reader are gendered male throughout this discussion, to reflect the historical circumstances in which Blackstone lectured and wrote.

18. Bandes and Blumenthal, "Emotion and the Law," 164.

19. Ibid., 171. John Deigh similarly proposes an "emotion-based account of the law's authority," premised on "an emotional bond between the subjects and the law" analogous to "the bond children develop [with] their parents." As Deigh explains, "That such an emotional bond can explain this disposition [i.e., the legal subjects' willingness to subordinate their own ends to those of the law] is evident from the explanation its prototype supplies of a like disposition children acquire through socialization." John Deigh, "Emotion and the Authority of Law," in *The Passions of Law*, ed. Susan Bandes (New York: New York University Press, 1999), 295. Whereas Deigh imagines this bond attaching to the addressee of the law's demands, however, Blackstone's affective rhetoric also encourages the student to identify himself with the law's operations.

20. Bandes and Blumenthal, "Emotion and the Law," 171.

21. Blackstone, *Commentaries*, 2:44. Blackstone returns to these majestic ruins in volume three, when defending English law Latin as a language "calculated for eternal duration," just as "[t]he rude pyramids of Egypt have endured from the earliest ages, while the more modern and elegant structures of Attica, Rome, and Palmyra have sunk beneath the strokes of time." Blackstone, 3:320. As David Lieberman notes, in advocating this approach to the study of law, Blackstone draws on Lord Kames's view that "Law . . . becomes . . . only a rational study, when it is traced historically, from its first rudiments among savages, through successive changes, to its highest improvements in a civilized society." Henry Home, Lord Kames, *Historical Law-Tracts*, 2 vols. (Edinburgh: A. Kincaid,

1758), 1:v, cited in David Lieberman, "Blackstone's Science of Legislation," *Journal of British Studies* 27 (1988): 128. On Blackstone's invitations to contemplate the ruins of Rome and Palmyra, see also Prest, "Blackstone as Architect," 120; Kjell Å. Modéer, "Living Ruins of the Law: On Legal Change and Legal History in Late Modernity," *Scandinavian Studies in Law* 53 (2008): 223.

22. Peter S. du Ponceau, *A Dissertation on the Nature and Extent of the Jurisdiction of the Courts of the United States* (Philadelphia: A. Small, 1824), 130. Conversely, Hugh Henry Brackenridge could argue, around the same time, that judges were better positioned than legislatures to undertake legal reform precisely because "[t]he legislature can act only by details, and in particulars, whereas the able judge can remove at once, or alter, what was originally faulty or has become disproportioned in the building." Yet he warned that "no one but a *skilful architect*, and who can have the whole edifice in his mind . . . ought . . . to attempt this." Hugh Henry Brackenridge, *Law Miscellanies* (Philadelphia: P. Byrne, 1814), 75. For further discussion of this passage and its relation to early nineteenth-century American thought about legal reform, see Morton J. Horwitz, *The Transformation of American Law 1780–1860* (Cambridge, MA: Harvard University Press, 1977), 24.

23. Blackstone, *Commentaries*, 1:10.

24. Ibid., 1:30.

25. For a helpful summation of Blackstone's criticisms of the law, see Holdsworth, *A History of English Law*, XII: 728–29.

26. For example, in "demonstrat[ing] the utility of some acquaintance with the laws of the land," Blackstone mentions, among other benefits, the use of learning enough about real property to acquire "some check and guard upon a gentleman's inferior agents," and the value of understanding the "forms necessary in the wording of last wills and testaments." Blackstone, *Commentaries*, 2:6–7.

27. Dan M. Kahan and Martha C. Nussbaum, "Two Conceptions of Emotion in Criminal Law," *Columbia Law Review* 96 (1996): 273. For a helpful critique of this account, see Terry A. Maroney, "Law and Emotion: A Proposed Taxonomy of an Emerging Field," *Law and Human Behavior* 30 (2006): 128–29.

28. See Simon Stern, "Blackstone's Criminal Law: Common-Law Harmonization and Statutory Reform," in *Foundational Texts in Criminal Law*, ed. Markus D. Dubber (Oxford: Oxford University Press, 2014), 65–69; Nicola Lacey, "In Search of the Responsible Subject: History, Philosophy and Social Sciences in Criminal Law Theory," *Modern Law Review* 64 (2001): 359–60; Nicola Lacey, "Contingency, Coherence and Conceptualism: Reflections on the Encounter between 'Critique' and 'the Philosophy of the Criminal Law,'" in *Philosophy and the Criminal Law: Principle and Critique*, ed. Antony Duff (Cambridge: Cambridge University Press, 1998), 21–25.

29. Blackstone, *Commentaries*, 4:2.

30. To that extent, Blackstone anticipates modern scholarship that shows how "people tend to inaccurately predict how they . . . will be emotionally affected in the future by negative events such as harm or injury." Bandes and Blumenthal, "Emotion and the Law," 166 (citing Jeremy A. Blumenthal, "Law and the Emotions: The Problems of Affective Forecasting," *Indiana Law Journal* 80 [2005]: 155–238).

31. Blackstone, *Commentaries*, 4:15.

32. Ibid., 2:190.

33. Ibid., 2:191. Blackstone gives an equally matter-of-fact summation when explaining the doctrine of self-defense in analogous terms: "[T]his is what the law expresses by the word *chance-medley*, or (as some rather chuse to write it) *chaud-medley*: the former of which in its etymology signifies a

casual affray, the latter an affray in the *heat* of blood or passion: both of them of pretty much the same import." Ibid., 4:184. For a helpful discussion of the "heat of passion" defense and the social psychological research on the assumptions driving this defense; see Steven J. Sherman and Joseph L. Hoffman, "The Psychology and Law of Voluntary Manslaughter: What Can Psychology Teach Us about the 'Heat of Passion' Defense?" *Journal of Behavioral Decision Making* 20 (2007): 499–519.

34. Blackstone, *Commentaries*, 4:172.

35. Ibid., 4:4.

36. Ibid., 4:258.

37. These passions belong to the "set of emotional variables" that Susan Bandes associates with "the mainstream notion of the rule of law"; as she explains, "[T]he passion for predictability, . . . and mechanisms such as distancing, repressing, and isolating one's feelings from one's thought processes, are the emotional stances that have always driven mainstream legal thought; as a result, they avoid the stigma of 'emotionalism.'" Susan Bandes, "Empathy, Narrative, and Victim Impact Statements," *University of Chicago Law Review* 63 (1996): 368–69.

38. Blackstone, *Commentaries*, 2:2.

39. For example Jonathan B. Wiener observes that Blackstone presents "this absolutist conception as *merely* . . . [a] simplistic conception of property rights that people tend to imagine" (354). See Jonathan B. Wiener, "What Begat Property?" *History of Political Economy* 43 (2011): 353–60. Similarly, Carol Rose writes that "[i]f those who quote Blackstone's definition read further, they might come to think that Blackstone posed his definition more as a metaphor than as a literal description" (602). See Carol Rose, "Canons of Property Talk, or, Blackstone's Anxiety," *Yale Law Journal* 108 (1999): 601–32. Both scholars are responding to a frequently observed tendency to treat Blackstone's opening remarks literally.

40. In expounding on the affections that the gentleman-landowner cherishes when contemplating his property rights, Blackstone might almost be responding to Addison's comments about the property-inspired pleasures in store for the educated virtuoso, and reaffirming the class distinctions that inform those comments: "A Man of a Polite Imagination is let into a great many Pleasures, that the Vulgar are not capable of receiving. . . . It gives him, indeed, a kind of Property in every thing he sees." Joseph Addison, *The Spectator*, ed. Donald F. Bond, 5 vols. (Oxford: Oxford University Press, 1965), 1:288 (no. 411, June 21, 1712). Addison suggests that the imaginative capacity itself has an appropriative force, whereas for Blackstone, the property right is a spur to the imagination.

41. Blackstone, *Commentaries*, 1:7.

42. Ibid., 1:134.

Nancy E. Johnson

Narrative Sentiment in Adam Smith's *Lectures on Jurisprudence*

20 SCHOLARS OF ADAM SMITH'S PHILOSOPHY—FROM HIS FIRST biographer to his more recent critics—have noted Smith's ubiquitous use of stories.[1] As early as 1793, Dugald Stewart commented on the "variety and felicity" of Smith's "seducing" illustrations.[2] More recently, Charles Griswold has observed that "[s]o permeated with examples, stories, literary references and allusions and images is *The Theory of Moral Sentiments* that at times it presents the character of a novel."[3] Although one would never mistake Smith's dense and weighty *Lectures on Jurisprudence* for a novel, they are infused with, and utterly dependent on, narrative.[4]

The narratives that populate Smith's lectures are often historical. Smith traces the development of legal concepts from the Greeks and Romans to Modern Britain, culminating in the successes of the Glorious Revolution at reestablishing British liberty.[5] The narratives are also frequently hypothetical or conjectural, and therefore employ imagination and spectatorship. For example, when explaining "occupation" as a method of acquiring property legally, Smith asks us to imagine an earlier time of hunting and gathering. "If we should suppose 10 or 12 persons of different sexes settled in an uninhabited island, the first method they would fall upon for their substance would be to support themselves by the wild fruits and wild animals which the country afforded."[6] He then draws a vivid scene of life in "the Age of Hunters"—as he imagines it to have been—to conclude that law was far less necessary, than it is now, to protect property.

Smith's use of anecdotes is no doubt partly for pedagogical effectiveness. The now-published *Lectures on Jurisprudence* are "reports" of public lectures given at Glasgow University, where Smith was chair of moral philosophy from 1752 to 1764.[7] In addition, by using narrative, Smith is situating himself in the tradition of ancient rhetoricians, such as Tacitus and Quintilian, on whom he began lecturing in 1748.[8] However, the particular use of narrative in which I am interested is that which accounts for sentiment in the law. I will argue that as the law became increasingly secularized—when it began to lose its attachment to a divine knowledge that could speak to what is in the heart—Smith looked to narrative as a means to articulate the roles of imagination, emotion, and passion in an otherwise rational discourse. As Emma Rothschild has noted, Smith was keenly aware of the persuasive role of sentiment in political, moral, and economic theory. Defined as "feelings of which one is conscious, and on which one reflects," sentiments were for Smith "the traffic or commerce of modern life"; they were "the objective of economic striving, and . . . the adjunct of economic exchanges."[9] In keeping with Rothschild's observation, I will also argue that in his lectures on jurisprudence, narrative as a vehicle of sentiment became for Smith a valuable form of property—a form of cultural capital that engages with but also inheres in the law.[10] When narrative enables a discussion of sentiment within the confines of the rules of civil government, it satisfies two principles of Smith's economic and political philosophy in regard to property: utility and fluidity. Narrative is *useful* because it can account for sentiment, and narrative is *fluid* because it is a circulating, consumable good. After a brief discussion of narrative in Smith's *Lectures on Jurisprudence,* I will look at three instances of sentiments in the law—specifically in laws governing inheritance, marriage, and slavery—to discuss the use and value of narrative in Smith's *Lectures.* In the latter part of the essay, by way of conclusion, I will discuss Smith's treatment of narrative as property.

Narrative

In addition to serving as a source for anecdotes and illustrations, history provides the narrative frame for Smith's lectures,[11] a device that J. G. A. Pocock observes was a mark of eighteenth-century theories of jurisprudence.[12] He cites Smith's *Lectures* as an example of juridical theories that employ "complex historical schemes" and a "nascent historicism" to address "tensions between virtue and commerce, ancient and modern"; Smith's particular goal, Pocock contends, was to "defend commerce against ancient virtue."[13] The historical trajectory that becomes the master narrative of Smith's *Lectures on Jurisprudence*, and does indeed defend modern commerce, appears early on in the lecture dated "Tuesday. February 22d 1763," where Smith suggests that government has evolved organically and has taken its shape as a result of "the natural progress which men make in society" (207). The process begins in what he calls "the Age of Hunters," followed by "the Age of Shepherds," "the Age of Agriculture," and finally, "the Age of Commerce" (14). This narrative frame is subsequently illustrated by the opening story noted above that offers a conjectural history: "[i]f we should suppose 10 or 12 persons of different sexes settled in an uninhabited island . . ." (140). The illustrative story works with the master narrative to clarify, instruct, and justify the role of law in a society; it is also a means to blend his system of ethics from *The Theory of Moral Sentiments* with his theory about the law. When a property dispute occurs in this conjectural history, the impartial spectator appears to moderate the disagreement and help the parties reach a just conclusion. Whereas imagination and sympathy are the operations of the impartial spectator, they are thereby embedded in the judicial process.[14]

While narrative gives an overall shape to Smith's *Lectures on Jurisprudence*, it also operates on a micro level in the foundational activity of a contract—and here too we find the impartial spectator at work. A contract, in Smith's theory, is utterly dependent on narrative construction. The validity of a contract (which involves both a promise and a dependence) is a function of the intention of the promisor and the expectation of the promisee. The legitimacy of the agreement is determined once again by the impartial spectator who plays the role of judge. By way of another conjectural narrative, Smith explains the process.

> If I should say that I intend to give you voluntarily £100 next new years day, but make this declaration in such a manner as plainly shews I don't intend you should depend upon it, and expressly say, 'You need not depend upon it, but this is my present design', the [impartial] spectator could not here imagine that he to whom I made the promise would have any reasonable expectation; but this without doubt he would, if I should plainly declare that I meant that he should depend upon it. (87)

By here invoking the impartial spectator, Smith renders the legal contract a representation of intention and expectation, as well as an object of observation and interpretation when the impartial spectator assesses the legitimacy of the agreement.[15] Smith thus narrativizes the event of the contract, and certainly any discussion of it thereafter.

Narrative and Sentiment

When the impartial spectator is present, we find a story, and we find sentiment. In Smith's larger narrative scheme, sentiment accounts for the internal motivations behind the evolutionary developments of legislation, which are throughout tied to economic advancements. Smith examines sentiment—variously defined by him as "motivation," "passion," "feeling," and "natural human dispositions"—in relation to governance (customs, laws, and punishment) to explain why we regard a particular action as legally just and another unjust.[16]

One of the earliest examples that Smith provides of sentiment at work in the law, and the corresponding functionality of narrative, is in relation to "testamentary succession"—that is, laws governing inheritance. He begins his exploration of this topic with a clarification of the logic behind what he states simply as "the transference of property from the dead to the living" (37), and a description of practice among the ancients and moderns. Notably, he locates his study of inheritance within his master narrative. "In the age of hunters," he writes, "there could be no room for succession as there was no property. . . . In the age of shepherds, when property was greatly extended, the goods the deceased had been possessed of were too valuable to be all buried along with him . . . the rest would go to other members of the family," and thus the practice of bequeathing property commences (39). Once Smith exhausts the logical and historical discussion of laws of inheritance, he begins to consider the emotions involved in the process of testamentary succession in modern societies.

Smith poses the questions: why do we abide by the wishes—recorded in a legal will—of a deceased person who has no power or knowledge of events after his death? Why should any man have control of his goods after they are no longer in his possession—in other words, why these laws governing inheritance? He first cites Pufendorf, who credits "the immortality of the soul." We honor "the will of the deceased," Pufendorf suggests, "supposing that he is still alive and wills in the same manner" (63). While not dismissing this explanation but rather recasting it, Smith moves the discussion away from matters of the divine toward human behavior driven by emotion. Smith's answer to the questions raised above is sentiment. In response to Pufendorf, Smith argues that "[t]he *regard* we all naturaly [*sic*] have to the will of a dying person seems to be sufficient to explain it" (63–64, my italics). At the time of a man's death "[w]e have a great *reverence* for his commands," and

the "piety" we feel for the deceased obliges us to respect his intentions (64, my italics). Regardless of the economic soundness of a bequeathal, we respond with respect and veneration.

Narrative is the mechanism through which we process or conceptualize these sentiments; it is also a rhetorical device in Smith's argument. To explain how we respond to a dying man, Smith employs a conjectural story: "[s]uppose a man on his death bed calls his friends together and entreats, beseeches, and conjures them to dispose of his goods in such or such a manner. . . . They would afterwards be, as it were, forced by their piety to the deceased person to dispose of his goods as he desired" (64). In this conjectural narrative, immersed in the emotions of piety and reverence, we then use narrative to guide our response to the wishes of a dying man. We would "*imagine* what he would think were he to see them disposing of them in a manner contrary to what they were so solemnly intreated" (64, my italics). After a man's death, "we do not consider what he willd [*sic*] [i.e., the legal document], but what if he was then alive would be his will [i.e., his intention]: we think, as we say, what would be his will if he should look up from the grave and see things going contrary to what he had enjoined" (64). In other words, we construct an imaginary narrative in which we play the role of witness (similar to the impartial spectator of the contract—but not impartial). We observe the will (the determinations, the desires) of the deceased, as if he were alive, and consequently feel a sense of obligation and responsibility to honor his wishes. These sentiments, then, conceptualized through narrative, inform our laws of inheritance and deem them just forms of legislation (309).

Laws that govern marriage, according to Smith, are particularly prone to the powers of sentiment, as well as partiality and prejudice. As he does for the topic of testamentary succession, Smith begins his study with a narrative history, this time of marriage laws, and he incorporates into that narrative a study of the emotions—"jealousy" and "the passion of love" in particular—that influence legislation. When legislative power shifts from the clergy to secular legislators, Smith observes that it is nonclerical men who make the laws, and because these legislators are usually husbands, they are concerned parties when it comes to the governance of marriage. Whereas they were not allowed to marry, "clergy were much more impartiall [*sic*] judges" when it came to issues of matrimony such as infidelity. However, legislators, as married men, are "a party concerned" and "they generally will be inclined to curb the women as much as possible and give themselves the more indulgence" (147). In addition, Smith suggests that in contracts of marriage, the husband is justly superior to the wife because "the injury done to his honour and love will be more grievous, all injuries done to a superior by an inferior are more sensibly felt than those which are done to an inferior by one whom they look upon as above them" (147).

The acts of polygamy and incest have been rendered illegal, Smith argues, in part because of the emotions they provoke. Polygamy, according to Smith, is a "species of marriage" that has been allowed "[i]n all the eastern countries," though not in the west, nor in ancient Greece and Rome. "[W]hen polygamy is allowed," Smith writes, "the wife is taken to be one of 4, 5, 10, 20, 100 wives; this is the condition, and there can not be said to be any injury done her when she finds herself in that situation" (150). However, Smith admits, while polygamy may not be illegal in these cultures, "yet it is productive of many bad consequences" (151). For the wives it creates "the greatest misery, as jealousy of every sort, discord, and enmity must inevitably attend it." The children are "greatly neglected in every shape and lead but a very wretched life." The husband "to whose happiness or rather pleasure the good of all the rest seems to be sacrificed, . . . also has no great enjoyment. He is racked by the most tormenting jealousy and has little enjoyment from the affections of his family or the intercourse of other men" (159). The result is a family driven into "confusion and disorder" by the emotional workings of jealousy and an unproductive self-interest (152).

Degrees of consanguinity are deemed to be violations of the law because they transgress the natural hierarchy of the family and therefore elicit emotions either unnatural or contrary to the well-being of a family. Marriage to an ascendant or descendant turns the structure of a family upside down. A marriage between a mother and son renders the mother, who should be superior to her son, an inferior to him as a wife; less egregious is a father marrying a daughter because the daughter/wife, in both roles, is inferior to her father. The greatest danger is a relationship between brothers and sisters because of "[t]he constant intercourse betwixt them who generally are bred up together, and the many opportunities as well as the great incitements this connection would give them" (164). As the hierarchy of the family is disturbed, so would be the emotions that maintain the proper structure of the family. The father, whose responsibility it is to be a "guardian and tutor" to his daughter and "educate her in all sort of virtues and instill into her the purest morals and the chastest affections," would become her seducer, "for there is always some seduction necessary to persuade one to be a wife" (163). Both parents would see themselves as in competition with their children. "The mother would look on her daughter in a very dissagreable [*sic*] and even a jealous light when there was the least prospect that she might some time fill her place in the marriage bed, and in the same manner the father could not behold his son with pleasure when he thought there was a possibility of his taking his place as the husband of his wife" (164). Suitors would be reluctant to court a young woman with brothers for fear that she has been corrupted. Incest is illegal, therefore, not only because it runs counter to reason but also because it would be "shocking and abominable" (166).

Smith's narrative on the history of marriage evolves concomitantly with an analysis of shifting conceptions of the cultural role of love. On this occasion, rather than use conjectural stories, Smith turns to literature for evidence. In this relationship between law and literature, the law is the dominant agent, causing an alteration in the way society views love, which in turn is manifested in the literature of the time. In the midst of his history of marriage laws, Smith observes that in ancient cultures marriage was informally entered into, "there was no more required than the mutual consent of the parties" (148). It was also easily dissoluble; "[t]he choice of the person was of no very great importance, as the union might be dissolved at any time" (150). As a result, love was regarded as "very silly and ridiculous" (149). Smith points to literature as proof: "[w]e see that there [are] no poems of a serious nature grounded on that subject either amongst the Greeks or Romans" (149). Additionally, he notes that the passions depicted in the great tragedies and epic poems are "anger, hatred, revenge, [and] ambition," but rarely love—and when love is present as a subject, it is peripheral to other emotions and actions (149). The frequency and ease of divorce "made the gratification of it [love] of no great moment: it could be today, it might be to morrow, and if not this year it might be the next; and one might find another object as agreable [*sic*] as the former" (149–50).

However, when in modern times marriages became difficult to dissolve, the cultural conception of love changed. Smith notes that "[t]he choice of the object of this passion, which is commonly the forerunner of marriage, became a matter of the greatest importance. . . . From that time therefore we find that love makes the subject of all our tragedies and romances, a species of epic poems till this time" (150). Consequently, as love becomes more significant because laws governing marriage are much stricter, love plays a more prominent role in literature. "It is become from a contemptible a respectable passion," Smith argues, "as it leads to a union of such great importance, and accordingly makes the subject of all our publick entertainments, plays, operas, etc." (150). Narrative here provides the evidence of a shift in the sentiments of love.

The final example of sentiment, narrative, and the law that I will mention here is one of Smith's most compelling. Smith takes on the issue of slavery, and, though opposed generally to servitude that imposes dependence, he is largely pessimistic about the abolition of slaves. He comments on the negative economic impact of outlawing slavery: "To abolish slavery . . . would be to deprive the far greater part of the subjects, and the nobles in particular, of the chief and most valuable part of their substance" (187). Yet beyond the economic concerns, what remains a considerable hindrance to the abolition of slavery are the sentiments that attach to it—and thus we have another instance in which emotion influences the law and determines what actions a culture deems to be just. Smith sees man's natural disposition to dominate, control, and tyrannize as the primary operable force, and an impossible force to counter precisely because it is a natural propensity (187). Provocatively, Smith identifies the source of this disposition as "love," but it is the human "love of domination and tyrannizing," and that love, Smith argues, "will make it impossible for the slaves in a free country ever to recover their liberty" (186). The sentiment of pleasure is also to blame, "the pleasure men take in having every thing done by their express orders, rather than to condescend to bargain and treat with those whom they look upon as their inferiors and are inclined to use in a haughty way" (186). In

Smith's view of slavery, the love of domination and the pleasure derived from control over presumed inferiors take precedent over the more rational system of economic benefit that was so often used to justify slavery.

Still, economics does come into play when Smith examines variations in the treatment of slaves, which, Smith suggests, will be determined by economics. Smith addresses the more familiar sentiments of sympathy and compassion, associated with abolitionists' movements, when he notes that slavery can be more or less humane given the economic status of slave owners and the economic health of the nation at large. Slavery in a poor country, Smith argues, will be more tolerable than slavery in a rich nation because of a difference in sympathy. In a poor country a slave is not substantively very different from his master, who is likely to be a farmer. The farmer and the slave, Smith writes, "will eat at the same table, work together, and be cloathed [*sic*] in the same manner" (184). On this common ground, the master will be able to identify and sympathize with his slave, and he will be inclined to treat him more humanely. In a society where there is a wider gap in economic status, where "[a] man of great fortune, a nobleman, is much farther removed from the condition of his servant than a farmer," a slave is more likely to be mistreated because the master cannot sympathize or identify with the slave (184). It is a matter of economic and emotional proximity. "Those persons," Smith argues, "most excite our compassion and are most apt to affect our sympathy who most resemble ourselves, and the greater the difference the less we are affected by them" (184). Once Smith invokes sympathy, he also invokes imagination—and narrative. As we know from Smith's *The Theory of Moral Sentiments*, in sympathy, "we have no immediate experience of what other men feel, . . . but by conceiving what we ourselves should feel in the like situation."[17] This experience of fellow-feeling summons the imagination and requires the construction of a representation—that is, a story.[18] Smith uses a story—a conjectural anecdote—to explain the operations of sympathy; he asks us to imagine our brother on the rack, and while we cannot experience our brother's pain directly, we can imagine ourselves in his situation, we can "conceive ourselves enduring all the same torments."[19] We engage in a narrative process to understand the sufferings of slaves, to sympathize with them, and thus to treat them with more humanity. Narrative, therefore, functions to counterbalance the love and pleasure associated with domination. The story invoked in the act of sympathy might lead to more humane treatment, although it does not overwhelm our proclivity toward tyranny and control over perceived inferiors—and thus, according to Smith, slavery will persist.

Lastly, as he does for so many of his points, Smith uses narrative rhetorically in his review of slavery laws. As he does so, he complicates the operations of sentiment and offers us a possibly sanguine solution to the propensity of slavery. Smith tells one story of abolition—its success driven by one of the most powerful sentiments in Smith's juridical theory: self-interest. In this instance, the sentiment of self-interest proves to be more powerful than the love of tyranny alone. The narrative, which is a historical one, is set in feudal Europe, where the clergy's authority was chiefly over the slaves. To increase the power of the church (assuming they would enjoy complete control over these newly independent people), the clergy advocated for the slaves' emancipation. Likewise, the kings promoted abolition because they saw it as an opportunity to recover power from the nobles (who were the predominant slave owners). These two instances of self-interest coincide, and as a result, the kings' courts worked to decrease the authority of the nobles and to favor the slaves (in particular those designated as "speciall [*sic*] villains" or copyholders), and soon slavery was abolished. This historical narrative provides an exception to Smith's pessimistic view of the viability of abolition. It also allows him to demonstrate not only the power of self-interest, but also the social value of self-interest—its usefulness in advancing and modernizing a society.

Narrative as Property

As argued above, narrative is a distinguishing feature of Smith's *Lectures on Jurisprudence*; the integral presence of property is another.[20] Narrative in the *Lectures* is a property of great value because it aids in accounting for sentiment in the law and because it is versatile, temporal, and contingent and thus has the quality of fluidity that Smith identifies as a feature of the most beneficial property. For Smith, property is both the end (purpose) of law and the substance of juridical thought. Smith defines jurisprudence as "the theory of the rules" or "the general principles" by which "civil governments ought to be directed" (5). The design of civil government is composed of four branches, all of which are grounded in property: (1) to maintain justice (meaning, protecting property and rights); (2) to promote opulence through policing; (3) to encourage and protect the revenue of the state; (4) to establish laws of peace and war (to maintain or increase property), (5–7). In defining rights (specifically, "real rights" in civil law), Smith categorizes them in another group of four—and, once again, all have to do with property: (1) Dominion (of property); (2) Servitus (giving up some part of the full right of property); (3) Pignus (debt or pledge); (4) Haereditas (inheritance of property). Moreover, Smith provides several examples (in the form of cause-and-effect narratives) of how economic development generates changes in legislation and forms of civil government.

Smith's master narrative, Nicholas Phillipson argues, was a theorizing of Hume's theory of rights in which property emerges as "the mother of the civilizing process." Phillipson observes that Smith's jurisprudence was "derived from a conjectural history of property that explained the evolutionary process by which a society progresses from its savage to its pastoral, feudal and commercial stages of development."[21] In other words, Smith's master narrative is driven by Smith's interest in property and his view that it has been *the* central force in moving society forward. If we return to Smith's story of the ten or twelve persons on an uninhabited island, we see that each major shift, from the age of hunters to the age of shepherds, for example, is driven by the need to accumulate property—in this instance, animals. By the time populations increase and a society develops to the point of requiring agriculture and then a division of labor, the people "would exchange with one another what they produced more than was necessary for their support, and get in exchange for them the commodities they stood in need of and did not produce themselves." Property then moves from accumulation to trade—trade "not only betwixt the individuals of the same society but betwixt those of different nations" (15–16). This last step in Smith's narrative brings us to the age of commerce.

Jurisprudence emerges when property needs to be protected.[22] In his opening lecture, dated December 24, 1762, Smith proclaims that "[t]he first and chief design of every system of government is to maintain justice; to prevent the members of a society from encroaching on one anothers property, or seizing what is not their own." The purpose of the law is "to give each one the secure and peaceable possession of his own property" (5). Providing a hint of what is to come in his theory of government, Smith also suggests that when individual security is established, "the government will next be desirous of promoting the opulence of the state," which in turn will require police, who will be supported by "the revenue of the kingdom or the state" (5–6). By the time a society has developed into a modern one, protection of property is protection of liberty, and while a judge "will to such an early nation appear very terrible," he is "now rather a comfortable . . . sight as he is the source of our liberty, our independence, and our security" (313). Thus, embedded in Smith's juridical theory are the processes of the accumulation, trade, and protection of property.

In his master narrative, Smith posits a theory that works against the dominant contractarian theories of his time.[23] Smith takes issue with the idea that an initial contract, a "very figurative metaphoricall [*sic*] consent" between "first members" of a society, binds the generations that follow (316, 323). Having taken such a position, one might expect to see Smith align himself with a view of government and legislation dependent on prescription and precedent. However, Smith's focus on property as a catalyst for, and determinative force in, jurisprudence moves his theory into an economic terrain that privileges trade and embraces a principle of utility. Addressing the duties of citizenship within a community—such as loyalty to a sovereign and a compliance with the law—Smith argues that it is not allegiance to a preexisting contract but rather a natural disposition to respect authority that brings about obedience. The "duty of allegiance"—which, like respect and obedience, is a form of sentiment—is based, first, on a "principle of authority" that prevails both in the family (children respect the authority of parents) and in the state (subjects respect the monarchy). Allegiance is based, second, on "the principall [*sic*] of common or generall [*sic*] interest" (318), which leads to the principle of utility. The former prevails in a monarchy, the latter in a republic; both, one may conclude, are at work in a constitutional monarchy such as exists in Britain.[24] Though Smith acknowledges the foundational

function of the principle of authority, his interests clearly lie in the power of common or general interests. While self-interest operates in the principle of authority—families of fortune are best served by a monarchy rather than a republic—it has more range in the principle of utility or common interest. A population at large, he argues, will see that obeying authority will be to its personal advantage and that without law, "all will fall into confusion" (318–22). At stake for all is the security of property, including property in the self.

In his opposition to contractarianism and support of a monarchical authority modified by utility, Smith betrays a significant concern that colors much of his juridical theory—that is, a reluctance to bind government (and its legislation) too strongly to the past because economic interests necessitate looking and moving forward. The only contract that binds posterity, according to Smith, is a financial one: a debt that encumbers an estate and must be paid by heirs. Smith is averse to laws or customs that impede the movement of property. He refers to the custom of entails as "absurd" and of primogeniture as "contrary to nature, to reason, and to justice"—a throwback to feudal governance (49, 70). His opposition is grounded in the fact that both customs "exclude lands intirely [*sic*] from commerce" (70). He explains,

> The interest of the state requires that lands should be as much in commerce as any other goods. . . . the right of primogeniture and the power of making entails have been the causes of the almost total bad husbandry that prevails in those countrys [*sic*] where they are in use.—When land is in commerce and frequently changes hands it is most likely to be well managed; those who have raised a fortune by trade or otherwise have generally money besides what they lay out. They are generally also men of scheme and project, so that they for the most part have both the desire and the ability of improving. Those on the other hand who possess old family estates seldom have any money besides. . . . We see accordingly that lands which lie near great towns, which frequently change masters, are much better cultivated than those which lie at a distance from them and continue long in one family.—The estate of a great family stands very little chance of being farther improvd [*sic*] than it is at present. . . . If this estate was divided into a number of small possessions each having a separate master, it would soon be cultivated to a high degree. (70)

Thus, the property that is most fluid—that is dispersed, that is bought, sold, and circulated—is the most useful and the most valuable. Law, whose purpose it is to protect property, must respond to and embrace this fluidity.

In Smith's theory of jurisprudence, sentiment has a profound and lasting effect on the law and legislation; moreover, in some instances law has influenced cultural conceptions of sentiments. Narrative articulates sentiment—the workings of the heart—in the law; it is integral to juridical processes and influences our views of justice.[25] Narrative as a form of property proves itself valuable to Smith because in its various roles it meets the foundational principle of utility; it is useful to the "common or generall [*sic*] interest" (318). Historical narrative provides a helpful frame; it lends the stability of logic, reason, order, and a linear progression to a theory of jurisprudence. It clarifies and educates. For the contract, narrative offers a means to evaluate its legitimacy. When a promise is made between two parties, the impartial spectator not only witnesses the promise but also interprets it to assess its viability and justice. Laws of inheritance seem just to us because of the reverence and piety we feel and because we can construct an imaginary narrative in which we observe the will of the deceased as if he were alive. Shifts in conceptions of love, which guide laws of marriage, are evidenced by the literature of the time. Finally, laws of slavery may be driven by the human love of domination; however, the role of narrative in sympathy, along with the sentiment of self-interest, might serve to alter those laws governing slavery.

Narrative is useful to Smith, but for narrative as property to reach the height of its worth in Smith's economic design, it must also be fluid. Despite Smith's insistence that the clearest language is the best language[26] and that the rules of law should be modeled on the precise, stable rules of grammar,[27] narrative is of value to Smith because of the properties we now attribute to it: intertextuality, instability, and contingency. Much recent work on Smith finds continuity between his economic, ethical, juridical, and rhetorical theories. For example, economic historian Vivienne Brown borrows the Bakhtinian notions of dialogism and heteroglossia to make an argument about consistency between Smith's texts. *The Lectures on Jurisprudence*, in particular, support her claim because much that Smith says in the lectures is based on or replicates points made in *The Theory of Moral Sentiments* and anticipates arguments later developed in *The Wealth of Nations*.[28] David Lieberman sees *Lectures on Jurisprudence* to be "the illuminating collective tissue between Smith's two great and enduring published contributions to moral and social theory [TMS and WN]."[29] The replicated concepts and accompanying narratives circulate between texts—dialogue with each other—and thereby reinforce ideas and develop and clarify points.

The instability of the text is embedded in the publication story of *The Lectures on Jurisprudence*. Smith's lecture notes were burned in the week before his death (at his own request), and what have subsequently been published are rewritten notes taken at (or even after) the lectures. In the case of Smith's *Lectures on Rhetoric and Belles Lettres*, the manuscript, which is also composed of observers' notes, is written in different hands (primarily two).[30] Thus we have a case of mediated authorship that will always challenge fixed assumptions about Smith's intentions. This instability gives wide range to interpretation of Smith's theories and renders the two lecture series more dependent on Smith's other published works, such as *The Theory of Moral Sentiments* and *The Wealth of Nations*, that corroborate ideas recorded in the lecture notes. The contingent reproduction of his lectures shatters any notion of a discernible truth, and in a parallel fashion, Smith's embrace of historicity in explaining the developments of jurisprudence casts the law as historically contingent and therefore subject to change.[31]

Narrative is valuable in Smith's jurisprudence because of its hermeneutical fluidity; it is also advantageous because of its authorial and physical fluidity. First, in the instance of the contract, the agreement must be "read" by the impartial spectator, thereby shifting the focus away from the author of the agreement to the reader of it. The meaning of the contract does not inhere in the promisor but in the reading of the promisor's intentions by the impartial spectator. Second, in the numerous historical narratives of the lectures, we see the movement of circulation, which is so important to Smith's economic theory. Smith defines narrative as "facts," which are located in the public domain.[32] When narrativizing history, a historian appropriates the facts temporarily, applies his or her individual style (which, according to Smith, must be natural to the author), and presents those facts in keeping with his or her goal of informing, teaching, or persuading. Once transformed into discourse, the facts make their way back into the public domain. While Smith suggests what might be the most effective means of styling an historical narration, he always defers to what is the "natural disposition" of the author, validating multiple forms of narration for the same set of facts.[33] Third, and finally, narrative in its conjectural form becomes a consumable good. The numerous stories that begin "suppose a man lends another man . . . ," or "suppose a servant walks into a shop . . . ," are situational and temporal. They are created to serve a particular purpose, to answer a specific need of illustrating a point, and then they are, in a sense, abandoned—or, one might say, already consumed. Their value does not extend beyond the immediate conceptualization of an abstraction. However, these conjectural narratives are indeed valuable because as Smith argues, "[i]t is the consumptibility of a thing which makes it usefull [*sic*]" (390).

In the culminating stage of Smith's master narrative—the age of commerce—we see a particular instance of narrative satisfying Smith's two principles of utility and fluidity when he identifies as our natural disposition, our natural sentiment, for bartering or "trucking" (347).

Narrative, once again, situates the law in this age of commerce. We might say it acts as a bridge between the "rules of civil government" and what Smith designates as the ultimate purpose of law in the age of commerce: providing and protecting the everyday necessities of life, such as "meat, drink, raiment, and lodging for men" (338). Narrative, which inheres in and can meander through the general principles of jurisprudence, also grounds those principles in the material necessities of life—the very substance of commerce—and in doing so, enables the law to adjust itself to the ever-shifting demands of commerce. Narrative helps a society release itself from the restrictions of the past and move forward into a place where the traffic of sentiments is always moving and the corresponding law is always developing.

Notes

1. See Vivienne Brown, *Adam Smith's Discourse: Canonicity, Commerce, and Conscience* (New York: Routledge, 1994); Charles Griswold, Jr., *Adam Smith and the Virtues of Enlightenment* (Cambridge: Cambridge University Press, 1999); Emma Rothschild, *Economic Sentiments: Adam Smith, Condorcet, and the Enlightenment* (Cambridge, MA: Harvard University Press, 2001); Jerry Evensky, *Adam Smith's Moral Philosophy* (Cambridge: Cambridge University Press, 2005).

2. Dugald Stewart, "Account of the Life and Writings of Adam Smith, L.L.D.," in *Essays on Philosophical Subjects*, ed. W. P. D. Wightman and J. C. Bryce, vol. 3, *The Glasgow Edition of the Works and Correspondence of Adam Smith* (Oxford: Clarendon Press, 1980), 291.

3. Griswold, *Adam Smith*, 59–60.

4. I am using H. Porter Abbott's definition of narrative: "the representation of an event or a series of events." See H. Porter Abbott, *The Cambridge Introduction to Narrative* (Cambridge University Press, 2002), 12. Smith himself defines "narrative" as an unbiased account of facts; if a narrative deviates into "proposition" and "proof," it then becomes a didactic or oratorical composition. See Adam Smith, *Lectures on Rhetoric and Belles Lettres*, ed. J. C. Bryce, vol. 4, *The Glasgow Edition of the Works and Correspondence of Adam Smith* (Indianapolis, IN: Liberty Fund, 1985), 89–90.

5. Evensky, *Adam Smith's Moral Philosophy*, 16–19. Jerry Evensky has cited Smith's use of narrative history to examine the fundamental human principles behind "the broad flow of humankind's evolution." Fabrizio Simon notes Smith's use of "historical inquiry" as a means to "discover and underline the intimate link between rights—particularly acquired rights—the development of the institutional framework, and the evolution of economic conditions." See Fabrizio Simon, "Adam Smith and the Law," in *The Oxford Handbook of Adam Smith* (Oxford: Oxford University Press, 2013), 395. See also David Lieberman, "Adam Smith on Justice, Rights, and Law," in *The Cambridge Companion to Adam Smith*, ed. Knud Haakonssen (Cambridge: Cambridge University Press, 2006), 225–30.

6. Adam Smith, *Lectures on Jurisprudence*, ed. R. L. Meek, D. D. Raphael, and P. G. Stein, vol. 5, *The Glasgow Edition of the Works and Correspondence of Adam Smith* (Indianapolis, IN: Liberty Fund, 1982), 14. Subsequent references to this text will be given parenthetically. This story is an example of what Dugald Stewart called "conjectural history." See J. C. Bryce, introduction to *Lectures on Rhetoric and Belles Lettres* by Adam Smith (Indianapolis, IN: Liberty Fund, 1985), 24.

7. R. L. Meek, D. D. Raphael, and P. G. Stein, introduction to *Lectures on Jurisprudence* by Adam Smith (Indianapolis, IN: Liberty Fund, 1982), 1–42. The published *Lectures* are rewritten versions of notes taken at the lectures; therefore, while Smith's editors believe them to be highly accurate, they are not Smith's personal record. There are two reports, the first from the 1762–1763 session and the second most likely from the 1763–1764 session (5). Meek, Raphael, and Stein note that the primary difference is the order in which Smith covers the topics of property, domestic law, government, and police (22). Nicholas Phillipson suggests that Smith began working on his theory of jurisprudence in 1750–1751 when he lectured in Edinburgh. See Nicholas Phillipson, *Adam Smith: An Enlightened Life* (New Haven, CT: Yale University Press, 2010), 105, 108.

8. Phillipson, *Adam Smith*, 89.

9. Rothschild, *Economic Sentiments*, 9.

10. John Guillory notes both the "convergence" and "definitive separation" of aesthetics and political economy in Smith's "concept of the commodity." See John Guillory, *Cultural Capital: The Problem of Literary Canon Formation* (Chicago: The University of Chicago Press, 1993), 315.

11. Phillipson, *Adam Smith*, 101.

12. J. G. A. Pocock, *Virtue, Commerce, and History* (Cambridge: Cambridge University Press, 1985), 49.

13. Pocock, *Virtue, Commerce, and History*, 49–50.

14. Smith begins his exploration of "justice" in *The Theory of Moral Sentiments*. See Lieberman, 216.

15. For a discussion of the impartial spectator and justice in Smith's *The Theory of Moral Sentiments*, see Simon, "Adam Smith and the Law," 401–2. See also Lieberman, "Adam Smith on Justice, Rights, and Law," 216–18.

16. Rothschild, *Economic Sentiments*, 7–9; see also Simon, "Adam Smith and the Law," 400–408.

17. Adam Smith, *The Theory of Moral Sentiments*, ed. D. D. Raphael and A. L. Macfie, vol. 1, *The Glasgow Edition of the Works and Correspondence of Adam Smith* (Indianapolis, IN: Liberty Fund), 9.

18. Smith provides other instances of the effects of sympathy on the law. One is our response to punishment. In cases of property, he observes that trials can be protracted, but in cases of criminal violations, trials are often swift, and that is because the public sympathizes with the victim. This sympathy kicks into gear the subsequent emotions of passion, urgency, and gratification. "The whole of criminal law," Smith argues, "is founded on the fellow feeling we have with the resentment of the injured person. Revenge, as we commonly say, is a hasty passion: it wont [*sic*] wait for a delay of its gratification but demands it immediately, and the prosecution dictated by our fellow feellings [*sic*] partakes of the rapidity of the passion they were excited by. But there does not appear to be any thing so urgent in a demand for 40 shs." *Lectures on Jurisprudence*, 277. Sympathy and punishment are more thoroughly explored in part II of *The Theory of Moral Sentiments*.

19. Smith, *The Theory of Moral Sentiments*, 9–10.

20. Fabrizio Simon argues that in an analysis of Smith's juridical theory, as well as that of most other eighteenth-century jurists, "it would be unfair to dissect and separate economic, juridical, and political themes." While he distinguishes Smith from others such as Beccaria and Bentham, who offer a distinctly economic analysis of the law, he suggests that "in Smith, economy, law, and politics are all part of only one science: Jurisprudence." Simon, "Adam Smith and the Law," 412.

21. Phillipson, *Adam Smith*, 108.

22. Phillipson again notes the connection here to Hume, who claims that the goal of governance is to protect property. Phillipson, *Adam Smith*, 110.

23. Simon, "Adam Smith and the Law," 393, 410.

24. Smith draws party lines when he attributes the principle of authority to the Tories and the principle of utility, based on general interest, to the Whigs. He also reveals his skepticism when he writes that the Tories "pretend" the divine sanctioning of the king. Smith observes that the predilection for either principle has to do with money; those with a great fortune, who want to protect it, will no doubt prefer the principle of authority. *Lectures on Jurisprudence*, 319–20.

25. The vast body of work in the field of law and literature addresses the diverse roles of narrative in juridical processes and theory. See, for example, Anthony G. Amsterdam and Jerome S. Bruner, *Minding the Law* (Cambridge, MA: Harvard University Press, 2000); Peter Brooks and Paul Gewirtz, *Law's Stories: Narrative and Rhetoric in the Law* (New Haven, CT: Yale University Press, 1998); Jerome S. Bruner, *Making Stories: Law, Literature, Life* (Cambridge, MA: Harvard University Press, 2003); Richard A. Posner, *Law and Literature: A Misunderstood Relation*, 3rd ed. (Cambridge, MA: Harvard University Press, 2009); Austin Sarat, Matthew Anderson, and Catherine O. Frank, *Law and the Humanities: An Introduction* (Cambridge: Cambridge University Press, 2010); Ian Ward, *Law and Literature: Possibilities and Perspectives* (Cambridge: Cambridge University Press, 1995); James Boyd White, *The Legal Imagination: Studies in the Nature of Legal Thought and Expression* (Boston: Little Brown, 1973).

26. Smith, *Lectures on Jurisprudence*, 275.

27. Smith, *The Theory of Moral Sentiments*, 175.

28. Vivienne Brown notes that the lectures on jurisprudence have been considered an "interpretive bridge" between *The Theory of Moral Sentiments* and *The Wealth of Nations*. See Brown, *Adam Smith's Discourse*, 101.

29. Lieberman, "Adam Smith on Justice, Rights, and Law," 216.

30. Bryce, introduction to *Lectures on Rhetoric and Belles Lettres* by Adam Smith, 3. Bryce observes that there are minor emendations made by a third hand, probably a later owner of the manuscripts.

31. The exception for Smith, and many other theorists of the law, are those laws that protect natural rights. See Simon, "Adam Smith and the Law," 395. For a discussion of historical contingency in Smith's *Lectures on Jurisprudence*, see Lieberman, "Adam Smith on Justice, Rights, and Law," 225.

32. Smith, *Lectures on Rhetoric and Belles Lettres*, 149, 101.

33. Smith, *Lectures on Rhetoric and Belles Lettres*, 35, 55–56.

J. T. Scanlan

"How Like You the Eloquence of a Young Barrister?": Love and the Law in Boswell's Development as a Writer in the Late 1760s

I SUSPECT MOST READERS OF THIS COLLECTION WILL HAVE AT least a casual knowledge of Boswell's lubricious *London Journal 1762–1763*, first published to astonishing international popularity in late 1950—just about the same time, as the general editor of the Yale Boswell Editions Gordon Turnbull shrewdly notes, Alfred C. Kinsey's hugely successful *Sexual Behavior in the Human Male* (1948) appeared.[1] Boswell's energetic, comic, postadolescent depiction of himself among London actresses and ladies of quality has become standard fare in university courses in the English-speaking world. "You must know Madam, I run up & down this town, just like a wild colt." The response of the woman he designates "Lady Mirabel"? "Why Sir then, dont you stray into my stable, amongst others?"[2] Evidently, Boswell cut an appealing figure in London in his early twenties. In the words of Frederick Pottle, young James, after a timid and grave childhood, emerged into adulthood a "vain, noisy, bouncing, odd, comical, good humoured youth of manly features and masculine bearing whom many men and most women found immediately attractive."[3] It's worth reminding ourselves that a good number of the best writers and scholars of the day liked him, too. Johnson was not alone in his love for "Bozzy." And Boswell's friendships lasted for many years. Two days after Boswell died suddenly on

May 19, 1795, in his mid-fifties, Edmond Malone, the great Shakespearean scholar and Irish lawyer, wrote a letter to another friend, confessing what Boswell had meant to him over the course of a long friendship: "I shall miss him more and more every day. He was in the constant habit of calling upon me almost daily, and I used to grumble sometimes at his turbulence; but now miss and regret his noise and his hilarity and his perpetual good humour, which had no bounds. Poor fellow, he has somehow stolen away from us without any notice, and without my being at all prepared for it."[4] Malone's words capture what many literary men felt about Boswell.

But Boswell's many demons hint at a troubled life. Boswell did stray into many stables when in London, but often into the stables of common prostitutes, not Lady Mirabel's. Boswell typically fell, perhaps literally, toward one of them after a night of many toasts and protracted wine or port drinking. Boswell's many cases of gonorrhea, probably contracted from women from a range of backgrounds, demanded that he spend an astonishing amount of his life "confined," as he puts it, waiting for the symptoms to subside. Prone to extended periods of "melancholy," Boswell had other debilitating, unattractive traits. Commenting on Macaulay's condemnatory perspective on Boswell, Russell Fraser in the *Sewanee Review* writes that Boswell was "impertinent, shallow, servile, and pedantic, a bigot and a sot, a talebearer, an eavesdropper, and a common butt."[5] Although Fraser is perhaps excessively combative in pungently listing Boswell's weaknesses, he does capture an underside of Boswell's life that tends not to receive much sustained attention—an underside consisting of habits that, as he got older, certainly didn't nurture his writing. As many scholars have pointed out, Boswell's life was so troubled during the 1780s that without the encouragement and help of his dear friend Malone, Boswell undoubtedly never would have finished "my Life of Dr. Johnson the most important, perhaps *now* the only concern of any consequence that I ever shall have in this world,"[6] as he wrote in a letter to Malone. That said, Malone's inestimable contribution to his fascinating but radically flawed friend leaves unanswered a crucial question that has perplexed scholars for years: How, really, could such a man have written such a great book?

To be sure, many scholars have wrestled with this question. Some have accentuated Boswell's longstanding interest in theater, and more broadly, narrative, underscoring Boswell's own statement in the *Life of Johnson* that he's attempting to write a life "in scenes." But explanations of Boswell as quasi-dramatist or quasi-novelist, while extremely valuable, go only so far in capturing the essence of the *Life of Johnson* and Boswell's ability to create a great work of biographical art.[7] And they tend not to confront the implications of an important lacuna in the vast treasure trove of Boswelliana that Geoffrey Scott, one of the great Boswellians, noticed long ago: in all the piles of Boswell's papers, "we overhear the groans of authorship; but we are witnessing the contrition of an idler or perplexities of a scholar, never the doubts, still less the despairs of an artist. . . . Of his power to give life to the vast pile [of his Johnsonian materials] he never hints one doubt."[8] When Boswell does write about his own writing, his writes mainly about authentic, reliable documents. His approach, if that's even the right word, seems oddly prosaic. So what in his upbringing or his education or his personal life prepared him to present to the world such a lasting, magisterial achievement? How, really, did he manage to do it?

In my view, the underestimated element is his life in the law, which required him to develop skills in just the kinds of intellectual tasks that enabled him to shape his material into a work of permanent literature: detailed, argumentative writing and a comprehensive presentation of reliable, relevant evidence. The years he spent in the late 1760s as a young lawyer in Edinburgh, scurrying about for business and writing page after page of legal petitions, answers, replies, memorials, and other exacting legal prose works, mark an important moment in his literary education. All these works conditioned him to write about the world in part through a legal lens, and this habit never left him. His developing skill in speaking in public on legal issues—to clients, judges, and fellow lawyers—also honed at this time in various legal settings in Edinburgh—strengthened his ability to draw out people. This work schooled him in interpreting specific people for others, and this characteristic of his legal work also never left him. And while scholars have obviously examined his work in the law, most have tended to present it as in conflict somehow with his work in "literature." But that's the problem. To be sure, Boswell himself distinguished between a legal career and a career loosely defined as connected to other kinds of writing, including poetry. Without a doubt, Boswell, perhaps like all lawyers at all times, complained of how plodding legal business can be. But as a long line of criticism has taught us, biographers, critics, and literary historians should view with suspicion what authors say about themselves and their own habits of writing. A better strategy is to look at the writing itself and see what it can tell us. And if we look at Boswell's writing in his Journal in the late 1760s, and align it with the vast outpouring of legal writing he completed in the late 1760s, a different picture of Boswell in his late twenties emerges. These are the years that for Boswell constitute a gradual turning point in his life of writing.

Certainly Boswell's doubts about beginning a long career in the law are directly associated with the strong presence, in public and in private, of his father, Alexander Boswell, who was one of the most important legal figures in Scotland at the time Boswell had to decide on the choice of a career. His father's public presence, especially at this time, was surely imposing. Alexander Boswell (1706–1782) himself had a father who was an advocate, and like his own father, he attended the University of Leiden, a prominent center of both academic publishing and the so-called "New Science" in the early eighteenth century. In 1727, shortly before he graduated from the University of Leiden in December, he followed the path of his father and was admitted to the Faculty of Advocates in July. By 1754, he rose to become a justice in Scotland's Court of Session in Edinburgh, taking the title Lord Auchinleck. A year later he became a member of the Court of Justiciary, the criminal court. By all accounts, Alexander Boswell, Lord Auchinleck, was widely respected as a jurist. Notably, he rose to the Court of Session in the middle of the eighteenth century, when legal distinction, rather than political favor, characterized the principal qualifications of the justices.[9] And he was involved in important cases, some with shaping influence. *John Hinton v Alexander Donaldson and Others* (1773),[10] for example, held that perpetual copyright did not extend to London booksellers in Scotland. This cause, together with *Donaldson v Beckett* (1774), an English case in the House of Lords, became "the basis of modern copyright law in both countries."[11]

In private, Boswell's father could be imposing. He was well known to be rather distant and domineering to his three sons, and young James Boswell ran off to London in 1760 in part to escape his uncompromising father, who hoped his eldest son would follow him into the law. Lord Auchinleck, young Boswell often felt, in the words of Frank Brady, could be "cold and unimaginative."[12] In September of 1767, when Boswell was in his late twenties, he writes as much to William Johnson Temple, a friend from the University of Edinburgh: "How unaccountable is it that my father and I should be so ill together! He is a man of sense and a man of worth. But from some unhappy turn in his disposition, he is much dissatisfied with a son whom you know."[13] Irma Lustig summarizes what has become a widely held view on Boswell's relation with his father: "Since the publication of James Boswell's papers in the twentieth century Lord Auchinleck has been identified as the embittered father in a classic struggle: well-meaning and generous on his own terms but authoritarian, cold, and harsh—'If my sons are idiots, can I help it?' As he lay dying, his heir [James Boswell] 'wept; for alas! There was no affect between us.'"[14]

But as we shall see, on many occasions—and particularly when he was working on his legal writing—James Boswell felt differently about his father. In fact, he comes to respect, and comprehend and understand, his father's contributions to the law. And if we look at the relevant materials afresh—a good portion of which is newly published[15]—a different picture of Boswell comes into focus. And the picture is one of a young man hitting his stride as a writer, in part because of the help of his father. After some difficult times while studying at the University of Utrecht, James Boswell, with the help of his father, passes the Scots bar in July 1766 and becomes an advocate—a legal position similar to that of a barrister in English law. He then carves out for himself a solid career in the law. By the time Boswell was in his late twenties, the law had taken hold of him—for the better. And it shows in his writing. It shows in how he viewed the world and those close to him. The law—or more precisely, legal thinking—transforms his approach to rendering people. His "rational" legal life and his "passionate" love life: these are his two main themes in the late 1760s, and they merge in fascinating ways in his Journal and in a range of his other writing. To be sure, Boswell, being

Boswell, continued to say out late and sought out a variety of women for different purposes; but he writes about these activities in ways that exhibit the shaping influence of his legal work. Hour after hour, Boswell worked on performing legal tasks at this time, often dictating his written pleadings. This long-cultivated habit changes the way he thinks and writes. It not only guides him in his Journal of this time, but directs him, and maybe also stabilizes him, years later, when he designs and composes the *Life of Johnson*, his lasting achievement.

To explain this literary transformation in Boswell's early life and to indicate the importance of this legal orientation toward thinking and writing, I'll focus first on two powerful influences on his life in the mid- and late 1760s. I'll characterize legal Edinburgh during Boswell's time, and Boswell's immersion in that "hot-bed of genius," to use the phrase of the usually curmudgeonly Matthew Bramble in Smollett's *Humphry Clinker*. And I'll comment in detail on how love and the law merged in revealing ways for Boswell during these years. Afterward, I'll address, albeit in an introductory way, various fundamental aspects of the *Life of Johnson* that display habits of construction and composition that Boswell came to embrace when he worked as an advocate in Edinburgh in the late 1760s. This should be enough to underscore my conviction that when Boswell was in his mid- and late twenties—perhaps the most formative time for an author's intellectual development[16]—he learned legal habits of thinking and composition that quickly became second nature to him and that in time guided his greatest writing. For James Boswell, the late 1760s were a profound turning point in his life of writing.

Edinburgh, a "Hot-Bed of Genius"

Edinburgh in the eighteenth century has justifiably earned its reputation as a great center of intellect. Matthew Bramble may have been more exacting than he understood when he called eighteenth-century Edinburgh "a hot-bed of genius."[17] The list of significant, influential writers who found an intellectual home in Edinburgh is long. But as his phrase hints, eighteenth-century Edinburgh was also a relatively small place, geographically, especially if compared to eighteenth-century London. Consequently, Edinburgh writers lived and worked in close proximity to one another. James Boswell, in his mid-twenties, was the lucky beneficiary of all this. In July 1766, when Boswell successfully defended his Latin legal thesis for admission to the Faculty of Advocates, assumed his robe, and dictated his very first case, the section of the city called New Town—designed by the twenty-six-year-old James Craig and featuring elegant squares at the end of wide streets and stylish Georgian houses with both attractive stoops and large windows—was only in the planning stages. Boswell and others who were skeptical of all the new plans and building to the north preferred to live in the older, more compact area of the city to the south, not far from Parliament House, the center of Edinburgh legal life after the Act of Union in 1707. Of course Boswell had long nurtured his fascination with authors and "great men." But simply being a lawyer in Edinburgh placed Boswell near the very heart of the Scottish Enlightenment, intellectually and personally, for law seemed related to important social changes that were winning the day. Agricultural improvement, industrial and commercial development: both had important legal dimensions, requiring civil litigation and lawyers, and this is why, as one historian has said, "the law, lawyers and legal system were like a hub of a wheel in the eighteenth century, with spokes going out towards most areas of élite activity."[18] And the profession of law contributed heavily to that elite in Scotland: "it was the highest profession that the country knew; lawyers set the tone of society."[19] One can see why Boswell, whose focus was on civil litigation and who was always cognizant of his high social status, would have felt right at home in this literary-intellectual urban environment.

Boswell liked mingling with lawyers, not least because they had interests other than law. And Boswell doubtless respected their prominence. One example of such a figure is David Dalrymple, Lord Hailes, a judge as well as a historian of Scotland and a classicist; another is James Burnett, Lord Monboddo, a judge and also a wide-ranging scholar who contributed permanently to both historical linguistics and the theory of evolution. The achievements of these and other men indicate that law was not far removed from literature and authorship, broadly conceived. The Edinburgh legal-literary society was small enough to foster meaningful intellectual camaraderie, too. Monboddo, for example, was a curator of the Advocates' Library, one of the great legal and general libraries of the world at the time, and it was there that Monboddo first came to know David Hume, who served as librarian from 1754 to 1762.[20] Hume was a favorite of Boswell's, of course. Boswell was fascinated by that man and his works for many years. When Boswell finds himself "confined" in London with a bout of gonorrhea in January and February 1763, he tries to look on the bright side: he realizes he will now have more time to continue reading Hume's *History of England*. Boswell also records in extensive detail his correspondence with Hume at this time.[21] It is hardly a surprise, then, that when Boswell came to Edinburgh to work as an advocate in Parliament House, he rented rooms nearby that had been vacated by none other than David Hume. Boswell's association with Hume, though obviously in part a manifestation of Boswell's interest in literary celebrity, was also in keeping with broad, presiding assumptions in Scotland at this time: "the law was a profession congenial to the practice of literature and philosophy," as Anand C. Chitnis has noted.[22]

Lesser legal lights, just on the fringes of the most revered of the Scottish Enlightenment, would include two other friends of Boswell's at this time, Andrew Crosbie and John Maclaurin. "They were among the colleagues with whom Boswell associated and identified for much of his professional life in Edinburgh," writes Richard Sher, "and Boswell scholars have not fully grasped their importance in shaping and nurturing Boswell's personality."[23] As Sher observes, Crosbie's "impressive" library may well have been the model for the library of Sir Walter Scott's Pleydell, an advocate, who says, "A lawyer without history or literature is a mechanic, a mere working mason; if he possesses knowledge of these, he may venture to call himself an architect."[24] We might recall further that the word *literature* had not yet taken on associations of creativity, individual expressiveness, or imaginativeness. Johnson defines the word as follows: "learning; skill in letters."[25] To Boswell, an impressionable young advocate coming of age in a place where history, philosophy, and literature were the rage, all of these legal figures counted as "authors."

So when Boswell came to perform his legal work—in civil litigation mainly, which demanded that he write for an audience of learned judges and from time to time speak in public as well—he doubtless regarded his own toils in the law as part of the world inhabited by some of the leading writers and intellectuals of the day. This further helps explain why Boswell was on easy terms with a good number of them. And like them, Boswell made easy transitions shifting from one kind of writing to another. I doubt Boswell viewed his legal work as wholly in conflict with his more popular political work, *An Account of Corsica* (published in February 1768), or with his other occasional journalistic performances. Nor did he find writing in his Journal at odds with his legal work, as we'll see. In fact, all these different activities in Boswell's life of writing nurtured one another, regardless of whether he fully understood this interplay.

But it was as an Edinburgh advocate that he gradually came to define himself, a reality that pleased him at this time of his life. His friends were happy to notice this, too. His friend Temple, who after the University of Edinburgh had studied law at Cambridge before deciding to pursue holy orders, writes to him warmly in late June 1767: "Would you believe it, but I really tremble to think of hearing you at the bar. 'Tis childish, for I have been told by several people that you are beginning to make a figure. Persevere in the glorious career, my dear Boswell, and be the joy and boast of your worthy father's old age."[26] Johnson offered similar support. Boswell embraced their good wishes for his legal career, as he did others' similarly benevolent encouragements. Boswell embraces the social dimension of his trade as well. On January 19, 1768, he registers a strong sense of contentment after a social gathering of his fellow advocates. "Was at the anniversary meeting of the Faculty of Advocates. Had the true old sensations, and felt myself *Mr. James Boswell,* comfortable and secure. Recollected how formerly I should have been wretched with a life so void of vivid enjoyment, about now had force of mind enough to be content."[27] After the usual rituals, he joins his fellows at an Edinburgh tavern popular among lawyers, Clerihue's, where, he writes, "we were very well." A few weeks later, on February 5, 1768, he "supped at Lord Monboddo's" with a few other legal luminaries. "I was quite easy. I saw lords of session in a quite different light from what I have done by looking only at awful judges."[28] The very next day he writes of himself with a sense of personal achievement: "Considered the law is my profession, my occupation in life. Saw it not to be such a mystery as I apprehended."[29]

Boswell did have a tough time studying the law at the University of Utrecht in the early 1760s, as is well known. (Nevertheless, he ruminated on translating John Erskine's *Principles of the Laws of Scotland* into Latin—the language of the learned.) But when he returned home and prepared for entering the Faculty of Advocates, he observes, "I have studied Scots Law with a good deal of care under as good a Professor as ever lived My Worthy father . . . I have had more real satisfaction these two months past, than I had for years before. I have been doing my duty. . . . I would fain hope that my idle days are now over, and that the rest of my life shall be employed as it ought to be."[30] And by 1767 or 1768, whatever bad feelings he had about his legal studies in Utrecht are evidently behind him, as he settles into everyday legal work. Like young lawyers today who wisely avoid revisiting their secret failures in law school and just get on with their work, Boswell evidently buried himself in his work—for the better. A thoroughly typical entry in his Journal at this time is that of February 1: "Was busy all day with law till five, when I drank tea at Miss Montgomerie's. At seven consulted at Solicitor's."[31] As these passages from his Journal suggest, Boswell seems aware of this positive change in his life. Long gone, apparently, is his relish, first, for playing the Man of Pleasure, as he did so eagerly in London, and second, for amply extending the theatrical dimension of it all in extended, stylized narrative in his Journal. He perceives his own change in outlook. In early March, in Edinburgh, he takes in *The Beggar's Opera*. "The songs revived London ideas, and my old intrigues with actresses."[32] Near the end of March 1768, he returns to London, stopping first at the Star and Garter in Bond Street, near Picadilly. But the "streets and squares of the metropolis with all the hurry and variety struck me to a certain degree, but by no means as they had once done, and I contentedly felt myself an Edinburgh advocate."[33] He still "patrols": that very night, "I sallied forth like a roaring lion after girls, blending philosophy and raking. I had a neat little lass *in armour* [that is, he deployed an eighteenth-century condom—a reusable sheath, probably made from the intestine of an animal] at a tavern in the Strand,"[34] but his thoughts, and his literary energies, are elsewhere. The description of the evening is brief. The next morning he watches at Tyburn the executions of an attorney, convicted for forgery, and of another person, convicted for highway robbery. "It is a curious turn, but I never can resist seeing executions."[35] His mind was mainly full of law.

When he first came to London this time, he sought out Johnson but was told that Johnson had gone to Oxford. So on March 26, only four days after arriving in London, Boswell decamps and journeys up to Oxford, where he finds, significantly, that Johnson is in New Hall Inn with the second Vinerian Professor of English Law, Robert Chambers, whom Johnson was then helping complete overdue legal lectures.[36] Boswell relishes this opportunity. After Boswell has tea with the Vinerian Professor of English Law, Johnson arrives. Boswell is bursting to tell Johnson about new developments in his life. "I told him how I was settled as a lawyer and how I had two hundred pounds by the law this year. He grumbled and laughed and was wonderfully pleased. 'What Bozzy? Two hundred pounds! A great deal.'"[37] They then settle down a bit and talk about law and morality. It is in this context that Boswell and Johnson discuss, at length, whether the profession of law, in Boswell's words, "hurt the principles of honesty; and I asked him if it did not."

> "Why, no, Sir," said he, "if you act properly. You are not to deceive your clients with false representations of your opinion. You are not to tell lies to a judge." "But," said I, "what do you think of pleading a cause which you know to be bad?" "Sir, you don't know it to be bad till the judge determines it. I have said that you are to state your facts fairly; so that your thinking, or what you call knowing, a cause to be bad must be from reasoning, must be from thinking your arguments weak and inconclusive. But, Sir, that is not enough. An argument which does not convince you yourself may convince the judge before whom you plead it; and if it does convince him, why, then, Sir, you are wrong and he is right. It is his business to judge, and you are not to be confident in your opinion, but to say all you can for your client and then hear the judge's opinion." "But, Sir," said I, "does not the putting on a warmth when you have no warmth, and appearing to be clearly one opinion when you are in reality of another, does not such dissimulation hurt one's honesty? Is there not some danger that one may put on the same mask in common life, in the intercourse with one's friends?" "Why, no, Sir. Everybody knows you are paid for putting on a warmth for your client, and it is properly no dissimulation.

> The moment you come from the bar you resume your usual behavior. Sir, a man will no more carry the artifice of the bar into the common intercourse of society than a man who is paid for tumbling upon his hands will continue tumbling upon his hands when he ought to be walking on his feet." Wonderful force and fancy. At once he satisfied me as to a thing which had often and often perplexed me.[38]

This is a remarkable passage for a number of reasons. First, its sheer length indicates just how important Boswell viewed, at this time of his life, the subtle but clearheaded reasoning Johnson provided on a matter that evidently did indeed perplex the youthful advocate. Second, Johnson is in essence granting approval, from a moral standpoint, of the very heart of Boswell's day-to-day activities as an Edinburgh advocate. Boswell is not doing harm, morally, from Johnson's point of view. And this meant the world to Boswell, as he settled into his legal career. Third, Boswell casts this passage very much in the form of a public legal proceeding, with Boswell playing the role of the advocate, asking the questions and drawing out the witness. Each successive question, followed by each of Johnson's responses, enriches the general proposition that the profession of law does not hurt the principles of honesty. Finally, Boswell's concise reaction to the conversation—"Wonderful force and fancy"—indicates the high estimation he gives to this discussion in general. I think it is fair to say that by the time of this conversation in the Oxford rooms of Sir Robert Chambers—the man who followed Sir William Blackstone as the Vinerian Professor of English Law—James Boswell had determined, with more than a little pleasure, that he would indeed follow his father into the law. With confidence he had made his choice of life.

A few days later, on March 28, Boswell and a friend call on Johnson and Chambers. Boswell reconfirms his decision to become an advocate and recognizes how much he has changed in only a few years. "I then talked of law and of our courts of justice in Scotland, of which I gave a very good account. I found that having been two years a lawyer in real business had given me great force." In short, London is no longer Boswell's center of activity in his own mind. As he says to his friend George Dempster, also a lawyer, in September 1769, "the Outer House of the Court of Session was a good house for me, but it required a garden, and the amusement of London was my garden."[39] As Boswell nears age thirty, London had ceased to be his proving ground for self-definition. It had evolved into a place for play—and for seeing Johnson and his literary friends. Edinburgh was the place for work.

And work Boswell did, notably without much complaining. His Journal and correspondence of the late 1760s are full of short, meaningful entries attesting to how much time he spent on legal matters. "Busy with election law," writes Boswell in early January 1768. "At home all day consulting and writing law papers." Monday, January 11: "Busy with law." On Sunday, January 17, he works on a forgery case, "as I allow myself to consult on criminal business on Sundays. Went to bed at nine that I might be up early next morning." And Boswell stuck to this resolution. Monday, January 18: "Rose at three. Wrote a reply . . . and prepared a charge to the jury. Went to the Justiciary Court at nine. . . . At two I went home and drank a glass or two of Malaga [fortified wine], and wrote another reply. Returned to the court. . . . At eight had tea . . . and a consultation with Mr. James Hay, Writer to the Signet,"[40] that is, a consultation with the most prominent of the Scottish equivalent of solicitors. As numerous similar depositions attest, Boswell adheres to this schedule, at least during term time, throughout his late twenties.

And interestingly enough, such work brings him closer to his father at moments. In August of 1769, he muses on all this legal work.

> Having from this day till Thursday . . . omitted to mark what passed every day, it is enough to say that I have . . . written a great many pages of law papers, and been employed several hours for several evenings in sorting a large mass of session papers belonging to my father and selecting said as worth binding; and, to show the force of custom, I have been very fond of this business.[41]

All such passages hint at the deep influence his legal work was having on his daily life and how he viewed the world.

Ours Is a Court of Papers

What sort of legal work, specifically, did Boswell perform? As a recently published collection of his assorted legal writings indicates, an enormous amount of Boswell's work consisted of written pleadings of various kinds. His work in the court concentrated on civil litigation, and while a handful of legal papers address criminal law, many of his cases addressed matters in property law, one of the most complex, and important, areas of law in the eighteenth century. As Hugh Milne has indicated in detail, his writings may be classified according to accepted forms of legal composition at the time, among them petitions, reclaiming petitions, the answer, replies, memorials, and so on. But more important than anything was the sheer significance of such writing itself. Milne underscores in importance what Boswell himself writes in February 1776: "so little attention is paid to pleading in the Court of Session that I was the only lawyer who attended today from beginning to end; and for long intervals there was an absolute void in the benches. Ours is a court of *papers*. We are never seriously engaged but when we write. . . . We do not fall heartily to work till we take to our pens. . . ."[42]

It is difficult to deliver briefly a feel for the character of Boswell's legal expression because the corpus is so vast. Suffice it to say, any selection is bound to overlook an important dimension of his overall achievement, and certainly this essay is not the place for a comprehensive survey of his achievements as a legal writer. That topic demands another essay. Still, a few salient traits of Boswell's legal papers are worth noticing, especially in that they help shape how he writes on ostensibly nonlegal matters.

First of all, Boswell is completely at home with precise legal terminology. He deploys it deftly and confidently. Certainly all lawyers learn to deploy this language early in their legal educations, and Boswell, apparently, is able to do this well. For example, he exhibits his skill at this in one memorial—a written pleading, an argumentative summary of the relevant facts and issues—for the Countess of Caithness, outlining her understanding of what she deserves upon the death of the Earl of Fife. As it turns out, she must bring this process against her own daughter. As Boswell explains in his memorial in *Countess of Caithness v Countess Fife and Earl Fife and Sir John Sinclair* (1767), the Countess of Caithness, among other things, believes she deserves a jointure house—a house to be used by the widow for life. In the course of arguing this issue, he begins by saying that she "has an express clause in her contract of marriage," and he quotes the contract (sort of like a modern-day "prenup"). But the lawyer on the other side, according to Boswell, is pretty shrewd: "the ingenuity of their able counsel, after beating about a long time, fell at last upon a most extraordinary device: They found out that there are two sort of houses upon the estate of Caithness, when in reality there is only one which is even tolerable, . . . And upon this conceit . . . did Sir John Sinclair's learned lawyer gravely plead, that as the marriage contract is silent as to any sum in lieu of the jointure house, so he must interpret the Earl's intention, as if it was understood, that the principal messuage should go to the heir, and the other go to the widow. . . ." *Messuage*? That's an English legal term, "meaning a house, outbuildings and adjacent land."[43] What is significant here is how easily Boswell deploys this term to great argumentative effect. After presenting this, Boswell writes, "The memorialist will not take up your Lordships time with a serious refutation of this most extraordinary defence." As even this brief passage indicates, Boswell's writing from beginning to end of this eleven-page memorial is clear, fluid, reasonable, and in places, appropriately light in tone. His deployment of specific legal terms in no way cuts against, or obscures, the essential force of his carefully structured argument. Boswell won the case, with the Countess receiving a sum in place of the jointure house.

Second, Boswell early on learned how indeterminate evidence can seem in a formal legal context when the evidence is not reliable and authentic. In a case involving Boswell's friend and publisher, Alexander Donaldson, Boswell argues vehemently against John Reid's representation—a written pleading requesting a change in the documents of a case—that there are new documents in the case. Boswell, in his answer—a written response to a representation—completely rejects the premise of the representation. With fire in the belly, Boswell writes,

> But upon perusal, it appears these new facts are drawn from the old Bill Book, which has been in the Representer's hands every Day for nine years past. . . . The truth is, every Material fact in the Cause seems to be exhausted by former papers—how many new Fables the Representer has yet to produce, the Respondent cannot Guess.
>
> On the 4th page of this Representation there is a Conversation betwixt the Representer and the Respondent which seemed intended

> for your Lordships particular attention. But where this important Dialogue has been treasured up since November 1760, when it must have happened, is certainly subject for speculation. The Representer has blacked two pages in one of his papers, four in another, and eight in a third, yet not a Syllable in any of them like what we are here informed of: This "*Genuine account of the matter*" has been reserved for the Coup-de-Grace! When facts are to be collected from a variety of Extraneous discoveries at any period of a Cause, but after repeated Decisions against him, when a party introduces Conversations and allegations which if true he might have recollected from the beginning, one is rather apt to ascribe them to the fertility of the imagination, than the fidelity of the memory.[44]

In this passage Boswell reveals his training in the handling of documents, his conviction that bad documents are in themselves not to be relied upon, and his perhaps overstated zealousness. This strong interest in the quality of evidence itself is a preoccupation in much of his writing, both public and private, throughout his life. Most importantly, as this document indicates, Boswell had developed these views about evidence—and wrote strongly about them—by at least 1769, when he was in his late twenties.

And finally, while Boswell's early days in the law in Edinburgh demanded that he spend many hours writing, he also spent a lot of time speaking both in public and in private about legal matters. And although pleading in person before judges was not his primary business, he did it often, and he was pretty good at it, evidently. In a famous case on copyright featuring yet again his friend from publishing, *John Hinton v Alexander Donaldson* (1773), it was Boswell, a member of a team of lawyers defending Donaldson, who made the opening speech. Several judges praised the speeches of both sides.[45] But by then, he was well practiced at public speaking. As he writes with satisfaction in a letter to Temple in early 1767, more than five years earlier, "I am surprised at myself, I allready speak with so much ease and boldness, and have allready the Language of the Bar so much at command."[46] And of course Boswell also spent much time meeting with clients, often in taverns and inns, asking probing questions about their legal problems and providing advice.

Love and the Law

So how did all this legal work affect Boswell's other writing? How did his legal thinking color his view of his friends and lovers—two of his favorite topics in his Journal? Although Boswell was a hardworking young advocate and spent more time with legal affairs than we might be accustomed to remember, he certainly managed to reserve time for nonlegal amusements—just as lawyers who complain about relentless work do today. But unlike contemporary lawyers perhaps, Boswell didn't "compartmentalize" his life, as many lawyers claim to do today; and as a writer coming of age—as a man who *liked* to write!—Boswell clearly enjoyed deploying legal diction and legal rhetoric to the materials of his everyday life. He didn't entirely separate his legal life from his love life, and this literary habit had beneficial, lasting, and often comic effects on his writing overall. For example, in 1767 he writes to Temple complaining that he has not heard from him "with regard to my amiable Miss Blair." Boswell's explanation of the silence? "I conclude . . . you are not able to make an apology for the conduct of a lady for whom you are a kind of surety."[47] *Surety* is a normal English word, but like many normal English words, when used in a legal context, it takes on highly specific meaning. To give a *simple* legal definition: a surety is "One who at the request of another, and for the purpose of securing to him a benefit, becomes responsible for the performance of the latter of some act in favor of a third person, or hypothecates property as security therefor."[48] (There is actually a subfield of legal work today, suretyship.) In this particular passage in his letter to Temple, Boswell is deploying his skill in legal terms and definitions, which he was then in the process of honing as his legal practice was picking up steam. This little joke about *surety* would not be lost on Temple, who, as noted earlier, studied law at Cambridge.

Elsewhere in his Journal of this time Boswell applies his emerging analytical-legal skills. Many of his conversations with Johnson in the late 1760s tend to take the form of a legal proceeding, with Boswell asking the questions and Johnson providing the answers. One example would be their conversation about suicide, on October 17, 1769.

> Called Mr. Johnson. Talk of suicide, if a crime. He said, "Yes. Thought so by all Christians. Saul forsaken of God. Cut off leg to preserve life."

> BOSWELL. But may it not be done to save many lives, if you can't bear torture and would discover?" JOHNSON. "Why, Sir, there's no end of arguing on improbable suppositions. And after all, you do make out that what you allow is not vicious. Only this, that in a supposable case, a smaller vice is to be chosen rather than a greater." . . . BOSWELL. "If you promise to a highwayman £100, should you keep it?" JOHNSON. "Why, yes. It is binding not as an obligation with respect to the highwayman but with respect to society, which has an interest that promises be kept and men do not explain them away." BOSWELL. "But, Sir, if £10,000?" JOHNSON. "Why, then, Sir, a man is to balance the circumstances. If himself concerned, 'tis binding." BOSWELL. "But he has perhaps a wife and family." JOHNSON. "Why, then, their claim in justice may be preferable. But, Sir, that kind of casuistical reasoning is very pernicious. Rules cannot be given for improbable cases. One must judge when they happen."[49]

This passage presents Boswell very much as the advocate, asking the penetrating questions and follow-up questions, pressing and leading Johnson. Toward the end of the passage, Johnson acts just as normal people do who are pressed in this legal way outside of a legal setting: he becomes frustrated and tries to shut down the argument. Notably, Johnson strikes against Boswell's legal instinct to try to find or to shape the rules that can be applied to messy daily experience. Since Johnson had from an early age a strong interest in law, the application of legal thinking here yields a special excitement to the conversation.[50]

As a young man growing in professional confidence, Boswell doesn't stint in exercising his abilities as a legal writer. As readers have long delighted to see, the arch and formulaic elements of legal writing contrast vividly with the low actualities of human life, and when the legal language is applied to such low materials outside of a legal context, a somewhat comic effect typically emerges. Boswell undoubtedly understood this. Perhaps to explore his abilities in this way, and certainly to show off his dexterity with legal language, Boswell applies his legal understanding to many areas of his life. In one passage in his Journal, he depends on his secure understanding of the legal pleading to try to come to terms with one of his bouts of venereal disease. He writes to Temple that after a "debauch," as he puts it, he resumed his affair with his current mistress; but he's worried that she has become infected, since his own symptoms were "long of appearing." He writes: "Will you forgive me, Temple, for exclaiming that all this evil is too much for the offence of my getting drunk because I would drink Miss Blair's health in a large bumper? But general laws often seem hard in particular cases."[51] Determining how a general rule relates to the contested facts of human existence—and more specifically in this case, whether the punishment fits the crime—is at the very heart of legal reasoning, as everyone who has ever studied law at all knows. Hence the comic effect. Perhaps, too, such ostensibly formal legal reasoning—his quick shift of topic to whether the punishment fits the crime—allows him to avoid taking responsibility for his bad behavior. If so, then all the more reason to view the passage as important and revealing. Indeed, for Boswell, at this time of his life, legal thought may be a kind of crutch, a way of thinking or viewing the world that is, for better or worse, becoming second nature to him. It's worth adding that viewing the world through a legal lens is entirely normal among young people who immerse themselves in the law. To use a modern example: a broken-down old refrigerator at curbside for special trash collection in a suburban neighborhood is just that to an average person; to a lawyer, such an item is an "attractive nuisance": some neighborhood kid might jump inside while playing hide-and-seek, find himself locked inside, and suffocate to death. And the owner of the fridge would be liable.

In a more extensive passage arising from a similar act of bad behavior, Boswell reverts to law again, but this time to a different dimension of his legal work. Again, he writes to Temple.

> That very evening I gave supper to two or three of my acquaintance, having before I left Scotland laid a guinea that I should not catch the venereal disorder for three years, which bet I had most certainly lost and now was paying. We drank a great deal till I was so much intoxicated that instead of going home, I went to a low house in one of the alleys of Edinburgh where I knew a common girl lodged, and like a brute as I was I lay all night with her. I had still so much reason left as not to "dive into the bottom of the deep" [an allusion to the hot-tempered Hotspur in *Henry IV, Part One*], but I gratified my coarse desires by tumbling about on the brink of

> destruction. Next morning I was like a man ordered for ignominious execution. But by noon I was worse, for I discovered that some infection had reached me. Was not this dreadful? I had an assignation in the evening with my charmer. . . . But how could I tell her my shocking story? I took courage. I told how drunk I had been. I told the consequences. I lay down and kissed her feet. I said I was unworthy of any other fortune. I gloried that I had ever been firmly constant to her while I was myself. I hoped she would consider my being drunk as a fatal accident which I should never again fall into. I called her my friend in whom I had confidence, and entreated she would comfort me.
>
> How like you the eloquence of a young barrister? It was truly the eloquence of love. She bid me rise; she took me by the hand. She said she forgave me.[52]

In this recap, Boswell is unmistakably *pleading*, and not simply in the ordinary sense of that word. As an advocate, Boswell's job before the Court of Justiciary often enjoined him to plead in the defense of various malefactors, and Boswell here is displaying his skills as a legal rhetorician. Boswell is both the accused *and* the lawyer for the defense, which lends a light touch to the narrative. And he wins his case—and his client gets off, sort of. In other words, Boswell is playfully bragging a bit. He's showing off. "How like you the eloquence of a young barrister?": Boswell is hitting his stride, albeit in his typically bizarre ways, as a legal professional.

It's instructive to compare this passage to his more famous rendering of his affair four years earlier with Louisa in the *London Journal*. The differences are remarkable. The Boswell of the Louisa episode is a theatrical character in a Restoration play. After a night during which he was (he claims) "five times . . . fairly lost in supreme rapture," he considers himself as "one of the wits in King Charles the Second's time" and compares himself to Captain Plume, a character in George Farquhar's *The Recruiting Officer*.[53] His infection from "Signor Gonorrhoea," as he puts it, appears a surprise in the journal, an effect which depends on Boswell's shrewd use of his materials to emphasize plot—and the situational comedy of the entire episode. It is notable, too, that the day after his night of "luscious fatigues" with Louisa, January 13, 1763, he calls upon David Garrick and tells him that he's still hoping to get into the Guards. "The

Law requires a sad deal of plodding," he adds.[54] In the letter to Temple written more than four years later on March 8, 1767, few if any of these theatrical-narrative flourishes are to be found. While Boswell was still sometimes pretty reckless in his personal life, his way of presenting that recklessness has changed. At the conclusion of the passage, he styles himself not a wit in "Charles the Second's time," but a "young barrister." By 1767, his life in the law had changed his habits of composition.

The "Life of Johnson"

If the law helped Boswell become a different kind of writer in the late 1760s, then what was the effect of this transformation on his later writing? How did it influence his work on the *Life of Johnson*? Boswell's great book is saturated in law and legal topics. The book teems with legal figures, legal argument, discussion of particular cases, and commentary on legal writings past and present, both famous and largely forgotten. A full examination of the legal dimensions of the book are beyond the scope of this essay. Still, for our purposes, it may be helpful to point out three fundamental legal dimensions of the book that may be traced to the late 1760s in Boswell's life of writing, legal-literary orientations that by the mid-1780s, when he was working on the *Life*, he had long nurtured.

First, and most obviously, Boswell thinks of his act of writing Johnson's life as primarily a matter of sifting and sorting a huge mass of materials, all of which he needed to be checked for their reliability and authenticity. As he says in the Advertisement to the First Edition,

> *I must be allowed to suggest, that the nature of the work, in other respects, as it consists of innumerable detached particulars, all which, even the most minute, I have spared no pains to ascertain with a scrupulous authenticity, has occasioned a degree of trouble far beyond that of any other species of composition. . . . Let me only observe, as a specimen of my trouble, that I have sometimes been obliged to run half over London, in order to fix a date correctly. . . . I have also been extremely careful as to the exactness of my quotations. . . . and never to presume to introduce them with,*—"I think I have read;"—or,—"If I remember right;"—*when the originals may be examined.*[55]

That's his legal training in documentation coming to bear on his literary magnum opus. He also presents these documents with an eye to how others might use these same, or similar, documents. As scholars have noted, Boswell's *Life of Johnson* was conceived and written in part as a rejoinder to other planned biographies of Johnson. In the end, all this sifting and sorting served Boswell and his readers well. The care with which Boswell presents his evidence about Johnson stands to this day as one of the hallmarks of Boswell's achievement in the book.

Second, and perhaps more important, one of Boswell's supreme talents in the *Life of Johnson* is drawing out people, charging the conversation, and simply getting people to say things that they hadn't expected to say. In many memorable passages in the *Life of Johnson*, Boswell depends on his long experience as an advocate, who questions and probes to elicit revealing statements. Such passages are at the core of Boswell's success in the *Life of Johnson*. Consider this short example, drawn from a meeting between the two men in October of 1769—at just the time Boswell was honing his legal abilities.

> I had hired a bohemian as my servant while I remained in London, and being much pleased with him, as I asked Dr. Johnson if his being a Roman Catholic should prevent my taking him home to my family. JOHNSON. "Why, Sir. If *he* had no objection, you can have no objection." BOSWELL. "So, Sir, you are no great enemy to the Popish religion?" JOHNSON. "No more, Sir, than to the Presbyterian religion." BOSWELL. "You are joking." JOHNSON. "No, Sir, upon honour I think so. Nay, Sir, of the two, I prefer the Popish." . . . BOSWELL. "Is it necessary, Sir, to believe all the Thirty-nine Articles?" JOHNSON. "Why, Sir, that is a question which has been much agitated. Some have thought. . . ."[56]

Boswell is operating as an advocate, or a barrister, here, trying to draw out from Johnson what he thinks Johnson will say. But Johnson, recognizing what Boswell is doing, fools him and offers answers that Boswell didn't expect—and that show Johnson's own familiarity with legal questioning. Johnson cleverly tries to disrupt Boswell's questioning by saying he prefers Roman Catholicism to Presbyterianism. Boswell doesn't take the bait, though, and continues the questioning. The entire passage is exciting for us not only because we hear Johnson on a subject he really cares about—religion—but because the two are sparring, like dueling lawyers. While Johnson seems to win the contest because of his superior mind, perhaps Boswell wins, too, for Boswell shows his readers how kinetic Johnson's mind can be—one of the main themes in the biography. As he puts it at the very end of the *Life*, Johnson's "superiority over other learned men consisted chiefly in what may be called the art of thinking, the art of using his mind."[57] As a biographer, Boswell wants to put on display Johnson's intellectual dexterity. Setting up a legal forum is exactly the right way to do this.

Third, if law is integral to the patterns of many of Johnson's memorable conversations as Boswell presents them in the *Life of Johnson*, so is law—and especially legal terminology—a more prominent feature of the book than we might at first recognize. The book is full of specialized legal topics, and in more than a handful of places, Boswell is quite unashamed in using precise legal terms. An example occurs in one of the passages in which Johnson combatively challenges the reputation of Swift. During the summer of 1768, Johnson and a range of "eminent Scotch literati," as Boswell puts it, meet for conversation at the Crown and Anchor. The group included Hugh Blair, William Robertson, and others, including Dr. Douglas, Bishop of Salisbury, as well as Boswell himself, who "collected" the company, as he writes with obvious satisfaction.

> Swift having been mentioned, Johnson, as usual, treated him with little respect as an author. Some of us endeavoured to support the Dean of St. Patrick's by various arguments. One in particular praised his *Conduct of the Allies*. JOHNSON. "Sir, his Conduct of the Allies is a performance of very little ability." "Surely Sir, (said Dr. Douglas,) you must allow it has strong facts."[58]

Boswell places a footnote after this last statement (in the second edition) and enters into a long discussion about the authenticity and reliability of this statement. And in the course of explaining everything, he introduces and highlights a very precise legal term.

> My respectable friend [Douglas], upon reading this passage, observed, that he probably must have said not simply, "Strong facts," but "strong facts well arranged." His lordship, however, knows too well the value of written documents to insist on setting his recollection against my notes taken at the time. He does not attempt to *traverse the record*. The fact, perhaps, may have

> been, either that the additional words escaped me in the noise of a numerous company, or that Dr. Johnson, from his impetuosity, and eagerness to seize an opportunity to make a lively retort, did not allow Dr. Douglas to finish his sentence.[59]

"Traverse the record": the phrase is a legal one and might be classified among the many different kinds of "traverse," which in general suggests a denial. In this instance, when Boswell writes that Douglas "does not attempt to *traverse the record*," he is saying that Douglas knows he can't make a pleading that challenges the completeness of Boswell's record on the mere grounds of his own memory. Written records, even if incomplete, are much more reliable than one person's memory. That's true in the law, Boswell suggests with inclusion of the legal term, and if it's true there, then it surely is true for this biography. In fact, the passage seems strikingly similar to what an advocate would say or write in a formal legal context. To be sure, the footnote is clever: it may deliver a special charge to readers familiar with the legal pleading. But the footnote is not merely an opportunity for wit, for it reveals nakedly the extent to which Boswell believed in his written sources. What he writes in the text proper of the biography holds up because he had good written notes. The passage should stand because it has met the high standards of legal scrutiny—even when questioned by someone who was there.

There are many other similarly legal passages in the *Life of Johnson*. But a comprehensive examination of the legal dimension of Boswell's *Life of Johnson* demands another essay. For our current purposes, it's enough to say that Boswell would *not* have been able to present these passages in the first place had he not taken his career in the law seriously, which he began to do when he was in his late twenties, in the late 1760s. And we should be glad he did. For in taking himself seriously as a lawyer at this time, he was concurrently preparing himself to be taken seriously as a writer, not only by his contemporaries, but also by posterity.

Notes

I wish to thank Professor John J. Burke of the University of Alabama for his kind and learned comments on an early version of this essay. I also owe much to my students in the spring 2014 version of my course at Providence College, The Age of Johnson. The students' lively questions and comments—and particularly the acute observations of Jessica Rotundo—both sharpened and expanded my understanding of the legal dimension of the *Life of Johnson*. Finally, various materials of the Hyde Collection, now in the

Houghton Library at Harvard University, as well as the deep and up-to-date collection of eighteenth-century Scottish legal materials in the Harvard Law Library, proved to be invaluable.

1. Gordon Turnbull, in conversation with the author, more than once.

2. James Boswell, *London Journal, 1762–63*, ed. Gordon Turnbull (New York: Penguin Books, 2010), 96. Subsequent references to this work will be abbreviated *London Journal*.

3. Frederick Pottle, *James Boswell: The Earlier Years, 1740–1769* (New York: McGraw-Hill, 1966), 35.

4. May 21, 1795, *The Windham Papers*, ed. Lewis Melville, 2 vols. (Boston: Small, Maynard, 1913), 1:297–98.

5. Russell Fraser, "Boswell the Retailer of Phrases," *Sewanee Review* 111:4 (2003): 603.

6. James Boswell to Edmond Malone, June 30, 1790. *The Correspondence of James Boswell with David Garrick, Edmond Burke, and Edmond Malone*, ed. Peter S. Baker et al. (London: Heinemann, 1986), 369.

7. Two collections of essays present explorations of these issues: *Boswell's "Life of Johnson": New Questions, New Answers*, ed. John A. Vance (Athens: University of Georgia Press, 1985), and *New Light on Boswell: Critical and Historical Essays on the Occasion of the Bicentenary of the "Life of Johnson,"* ed. Greg Clingham (Cambridge: Cambridge University Press, 1991). Among the many compelling essays in these collections on the "art" of the *Life of Johnson*, perhaps the most wide-ranging is Ralph Rader, "Literary Form in Factual Narrative: The Example of Boswell's *Johnson*," in Vance, 25–52.

8. Geoffrey Scott, "The Making of the *Life of Johnson* as Shown in Boswell's First Notes," in *Twentieth Century Interpretations of Boswell's "Life of Johnson": A Collection of Critical Essays*, ed. James L. Clifford (Englewood Cliffs, NJ: Prentice-Hall, 1970), 27–28.

9. See David M. Walker, *A Legal History of Scotland, Vol. V, The Eighteenth Century* (Edinburgh: T. & T. Clark, 1998), 454.

10. In placing the title of Scottish causes (i.e., cases) in italics, and without a period after "v," I adhere to the usage in *Legal Papers*, which follows standard practice in British legal publications.

11. Hugh M. Milne, introduction to *The Legal Papers of James Boswell*, ed. Hugh M. Milne, vol. 1 (Edinburgh: The Stair Society, 2013), liii. Subsequent references to this book will be abbreviated *Legal Papers*.

12. Frank Brady, introduction to *Boswell in Search of a Wife*, by James Boswell, ed. Frank Brady and Frederick A. Pottle (New York: McGraw-Hill, 1956), x. Subsequent references to this book will be abbreviated *Wife*.

13. Boswell, *Wife*, 89.

14. Irma Lustig, "Boswell, Alexander, Lord Auchinleck (1707–1782)," *Oxford Dictionary of National Biography*. (Oxford: Oxford University Press, 2004); online edition, May 2005. The phrasing of Lustig's entry indicates she depended closely on Pottle, *James Boswell: The Earlier Years*.

15. See Boswell, *Legal Papers*.

16. Alfred North Whitehead offers a related discussion of this issue in *The Aims of Education*. In discussing the importance of culture and expert knowledge in the education of young men, Whitehead writes, "Their expert knowledge will give them the ground to start from, and their culture will lead them as deep as philosophy and as high as art. We have to remember that the valuable intellectual development is self-development, and that it mostly takes place between the ages of sixteen and thirty." A. N. Whitehead, *The Aims of Education* (New York: The Free Press, 1927), 1.

17. Tobias Smollett, *The Expedition of Humphry Clinker*, ed. Lewis M. Knapp (Oxford: Oxford University Press, 1966), 233.

18. Anand C. Chitnis, *The Scottish Enlightenment: A Social History* (Lanham, MD: Rowan and Littlefield, 1976), 75.

19. Chitnis, *The Scottish Enlightenment*, 78.

20. For more on Hume the librarian, see Adam Potkay, *The Passion for Happiness: Samuel Johnson and David Hume* (Ithaca, NY: Cornell University Press, 2000), 42.

21. See Boswell, *London Journal*, 122–23; 132; 139–42; 144–45; 147; 149–51; 159–60; 160–62.

22. Chitnis, *The Scottish Enlightenment*, 85.

23. Richard B. Sher, "Scottish Divines and Legal Lairds: Boswell's Scots Presbyterian Identity," in *New Light on Boswell*, 35.

24. Quoted in Sher, "Scottish Divines and Legal Lairds," 36. For more on the influence of Crosbie and Maclaurin, see 35–49.

25. Samuel Johnson, *A Dictionary of the English Language* (W. Strahan: London, 1755), s.v. "literature."

26. *Wife*, 77–78.

27. *Wife*, 120–21.

28. *Wife*, 123–24.

29. *Wife*, 124.

30. Milne, *Legal Papers*, xlv.

31. *Wife*, 123.

32. *Wife*, 132–33.

33. *Wife*, 139.

34. *Wife*, 140.

35. *Wife*, 140. Hugh Milne speculates that Boswell as a child "may well have seen from [his] school windows men being led to execution at the gallows erected at the east end of the Grassmarket," in Edinburgh. See Milne, introduction to *Legal Papers*, xxxix n. 2.

36. For the most comprehensive account of the extent of Johnson's help with the law lectures of Sir Robert Chambers, see Thomas M. Curley, "Editor's Introduction," in Sir Robert Chambers, *A Course of Lectures on the English Law*, ed. Thomas M. Curley (Madison: University of Wisconsin Press, 1986), 3–79.

37. *Wife*, 146–47.

38. *Wife*, 147.

39. *Wife*, 298.

40. *Wife*, 118–19.

41. *Wife*, 256.

42. See Milne, introduction to *James Boswell's Legal Papers*, p. lvi; James Boswell, *Boswell: The Ominous Years, 1774–1776*, ed. Charles Ryskamp and Frederick A. Pottle (New York: McGraw-Hill, 1963), 228.

43. Milne, *Legal Papers*, 91 n. 322.

44. Boswell, *Legal Papers*, 71.

45. Milne, *Legal Papers*, liii.

46. Quoted in Milne, *Legal Papers*, xlviii.

47. *Wife*, 84.

48. *Black's Law Dictionary, Standard Ninth Edition*, ed. Bryan Garner (St. Paul, MN: West Publishing, 2009), s.v. "surety."

49. *Wife*, 321–22.

50. For more on Johnson's long-standing interest in the law, see J. T. Scanlan, "Law," in *Samuel Johnson's Legal Context*, ed. Jack Lynch (Cambridge: Cambridge University Press, 2012), 225–33.

51. *Wife*, 80–81.

52. *Wife*, 37.

53. Boswell, *London Journal*, 92–95.

54. Boswell, *London Journal*, 95.

55. James Boswell, *Boswell's Life of Johnson*, 6 vols., ed. G. B. Hill, rev. and enlg., L. F. Powell (Oxford: Clarendon Press, 1934–1950), 1:7. Subsequent quotations from the *Life of Johnson* will be taken from this edition, which will be abbreviated *Life*.

56. Boswell, *Life*, 2:103–4.

57. Boswell, *Life*, 4:427–28.

58. Boswell, *Life*, 2:65.

59. Boswell, *Life*, 2:65, n. 2.

Melissa J. Ganz

Freedom and Fetters: Nuptial Law in Burney's *The Wanderer*

THE SECRET OF JULIET GRANVILLE'S COERCED MARRIAGE LIES at the heart of Frances Burney's *The Wanderer; or, Female Difficulties* (1814), but we do not learn of this union until the fifth and final volume of the text. In the winter of 1793, at the height of the Terror in France, Juliet eventually reveals, one of Maximilien Robespierre's ruthless commissaries seizes a promissory note from her guardian, a French bishop, while conducting a raid on their town. In the note, Juliet's paternal grandfather, the Earl of Melbury, promises to pay six thousand pounds "on the day of her marriage with a native of France, resident in that country."[1] Eager to profit from this discovery, the commissary demands that Juliet immediately marry him. If she refuses to comply, he tells her, he will execute her guardian. The bishop counsels Juliet not to take such a drastic action, but when she sees him standing in line for the guillotine, she cries out for his release. An officer promptly takes her to a room in the mayor's office, where—surrounded by noise and confusion—the commissary repeats his part of the ceremony. Before the formalities are finished, he rushes off to quash an uprising, enabling Juliet to slip away. But the ceremony continues to haunt her. She feels that she is "so irreligiously tied, that she could not, even if she wished it, regard herself as [the commissary's] lawful wife; though so entangled, that her fetters seemed to be linked with duty and honour" (816).

Juliet's plight raises questions about marriage that preoccupied jurists, legislators, and social observers in the late eighteenth and early nineteenth centuries. Begun in the 1790s and drafted between 1802 and 1812, during Burney's ten-year "seclusion in France," the novel responds to the National Assembly's redefinition of marriage as a civil contract and to feminists' calls to extend liberal principles to women and the family.[2] After 1792, couples could form unions fairly easily in France. In England, however, Parliament continued to exert considerable control over the nuptial tie. Lord Hardwicke's 1753 Marriage Act required couples to solemnize their vows in formal, religious ceremonies and required minors to obtain the consent of their fathers or guardians or mothers (in that order) before they could receive licenses to wed. Unions that failed to comply with these formalities were deemed void.[3] The Act sparked considerable controversy, much as did France's new law. Edmund Burke, for one, spoke out against the contractual model of marriage and in favor of Hardwicke's Act, arguing that England's law was crucial to maintaining the stability of family and society. Others, however, opposed the Act's stringent requirements, maintaining that it wrongly limited individual freedom. In the decades following its passage, MPs such as Charles James Fox sought to repeal or modify the law on numerous occasions; legislators introduced similar bills in 1812 and 1813.[4] Published in the midst of—and shaped by—these controversies, *The Wanderer* participates in heated debates about the contractual nature of the nuptial tie.

Critics remain sharply divided about the novel's treatment of marriage, but few scholars have looked closely at the legal questions raised by the text. Tara Ghoshal Wallace and Margaret Anne Doody read the novel as largely endorsing revolutionary feminism. According to Wallace, Burney "thematizes and advances, in subterranean ways, the specific feminist agenda proposed in [Mary] Wollstonecraft's posthumous novel," exposing and criticizing "oppressive laws governing marriage."[5] Darryl Jones emphasizes the text's ambivalent treatment of radicalism but concludes that it is "if not precisely a late Jacobin novel, then certainly a novel of 1814 which looks back on 1790s Jacobinism with relative sympathy."[6] Claudia L. Johnson, by contrast, argues that the novel "treats women as scapegoats for men, and as a result averts radical social criticism."[7] In presenting "social problems as the result of female excess," Johnson claims, "the institutional power of patriarchy is spared direct criticism despite its ultimate responsibility for [Juliet's] trials as a woman without a father's name."[8] Miranda J. Burgess reads the novel even more conservatively than Johnson does. According to Burgess, Burney "conceives her ideal society . . . as a return to a world in which . . . marriage is a private agreement between a woman's father and the suitor he approves."[9] "This is the world," Burgess claims, "of Hardwicke's Marriage Act, respected and rigorously enforced."[10]

While Wallace and Doody overstate the novel's radical sympathies, Johnson and Burgess underestimate the novel's challenge to patriarchal culture. In this essay, I read Burney's treatment of marriage alongside the era's heated nuptial controversies, revealing the novel's anxieties about both French and English law. Like anti-Jacobins such as Burke and Hannah More, I will argue, Burney offers a sharp critique of France's nuptial practices: Juliet's forced union with the commissary shows that, far from promoting love and liberty, the contractual model of marriage enables coercion and fraud by individuals and the state. The novel likewise demonstrates the dangers of radical marriage through Juliet's outspoken friend, Elinor Joddrel, who attempts to apply revolutionary principles to her personal life. At the same time that the novel shores up the idea of marriage as a public institution subject to regulation by church and state, however, it contests the patriarchal principle that underlies England's own law. Juliet's troubles, Burney shows, result not only from lax laws abroad but from stubborn patriarchs at home. While French revolutionaries and English aristocrats alike view marriage as an exchange between men, Burney imagines matrimony as an affective tie between two equal agents. Through Juliet's union with Albert Harleigh, the novel affirms the sacred and public nature of the conjugal bond while subverting the traffic in women.

"Liberation from All Shackles": Radical Marriage

In her preface to *The Wanderer*, Burney explains that those who "expect to find here materials for political controversy; or fresh food for national animosity; must turn elsewhere their disappointed eyes." "I have felt, indeed, no disposition,—I ought rather, perhaps, to say talent—," she insists, "for venturing upon the stormy sea of politics" (4). As critics have noted, however, the novel begins precisely on that sea. The conjugal difficulties that necessitate Juliet's hasty departure from France are intimately connected to the country's political upheaval. Before turning to the novel, we thus need to review the changes that the Revolution brought in its wake.

In the Old Regime, the family was a profoundly hierarchical institution: children owed allegiance to their parents, much as wives owed allegiance to their husbands. Arranged matches were common; marriages motivated by love were rare. And, once solemnized, unions were binding for parties' lives. In the years preceding the Revolution, reformers began campaigning for a fundamental rethinking of the conjugal relationship. If the state was to be grounded in a contract, freely chosen by the people, reformers reasoned, so, too, marriage ought to rest on the free choice and consent of both parties.[11] The revolutionaries put these ideas into practice upon seizing power. In the Constitution of 1791, the National Assembly redefined marriage as a civil contract and the following year, the Legislative Assembly passed laws lowering the age of majority, reducing parental control of nuptial choices, and licensing divorce. In order to form unions, couples now simply had to exchange vows in a public room in their town hall in the presence of four witnesses after giving six days' public notice.[12] Couples could obtain divorces by mutual consent as well as the complaint of one spouse alleging grounds including incompatibility, mental breakdown, physical violence, abandonment for at least two years, and absence without news for at least five years.[13] Through these laws, the revolutionaries attempted to transform marriage into a secular civil contract between two free individuals. Unhappy spouses immediately took advantage of the new rules: more than 20,000 couples obtained divorces between 1792 and 1803, or roughly 1,800 couples per year.[14] Although Napoleon reversed many of the reforms—the Civil Code of 1804 made it more difficult for couples to obtain divorces, for example—marriage remained (and still remains) a secular contract in France.[15]

These changes worried observers in England. In *Reflections on the Revolution in France* (1790), Burke famously warned that the unleashing of individual desire threatened social ties. Likening the revolutionaries to rebellious children, he highlighted the ways in which the overthrow of political authority undermined the stability of both the family and society.[16] He developed this idea in *Letters on a Regicide Peace* (1796), denouncing the revolutionaries' "strange, uncalled-for declaration . . . that marriage was no better than a common, civil contract."[17] Burke objected to their decision not only to "license . . . divorce at the mere pleasure of either party, and at a month's notice," but also to give "women the same licentious power" that they gave men. "It appears," he charged, "as if the contract that renovates the world was under no law at all."[18] In *Village Politics* (1792), Hannah More similarly decried the ease with which couples dissolved their vows in France, connecting lax ties in the family to disorder in society. "[S]houldst [*sic*] [thou] like to get rid of thy wife for every little bit of a tiff?" the conservative-minded blacksmith, Jack Anvil, asks his Francophile friend, Tom Hod, after the latter praises the "freedom and happiness . . . [that] they have got in France."[19] By the end of the dialogue, Tom realizes that he has confounded liberty with license, gratefully affirming the stability of English families. In the era's popular debating societies, men and women raised similar objections to France's law. At a meeting hosted by City Debates in November 1791, for example, participants considered whether the National Assembly had "[acted] wisely in degrading Marriage from a Divine Institution to a Civil Contract."[20] According to a notice in the *Daily Advertiser*, the group concluded that "the conduct of the National Assembly in rendering the Marriage Ceremony a mere Bargain between Party and Party, independent of all Divine Authority, justly begins to alarm all the European Ladies."[21]

Burney shared these concerns. She praised Burke's *Reflections* shortly after it appeared, describing it as "the noblest, deepest, most animated, and exalted work that . . . [she had] ever read."[22] She likewise echoed Burke's sentiments in a conversation with her father two years later, decrying the "feasibility of expunging all past experience, for the purpose of treating the World as if it were created yesterday, & every man, woman & Child, . . . loose to act from their [*sic*] immediate suggestion. . . ."[23] But where Burke and More emphasize the threat that French law poses to family and society in general, Burney focuses—as did City Debates—on the implications of the law for women. *The Wanderer* shows that, far from affirming individual liberty, the contractual model of marriage enables coercion and undermines women's consent. These problems are evident in the secret union that Juliet's parents contract in Flanders as well as the forced match that Juliet contracts with the commissary. The novel never makes fully clear what happened when Lord Granville took the penniless Miss Powel to Flanders in the late 1770s; Juliet's childhood friend, Gabriella, provides an incomplete account of the marriage in the fourth volume, and Juliet's long-lost uncle, Admiral Powel, provides further details in the fifth. The uncertainty surrounding the union underscores the precarious position in which Lord Granville leaves his wife and daughter. Although the admiral eventually realizes that Lord Granville did not "over-persuade" (837) Miss Powel to marry him, as the admiral initially believed Granville to have done, her assent is still meaningless, as Granville delays telling his father of the match and dies in an accident without ever publicly acknowledging his union. (His wife, who predeceases him, spends her brief married life concealed in a retreat on the banks of the Tyne in France.) The codicil that Granville writes before his death granting Juliet an equal share of his property proves useless, for the certificate of his marriage is destroyed when the revolutionaries set the bishop's house on fire and, without proof of his son's union, the earl refuses to recognize Juliet's claim on the family's estate. The certificate's destruction in the revolutionary blaze underscores the twin dangers of political and sexual liberty; such bids for freedom, the novel suggests, only consume themselves. The inflexible earl contributes to the problem, prompting his son to contract the match in private; likewise, the novel faults the cowardly Lord Granville, who refuses to inform his father of his union before he comes of age. But the novel also insists on the dangers of secrecy. Clandestine marriage, Burney shows, enables men to undermine women's agency and consent.

Although Juliet does not contract her union in private, it proves to be even more problematic than her mother's match. Juliet's account of her experience at the mayor's office on that fateful day in 1793 underscores the problems with France's radical law. After the commissary forces her back to the mayoralty, she recounts:

> The civil ceremony, dreadful, dreadful! . . . was instantly begun; in the midst of the buz [*sic*] of business, the clamour of many tongues, the sneers of contempt, and the laughter of derision; with an irreverence that might

> have suited a theatre, and with a mockery of which the grossest buffoons would have been ashamed. Scared and disordered, I understood not,—I heard not a word; and my parched lips, and burning mouth, could not attempt any articulation.
>
> In a minute or two, this pretended formality was interrupted, by information that a new messenger from the Convention demanded immediate admittance. The commissary swore furiously that he should wait till the six thousand pounds were secured; and vociferously ordered that the ceremony should be hurried on. . . . [T]hough my quivering lips were never opened to pronounce an assenting syllable, the ceremony, the direful ceremony, was finished, and I was called,—Oh heaven and earth!—his wife! his married wife!— (745)

Unlike her mother's union, this match takes place in a formal, public—indeed a legal—space. But the civil servants who preside over the ceremony are representatives of the law in name only. In reality, they are tyrants who manipulate the law for their own ends. Juliet does not speak a word during the ceremony, nor does she show any signs of assent, but such expressions are not necessary to transform her into a "wife." There is, it seems, little difference between nuptial practices in the Old Regime and those of the new Republic. Like Juliet's friend Gabriella, who is "[m]arried before the Revolution, from a convent, and while yet a child; according to the general custom of her country, which rarely permits any choice even to the man; and to the female allows not even a negative" (622), Juliet is unable to express her dissent to the match. Although there are witnesses present, none of them takes the ceremony seriously; Juliet hears only "sneers" and "laughter" fit for the theater. Where the bishop reminds Juliet of the sanctity of oaths, pleading with her to let him die rather than bind herself for his sake, the civil servants show a complete disregard for the sacred nature of the nuptial vow. The Earl of Melbury, who writes the promissory note, and his son-in-law Lord Denmeath, who attempts to enforce it, are deeply implicated in the scheme. But French law enables the commissary to marry Juliet against her will. Civil marriage, Burney shows, enables greedy men to turn a sacred ceremony into a farce, replacing love and consent with coercion and fraud.

Burney reveals the devastating effects of this union through the novel's complicated form. *The Wanderer* opens "in the dead of night" (11) with a confusing exchange in which Juliet requests permission to board a vessel filled with Britons fleeing the Terror. The mystery and darkness enveloping the scene convey the heroine's fear and uncertainty; the hostile reactions of the passengers underscore Juliet's vulnerable position. When Juliet arrives in England, she is an anonymous "Wanderer" (59); her acquaintances refer to her as "the Incognita" (31). Even her race is uncertain; she arrives "black, patched, and pennyless [*sic*]" (28) and her fellow passengers believe that she is a runaway slave. Juliet's friends soon christen her "Ellis" (owing to the fact that the letters that she receives from her friends are directed to "L.S."), but the narrator does not refer to the heroine by her given name until the third volume, and Juliet does not own her surname until the fifth. For more than ten months, she remains in limbo, unable to confide in family or friends; for more than seven hundred pages, Burney maintains suspense about Juliet's past. By withholding the details of Juliet's history until late in the text, Burney evokes both the emotional strain and the practical difficulties that Juliet experiences as a result of her coerced match.

Burney further undermines Juliet's union in the climactic scenes following the commissary's arrival in England. After a long chase, during which the commissary's agent pursues her through the New Forest, Juliet seeks refuge at an inn just as the commissary arrives there. Juliet's suitor Albert Harleigh happens to be staying at the inn, too; when he attempts to intervene on her behalf, the commissary bursts out, "*Oses tu nier mes droits?*"—or, "Darest thou deny my rights?" (726), as Burney translates in a note. Burney estranges the commissary by recording his threats in French; the narrator likewise refers to him as "the foreigner" (728), further distancing him from English readers. Much as in the ceremony at the mayor's office, Juliet remains silent when the commissary insists that she acknowledge their tie; she refuses either to concede or deny that he is her spouse. Unlike in the earlier episode, though, in this scene there are others present who shore up her will. Albert stands aside, distraught and helpless when the commissary claims Juliet as his "eloped wife" (728), but her elderly friend and admirer, Sir Jaspar Herrington, promptly arrives with a peace officer. Before Juliet can board the latter's coach, the officer arrests the Frenchman under the Aliens Act of 1793—or the "alien-bill" (756), as Sir Jaspar calls it—which gave the British government summary powers to deport foreigners.[24] The officer has no orders for Juliet's arrest and, "resolute against any resistance," he compels the commissary, "though storming, raging, and swearing, . . . to re-enter the inn" (734) without her. Through a law designed to defuse the French threat to English public life, the novel thus puts an end to Juliet's private terror. Contrary to Lord Denmeath's claims, the novel shows, the commissary—rather than Juliet—is the "criminal" (552) who must be expelled from the country. The Frenchman's arrest enables Juliet to regain her voice; she now recounts the history of her coerced match, exposing and condemning the violent constraints placed upon her will. Juliet's narrative affirms what the commissary's arrest has already shown: the need for legal authority to counter male violence and shore up women's agency.

Even as the novel undermines the commissary's claim over Juliet, however, it backs away from suggesting that she can simply ignore her vow. When Juliet finishes recounting her history, Sir Jaspar declares that she is "free as air" (753). Juliet's half-brother, Lord Melbury, later issues the same verdict; he insists that Juliet "had never really been married; that a forced, interrupted, and unfinished lay-ceremony, had mockingly been celebrated . . . and that the marriage could never have been valid, either in sight of the church, or of her own conscience" (856). Juliet is not willing to go this far. While she feels certain that her match cannot be valid—the "violent constraint, the forced rites, the interrupted ceremony, [and] the omission of every religious form" (845) convince her of that—she insists that her "violated freedom [has to] be legalized" (778) before she marries again. Her reluctance to heed her friends' advice stems primarily from her concern for the bishop, whose life depends upon her fidelity to her pledge. But this complication signals a reluctance on Burney's part to endorse even the specter of self-divorce. In England, marriage remained, in essence, an indissoluble tie; the idea of divorce sparked heated debates in this period.[25] Wallace argues that, in her portrait of Juliet's plight, Burney embraces the "radical feminist" position that Wollstonecraft offers in *Maria, or the Wrongs of Woman* (1798), implicitly sanctioning divorce for unhappy wives.[26] Unlike Wollstonecraft's novel, however, *The Wanderer* avoids confronting the problems experienced by women trapped in miserable matches. Where Wollstonecraft likens the plight of abused wives to that of slaves, Burney uses the language of "fetters" (816) and "shackles" (862) to describe Juliet's "marriage" only after she makes clear that Juliet's vows are not binding in the first place. Burney's focus is not the problems that stem from an unhappy union but the difficulties that attend a coerced and invalid match. So anxious is she to distance her treatment of marriage from that of the revolutionaries, as we will see, that, even after she establishes the match's illegitimacy, she puts an end to her heroine's difficulties by killing off the illicit "spouse."

Burney develops her critique of the contractual model of marriage through her portrait of Elinor Joddrel. Unlike the dutiful "Ellis," the outspoken Elinor eagerly embraces the idea of radical freedom. Elinor turns twenty-one shortly after the Revolution "burst[s] forth" (152); the political transformation inspires her to declare her own personal independence. She refuses to abide by her aunt's wishes now, determined to do "everything that she like[s]" (69). Her admiration for the Revolution creates tensions not only with her guardian but also her fiancé, the traditional-minded lawyer Dennis Harleigh. Where she views the uprising as "the finest thing in the world, . . . Mr. Dennis said [it] was the very worst" (69). Her enthusiasm for the Revolution becomes only stronger when—like Wollstonecraft—she goes to France to witness the conflict firsthand. Elinor's two-year stay there "luminously open[s] [her mind] to its own resources, and inherent right of choice" (156). Dennis's brother, Albert, who escorts her home, recoils at the "[u]nbridled liberty" (18) he sees there; Elinor relishes it.[27] Much as Wollstonecraft does, she applies the ideas that she encounters there to her personal life. Elinor goes abroad, in part, because she realizes that she loves Albert and wishes to put off her match with his brother. As her feelings for Albert remain the same when she returns, she informs her fiancé that she is no longer able to marry him. The Revolution provides the model for her breach. "But for the late glorious revolutionary shake given to the universe," Elinor tells Juliet, "I should, at this very moment, from mere cowardly conformity, be the wife of Dennis!—In spite of my repentance of the engagement, in spite of the aversion I have taken to him. . . , I must have been that poor man's despicable wife!" (154). Elinor looks forward to contracting a secret union with Albert now, and she advises Juliet to do the same with Lord Melbury. Teasing Juliet about the interest that the young nobleman has shown in her, Elinor "exhort[s] her [friend], now in raillery, now in earnest, but always with agitated vehemence, to make no scruple of going off with Lord Melbury to Gretna Green" (112; see also 148, 473). Elinor alludes here to the Scottish village that attracted English couples seeking to elude the restrictions of Hardwicke's Act. In Scotland, as in France, marriage remained a civil contract. Scottish law went even further than that of France in licensing individual freedom: couples could form binding unions there simply by exchanging consent before two witnesses.[28] For Elinor, as for the Scots and the French revolutionaries, marriage is, in essence, an affective agreement between two free individuals.

Although the novel affirms Elinor's sense of the centrality of love to marriage, it shows the dangers of turning the nuptial tie into a simple contract. Juliet's plight as the Earl of Melbury's unacknowledged granddaughter serves as a powerful rebuke to Elinor's "clandestine scheme" (201); Juliet's precarious position, as we have seen, is the direct consequence of her parents' secret match. Elinor's suggestion that Juliet elope with Lord Melbury raises even further difficulties, for Lord Melbury is Juliet's half-brother. Juliet knows that she and Lord Melbury are kin, and she promptly rejects the nobleman's proposals; as in *Evelina* (1778), there is no real danger of incest here. But Elinor's commitment to freedom licenses such transgressions. As Elinor sees it, one can marry whomever, whenever, and wherever one wishes to wed. Indeed, her own desire for Albert has incestuous overtones since she falls in love with him when she is engaged to his brother. In the end, Elinor's plan to run off with Albert backfires: after he rejects her suit, Elinor "elope[s]" (197) from her aunt's house with only a scared servant for company. Even as the novel defuses Elinor's threat, it shows the ethical and practical problems with her proposal.

The novel likewise undermines Elinor's attempt to seize control of courtship. Emboldened by her success directing a private performance of John Vanbrugh and Colley Cibber's *The Provoked Wife*, Elinor plans every encounter with Albert as if she were scripting a scene for the theater. When Juliet, acting under Elinor's direction, fails to elicit the hoped-for expressions of regard from Albert, Elinor approaches him herself. Echoing Wollstonecraft, she justifies her unconventional behavior by invoking the "Rights of woman" (175). In her "personal vindication" (175) of the principles upon which she acts, Elinor again applies the revolutionary ideals to her personal life. The novel shows, though, that—like the revolutionaries—she takes her commitment to freedom too far. No sooner does Elinor proclaim her love for Albert than she is overcome with shame. "How tenacious a tyrant is custom!" she laments. "Who should have told me, only five minutes ago, that, at an instant such as this; an instant of liberation from all shackles, of defiance to all forms; its antique prescriptions should still retain their power to confuse and torment me?" (174). Burney suggests here both the difficulty of escaping such prescriptions and the need to abide by them. Elinor's subsequent violence further reinforces the necessity of such restraints. When Albert rejects Elinor's advances and tacitly affirms her suspicion that he loves Juliet, Elinor pulls out a knife and threatens to end her own life with it. Juliet cries out for her friend to "forbear," assuring Elinor that Ellis (as Elinor calls Juliet) "never will be his!" (183). But this statement does not satisfy Elinor. She asks her friend again whether she would "refuse the hand of Harleigh, [if] he were to offer it to [her]," upon which Juliet declares that she will "never forget [her] engagement!" (185). In forcing this promise from Juliet by threatening to kill herself, Elinor embraces the coercive tactics that she claims to detest. As Andrea K. Henderson observes, Elinor's "theatrical display of desire rapidly becomes a miniature version of the Terror."[29] The promise that Elinor extracts from her friend stands in for Juliet's forced engagement to the commissary; Albert believes that Juliet refuses to marry him because she is bound by her promise to Elinor. Like the French politician and his ruthless agent, Elinor thinks only of her own needs and desires. Her vexed relationship with Albert and coercive dealings with Juliet highlight the problems that result from excess freedom in the negotiation of the nuptial tie.

The novel further shows the dangers of Elinor's approach to marriage when she lures Juliet and Albert to an isolated churchyard several weeks later. Once Elinor realizes that Juliet refuses to wed Albert, she becomes determined to bring them together so that Albert can experience the pain of rejection. After Juliet and Albert follow her inside the chapel, she throws off her veil, crying "Here! Harleigh, here! . . . 'tis here you must reciprocate your vows! Here is the spot! Here stands the altar for the happy;—here, the tomb for the hopeless!" (580). She then takes out a pistol and points it at her temple, imploring Ellis (as she still refers to Juliet) to come to the front of the chapel:

> Approach, Ellis, approach! . . . and let me sanction your nuptial contract! I here solemnly give you back your promise. I renounce all tie over your actions, your engagements, your choice. Approach, then, that I may join your hands, while I quaff my last draught of tender poison from the grateful eyes of Harleigh, whose happiness,—my own donation!—will cast a glory upon my exit! (580–81)

In Elinor's determination to "join" Juliet's and Albert's hands, Burney suggests a desire to solemnize—rather than simply authorize—their union. Such a desire is consistent with her view of marriage as a private contract.[30] The episode, though, highlights the limits of this approach. The union that Elinor attempts to stage does not affirm the love between two free individuals; it reflects Elinor's jealous rage. Even now, when Elinor claims to renounce all control over Juliet's actions, she resorts to violence. Elinor lures Juliet to the church, the novel suggests, to make a mockery of a sacred tie. (Elinor has, in fact, "publicly proclaimed her religious infidelity" [591].) The match, as she explains, is simply the "last act" in her lengthy "tragi-comedy" (581). Elinor predictably dispenses with all rules; although Juliet and Harleigh need to solemnize their vows in a formal, public ceremony and Juliet needs to obtain her guardian's assent before obtaining a license to wed, Elinor suggests that her own consent is all that Juliet needs to contract this match. The physical and emotional threats that permeate the proceeding underscore the necessity of such restraints.

In the end, Elinor's violence recoils back on herself. In this scene, she proposes to sacrifice her life for Albert: his joy, she explains, will be her bequest, his happiness her "donation" (581). She is motivated, of course, primarily by revenge; she wants Albert to feel the pain of her loss—wants him to regret loving and marrying Juliet. But Albert is impervious to her scheme: he thwarts her suicide by seizing her pistol and shows little sympathy for her "disordered . . . state" (582). Even afterward, when Elinor lies ill in bed, Albert refuses to visit her. Instead, he presses Juliet to marry him, elated that Elinor has "annulled [her] engagement" (595). At the same time that the novel exposes Albert's heartless treatment of Elinor, it highlights the costs of her uncontrollable passion.

Love and Law: Reimagining Marriage

Although the novel distances Juliet from her subversive double, it does not reject all of the ideas that Elinor espouses. Through Juliet's eventual union with Albert, Burney affirms the idea of marriage as a public institution subject to regulation by church and state, while criticizing the patriarchal principle inscribed in England's own nuptial law. Burgess suggests that Burney responds to the threat of French revolutionary ideals by invoking "an ancient ideal of marriage, a traditional contract between gentlemen, replacing circulating women and fluctuating worth with a stable system of value and exchange."[31] According to Burgess, this view of the nuptial tie accords precisely with that enshrined in Hardwicke's Act. For James Thompson, too, Burney presents marriage as an exchange between men; on his reading, Burney achieves closure by containing Juliet within domestic space, "moving [her] from . . . [an] exposed and vulnerable state . . . into the home of a new, protective male."[32] In *The Wanderer*, however, Burney undermines the patriarchal logic of the Act. Even as the novel shows the need for parental approval of children's matches, it shifts the focus of courtship from the wishes of fathers and guardians to those of the principal parties, affirming women's agency in the negotiation of the nuptial tie.

Until the middle of the eighteenth century, couples could form binding unions in England simply by exchanging vows before two witnesses. The canon law technically required couples to comply with certain formalities, such as publishing banns or purchasing a license and exchanging vows in church before witnesses during canonical hours. But the church courts rarely enforced penalties for violations of these requirements and the unions, if properly witnessed, remained valid.[33] Clerics, jurists, and social observers sharply criticized these matches, however, for enabling coercion, infidelity, and fraud. Legislators, for their part, introduced numerous bills seeking to outlaw clandestine unions in the Restoration and the early eighteenth century.[34] It took until 1753 for both Houses of Parliament to agree on the goals and terms of a law. In the spring of that year, Lord Chancellor Hardwicke introduced a bill that combined a host of restrictions with severe penalties for noncompliance. After nearly three months of heated debates and numerous revisions, the bill passed by a vote of 125 to 56.[35] As of March 25, 1754, the Marriage Act deemed all unions solemnized in England and Wales to be void unless they were preceded either by the calling of banns on three prior Sundays in the parish churches where each of the parties lived, or by the issue of an ecclesiastical license. Marriages had to be solemnized by authorized clergymen according to the form established in *The Book of Common Prayer* and, unless the parties obtained a Special License from the Archbishop of Canterbury, the ceremonies had to take place in one of the parish churches where banns had been called or where one of the parties had resided for four weeks before obtaining an ordinary license. The unions had to take place in the presence of at least two witnesses and had to be properly registered.[36] Individuals under the age of twenty-one, moreover, needed to obtain the consent of their fathers in order to proceed by license. If a minor's father was no longer living, she needed to obtain the assent of her guardian or—if she had no guardian—that of her mother. Without such permission, her union would be void.[37] In privileging the will of fathers over that of mothers, the law effectively turned marriage into an exchange between men.

Not surprisingly, these requirements sparked fierce controversy. During the debates in the Commons leading up to the law's passage, critics objected that the measure wrongly privileged familial and social stability over individual freedom. Charles Townshend warned that the bill would establish "such a tyrannical power in the father, as [would] . . . be the ruin of many children. . . ."[38] Robert Nugent likewise argued that the bill would enable the "quality and rich people" of England to "acquire the absolute disposal of their children in marriage."[39] After the law's passage, the Reverend Henry Stebbing published a series of treatises criticizing the nullity clauses and affirming individuals' natural right freely to form marriage; other observers denounced the Act on similar grounds.[40] In Parliament, meanwhile, Charles James Fox and other MPs attempted to repeal or modify the law. Legislators such as Burke and Richard Brinsley Sheridan, however, vigorously defended the measure. In his speech against Fox's 1781 repeal bill, Burke explained:

> The improvident marriage of one man becomes a tax upon the orderly and regular marriage of all the rest. . . . To give a man a family during his apprenticeship, whilst his very labor belongs to another; to give him a family when you do not give him a fortune to maintain it . . . would be to burden the state with families without any security for their maintenance. When parents themselves marry their children, they become in some sort security to prevent the ill consequences. You have this security in parental consent. . . .[41]

Much as in his treatise on the Revolution, in this speech Burke's main concern is ensuring stability and order in society. His focus on parental consent effectively erased that of the contracting parties, but he saw no reason to be concerned. In his view, critics like Fox needlessly worried about the "avaricious principle of fathers." "It is avarice by proxy," Burke maintained, "it is avarice not working by itself or for itself, but through the medium of parental affection, meaning to procure good to its offspring."[42] This argument ultimately prevailed: although the Commons voted to amend the Act, the Lords defeated the measure.[43]

In treatises, newspapers, and popular debating societies, however, men and women continued to question the restrictions that the Act placed on children's freedom. In *Letters on Love, Marriage, and Adultery* (1789), for example, one observer denounced the "unreasonable exercise of parental authority" in England, linking such authority to conjugal misery and infidelity.[44] The writer maintained that mutual affection was essential to marriage and insisted that "all connections, without that affection, which may be truly and properly called love; whether effected by the authority of parents, by views of interest, or by lust, however sanctified by superstition or legal forms, are PROSTITUTIONS."[45] Debating societies also considered the limits of the law. "Many are of Opinion, that the Marriage Act is repugnant to the Laws of Nature," the Coachmakers Hall Society declared in February 1790, "and has been a Bar to the Felicity of Thousands."[46] "Would it not be better," the society asked, "if young Men after the Age of 18, and young Women after the

Age of 16 could marry without being subject to any Censure from their Parents, their Friends, or the World?"[47] Legislators, too, worried about the law's effects on young people. Two years before the publication of Burney's novel, the House of Commons again considered proposals to repeal the provisions of the Act that voided the matches of minors who failed to obtain parental consent.[48]

In *The Wanderer*, Burney affirms critics' concerns about parents' and guardians' control over courtship. The earl's contract with the commissary shows the limits of Burke's faith in paternal benevolence. Rather than protect Juliet, as we have seen, the earl strips her of her inheritance, making her over to the most dangerous and unprincipled of men. The earl gives Juliet no power to dissent to the union; he assumes the right—as her closest living male relative—to negotiate a match on her behalf. After he dies, his son-in-law, Lord Denmeath, presumes to enforce the agreement, pledging to give the commissary "his assistance and [Juliet's] portion" (729). In their effort to make Juliet an "alien to [her] country" (752), these men betray both their kinswoman and their nation. The kindhearted bishop—who constitutes himself Juliet's "guardian and protector" (644) when her maternal grandmother dies—is powerless to protect Juliet from the mercenary arrangements of her father's kin. The earl's and Lord Denmeath's role in Juliet's plight vividly shows the dangers of turning marriage into an exchange between men.

Through Juliet's union with Albert, Burney develops her critique of Hardwicke's Act, while distancing English law from that of France. After Juliet is reunited with her guardian and her uncle, Albert offers her his hand once more. Where Albert previously attempts to pressure Juliet into marrying him, he begins his proposal now by assuring her that she "can have no tie but what is voluntary" (860). Before Lord Melbury obtains the assent of the bishop and the admiral on Albert's behalf, Juliet gives her own consent to the match. The novel thus shifts the focus from Melbury's discussions with the men to her own dialogue with Albert. In response to Melbury's petition, we learn only that the bishop feels "an implicit trust in the known judgment and tried discretion of his ward" (864). The admiral, too, approves of the union, for he holds that "a female, as the weaker vessel, could never properly, nor even honourably, make the voyage of life, but under the safe convoy of a good husband" (864). His paternalistic remarks, though, have been the object of satire from the beginning. While the admiral's and the bishop's presence is important to the resolution of Juliet's difficulties—the admiral possesses a duplicate copy of the codicil to Lord Granville's will, and he uses it to demand that Lord Denmeath restore Juliet's inheritance—their wishes do not trump those of Juliet.

At the same time that Burney affirms women's agency in the negotiation of the nuptial tie, she reminds us of the importance of formal, public marriage. At a dinner celebrating Juliet's engagement, the admiral recalls the plight of his deceased sister and inquiries into the motives for Lord Granville's secrecy. The bishop explains that if his friend could have "foreseen the innumerable hardships, the endless distresses, from which neither prudence nor innocence could guard the helpless offspring of an unacknowledged union, he would either, at once and nobly, have conquered his early passion; or courageously have sustained and avowed its object" (869). Albert, too, observes that, when Lord Granville sent his daughter to France, he could not have foreseen the upheaval that would result from the revolutionaries' "new doctrines" and their misguided attempts to emancipate individuals from all social ties (869). Through this exchange, the novel summons up the dangers of unregulated passion, distinguishing England's approach to marriage from that of France. In Juliet's union with Albert, Burney ultimately imagines marriage as an affective agreement, sealed by parental consent.

At the same time that the novel celebrates Juliet's union, however, it acknowledges her loss of freedom as a wife. After describing Juliet's first few years of marriage and describing Elinor's reaction to her friend's match, the narrator concludes by affirming the courage, ingenuity, and independence that Juliet has shown in the face of all of her challenges:

> Here, and thus felicitously, ended, with the acknowledgment of her name, and her family, the DIFFICULTIES of the WANDERER;—a being who had been cast upon herself; a female Robinson Crusoe, as unaided and unprotected, though in the midst of the world, as that imaginary hero in his uninhabited island; and reduced either to sink, through inanition, to nonentity, or to be rescued from famine and death by such resources as she could find, independently, in herself. (873)

In this passage, immediately after the narrator suggests that the heroine's "difficulties" have ended, she invokes them again, likening her own fictional wanderer to Daniel Defoe's famously autonomous hero. Even as Burney affirms Juliet's legitimacy and recounts the happiness that Juliet enjoys as Albert's wife, she reminds us of the lengthy ordeal that her heroine has "independently" survived. Nor does she stop there; the narrator goes on to lament "the DIFFICULTIES with which a FEMALE has to struggle" and to applaud her ability to overcome them (873). "Yet even DIFFICULTIES such as these are not insurmountable," the narrator insists, "where mental courage, operating through patience, prudence, and principle, supply physical force, combat disappointment, and keep the untamed spirits superior to failure, and ever alive to hope" (873). With these words, Burney summons up the specter of the heroine's rebellious friend, who advises Juliet, earlier in the novel, to "remember that [she is] an active human being" and that her "FEMALE DIFFICULTIES will vanish into the vapour of which they are formed" (397). Even as Burney writes Elinor out of the novel's end, then, she invokes her fiery spirit. Burney leaves us with a final image of Juliet as the Wanderer, running from the commissary, circulating through English society, relying on her own resources, and acting as an independent agent.

Notes

1. Frances Burney, *The Wanderer; or, Female Difficulties*, ed. Margaret Anne Doody, Robert L. Mack, and Peter Sabor (New York: Oxford University Press, 2001), 646. All further references will be noted in the text by page number to this edition.

2. Burney accompanied her husband, Alexandre d'Arblay, to his native country in 1802. The ongoing military conflict prevented her from returning to England until 1812 (see Margaret Anne Doody, *Frances Burney: The Life in the Works* [New Brunswick, NJ: Rutgers University Press, 1988], 313; Frances Burney to Dr. Burney, post September 23, 1813, in *Journals and Letters*, ed. Peter Sabor and Lars. E. Troide [New York: Penguin, 2001], 469).

3. On nuptial law in revolutionary France, see Suzanne Desan, *The Family on Trial in Revolutionary France* (Berkeley: University of California Press, 2006), 47–67; and James F. Traer, *Marriage and the Family in Eighteenth-Century France* (Ithaca, NY: Cornell University Press, 1980), 79–104. On the Marriage Act, see "An Act for the Better Preventing of Clandestine Marriages," 26 Geo. II cap. 33, in *The Statutes at Large*, ed. Danby Pickering, 42 vols. (Cambridge: Joseph Bentham, 1766), 21:124–30; and R. B. Outhwaite, *Clandestine Marriage in England, 1500–1850* (London: The Hambledon Press, 1995), 75–97.

4. For the debates over Hardwicke's bill, see "Debate in the Commons on the Clandestine Marriage Bill," in *The Parliamentary History of England*, 36 vols. (London: T. C. Hansard, 1813; reprint, New York: AMS Press, 1966), 15:1–84; and "Debate in the Lords on the Clandestine Marriage Bill," in *Parliamentary History*, 15:84–87. For Burke's defense of the law, see "Speech on the Second Reading of a Bill for the Repeal of the Marriage Act," in *The Works of Edmund Burke*, 9 vols. (Boston: Charles C. Little and James Brown, 1839), 5:431–35. Parliament considered bills to postpone, amend, or repeal the Act in 1754, 1765, 1772, and 1781 as well as 1812 and 1813 (Outhwaite, *Clandestine Marriage*, 112–16, 145).

5. Wallace, "Rewriting Radicalism: Wollstonecraft in Burney's *The Wanderer*," *Eighteenth-Century Fiction* 24 (2012): 488, 499. Doody similarly suggests that the novel "shows that Burney had . . . been listening, seriously listening, to the feminists of the '90s, to writers like Mary Hays and Mary Wollstonecraft" (*Frances Burney*, 334). According to Doody, the novel invites "a good deal of sympathy" for the radical-minded Elinor Joddrel, and Juliet's own "experiences offer a feminist and social view complementary to the theories of Elinor" (335, 350). For other readings of the novel as a feminist text, see Julia Epstein, *The Iron Pen: Frances Burney and the Politics of Women's Writing* (Madison: University of Wisconsin Press, 1989), 175–91; Barbara Zonitch, *Familiar Violence: Gender and Social Upheaval in the Novels of Frances Burney* (Newark: University of Delaware Press, 1997), 113–38; and Rose Marie Cutting, "Defiant Women: The Growth of Feminism in Fanny Burney's Novels," *SEL* 17 (1977): 525–30.

6. Darryl Jones, "Radical Ambivalence: Frances Burney, Jacobinism, and the Politics of Romantic Fiction," *Women's Writing* 10 (2003): 19. For similar readings of the novel's ambivalence, see Amanda K. Henderson, *Romanticism and the Painful Pleasures of Modern Life* (Cambridge: Cambridge University Press, 2008), 101–24; Katharine M. Rogers, *Frances Burney: The World of 'Female Difficulties'* (New York: Harvester Wheatsheaf, 1990), 131–66; Kristina Straub, *Divided Fictions: Fanny Burney and Feminine Strategy* (Lexington: University Press of Kentucky, 1987), 182–220; Justine Crump, "'Turning the World Upside Down': Madness, Moral Management, and Frances Burney's *The Wanderer*," *Eighteenth-Century Fiction* 10 (1998): 325–40; and Pam Perkins, "Private Men and Public Women: Social Criticism in Fanny Burney's *The Wanderer*," *Essays in Literature* 23 (1996): 69–83.

7. Claudia Johnson, *Equivocal Beings: Politics, Gender, and Sentimentality in the 1790s* (Chicago: The University of Chicago Press, 1995), 178.

8. Ibid.

9. Burgess, *British Fiction and the Production of Social Order, 1740–1830* (Cambridge: Cambridge University Press, 2000), 110.

10. Ibid. For James Thompson, too, Burney imagines marriage as an exchange between men (see *Models of Value: Eighteenth-Century Political Economy and the Novel* [Durham, NC: Duke University Press, 1996], 156–58, 174–84).

11. Desan, *Family on Trial*, 15–46.

12. Ibid., 16; Traer, *Marriage and the Family*, 95. Previously sons under the age of thirty and daughters under twenty-five had to obtain their fathers' consent to marry; the new law required children under twenty-one to obtain the assent of their fathers or—if their fathers were dead or unable to act—their mothers (Traer, *Marriage and the Family*, 95, 139).

13. Desan, *Family on Trial*, 96–99; Traer, *Marriage and the Family*, 105–36.

14. Lynn Hunt, *Inventing Human Rights: A History* (New York: W. W. Norton, 2007), 63.

15. On civil marriage under the Napoleonic Code and the reaction against the contractual model, see Desan, *Family on Trial*, 283–310; and Ursula Vogel, "The Fear of Public Disorder: Marriage between Revolution and Reaction," in *Shifting the Boundaries: Transformation of the Languages of Public and Private in the Eighteenth Century*, ed. Dario Castiglione and Lesley Sharpe (Exeter: University of Exeter Press, 1995), 71–88.

16. *Reflections on the Revolution in France*, ed. Conor Cruise O'Brien (New York: Penguin, 1986), 191–95.

17. *Three Letters Addressed to a Member of the Present Parliament, on the Proposals for Peace with the Regicide Directory of France*, in *Works of Edmund Burke*, 4:394. On Burke's anxiety about female sexuality, see

Deidre Lynch, "Domesticating Fictions and Nationalizing Women: Edmund Burke, Property, and the Reproduction of Englishness," in *Romanticism, Race, and Imperial Culture, 1780–1834*, ed. Alan Richardson and Sonia Hofkosh (Bloomington: Indiana University Press, 1996), 40–71.

18. Burke, *Three Letters*, 394, 396.

19. Hannah More, *Village Politics*, in *The Impact of the French Revolution: Texts from Britain in the 1790s*, ed. Iain Hampsher-Monk (Cambridge: Cambridge University Press, 2005), 197, 202.

20. "City Debates," *Daily Advertiser*, November 9, 1791.

21. Ibid. According to another advertisement, the debates typically attracted "from 400 to 600 respectable Citizens of this great Metropolis" ("City Debates," *Daily Advertiser*, February 13, 1790). On the rise of debating societies and a helpful listing of their debates, see Donna T. Andrew, comp., *London Debating Societies, 1776–1799* (London: London Record Society, 1994).

22. Frances Burney to Georgiana Waddington, November 23, 1790, in *Journals and Letters*, 307.

23. Frances Burney to Doctor Burney, October 2, 1792, in *The Journals and Letters of Fanny Burney (Madame D'Arblay)*, vol. 1, *1791–1792*, ed. Joyce Hemlow with Curtis D. Cecil and Althea Douglas (Oxford: Clarendon Press, 1972), 230. Earlier in 1792, though, Burney had distanced herself from Burke's dire predictions concerning that "most violent concussion of principle & order" (Burney to Mrs. Phillips and The Lockes of Norbury Park, June 18, 1792, in *Journals and Letters of Fanny Burney*, 195).

24. The Act, which received royal assent on January 8, 1793, required all foreigners landing in Britain "to register at the customs office on disembarking, give up any arms in their possession and then wait to be granted a passport by the Home Secretary or by a local magistrate" (Clive Emsley, *British Society and the French Wars, 1793–1815* [London: Rowman and Littlefield, 1979], 20). The law also gave the Home Secretary power to deport undesirable aliens (21).

25. The church courts granted separations for cruelty and adultery, but such separations did not dissolve the nuptial tie; they simply licensed spouses to live apart. In the late seventeenth century, Parliament began granting private acts of divorce to husbands whose wives committed adultery; such acts, though, were difficult and expensive to obtain (see Lawrence Stone, *Road to Divorce: A History of the Making and Breaking of Marriage in England, 1530–1987* [New York: Oxford University Press, 1995], 192, 301–46). For debates about divorce in the late eighteenth century, see "City Debates," *Daily Advertiser*, September 11, 1790; "London Forum," *Daily Advertiser*, February 12, 1794; and "How to Make All the World Happy," *Morning Chronicle*, December 5, 1796.

26. On Wallace's reading, Burney depicts "a woman almost literally 'Bastilled' in marriage," showing that "virtuous women must be freed from the chains binding them to marriages that contravene an English sense of justice" ("Rewriting Radicalism," 498). Emily Hodgson Anderson refers to Juliet as "a wife on the run," giving her an identity that Burney takes pains to deny (*Eighteenth-Century Authorship and the Play of Fiction: Novels and the Theater, Haywood to Austen* [New York: Routledge, 2009], 69; see also Straub, *Divided Fictions*, 219). Doody does not examine Burney's treatment of divorce in this novel but she notes that when Burney resided in France, she formed a close friendship with Mme. de Maisonneuve, herself a divorcée. Doody suggests that after the unhappy experiences of Burney's sisters in marriage, "Burney had no need to look harshly upon full legal separation of unhappy spouses" (*Frances Burney*, 314).

27. Wollstonecraft went to France in 1793 to observe the Revolution; upon her return, she published an optimistic account of its early stages (see Janet Todd, *Mary Wollstonecraft: A Revolutionary Life* [London: Weidenfeld and Nicholson, 2000], 195–202; Wollstonecraft, *An Historical and Moral View of the French Revolution* [1794], in *The Works of Mary Wollstonecraft*, ed. Janet Todd and Marilyn

Butler, 7 vols. [New York: New York University Press, 1989], 6:1–235). She had previously defended the principles of liberty and equality in her fiery reply to Burke's *Reflections* (see *A Vindication of the Rights of Men* [1790], in *A Vindication of the Rights of Men with A Vindication of the Rights of Woman and Hints*, ed. Sylvana Tomaselli [Cambridge: Cambridge University Press, 1995], 5–64).

28. Stone, *Road to Divorce*, 80–81. On Gretna Green's popularity with English couples, see Outhwaite, *Clandestine Marriage*, 132–35; and Stone, *Road to Divorce*, 130–31.

29. *Painful Pleasures*, 103–4.

30. According to the form of the ceremony set down in *The Book of Common Prayer*, the priest declares, "we are gathered together here in the sight of God, and in the face of this congregation, to join together this man and this woman in holy Matrimony"; at the end of the ceremony, he "join[s] their right hands together, and say[s], 'Those whom God hath joined together, let no man put asunder'" (*The Book of Common Prayer, and Administration of the Sacraments* [Oxford: W. Jackson and A. Hamilton, 1781], 193, 195). Burney's portrait of Elinor's performativity draws upon long-standing associations between clandestine marriage and the theater. For a discussion of these connections, see Lisa O'Connell, "Marriage Acts: Stages in the Transformation of Modern Nuptial Culture," *differences* 11 (1999): 68–111.

31. Burgess, *British Fiction*, 111–12.

32. Thompson, *Models of Value*, 178. Anderson likewise emphasizes Juliet's passivity; on her reading, "chance, and not her own agency, is responsible for [Juliet's] good fortune" (*Eighteenth-Century Authorship*, 68). Maria Jerinic, by contrast, argues that Burney shows that "English marriages are as suspect as the French ones." "Juliet," she claims, "falls back into her proper and accepted place within the English patriarchal family structure" at the novel's end ("Challenging Englishness: Frances Burney's *The Wanderer*," in *Rebellious Hearts: British Women Writers and the French Revolution*, ed. Adriana Craciun and Kari E. Lokke [Albany: State University of New York Press, 2001], 77). On this reading, Burney criticizes patriarchy but cannot imagine an alternative to it.

33. Outhwaite, *Clandestine Marriage*, 20; and Stone, *Road to Divorce*, 51–53, 72–73, 76–78, 96–97. The common law courts, which handled property disputes, recognized all unions solemnized by clergy (or individuals who at least purported to be clergy), no matter where or when the unions took place (*Road to Divorce*, 96–98). Rebecca Probert, however, emphasizes that clandestine matches did not confer on parties all of the same legal consequences as did regular marriages (see *Marriage Law and Practice in the Long Eighteenth Century: A Reassessment* [Cambridge: Cambridge University Press, 2009], 166–84).

34. On the campaign against clandestine marriage, see Henry Gally, *Some Considerations upon Clandestine Marriages*, 2nd ed. (London: J. Hughs, 1750); Outhwaite, *Clandestine Marriage*, 68–73; and Stone, *Road to Divorce*, 115–19.

35. Outhwaite, *Clandestine Marriage*, 75–97.

36. "An Act for the Better Preventing of Clandestine Marriages," 124–29.

37. Ibid., 127.

38. "Debate in the Commons," 59.

39. Ibid., 16.

40. See Stebbing, *An Enquiry into the Force and Operation of the Annulling Clauses in a Late Act for the Better Preventing of Clandestine Marriages, With Respect to Conscience* (London: M. Cooper, 1754), repr. in *The Marriage Act of 1753: Four Tracts* (New York: Garland, 1984); Stebbing, *A Dissertation on the*

Power of States to Deny Civil Protection to the Marriages of Minors Made without the Consent of their Parents or Guardians (London: C. Davis, 1755), repr. in *The Marriage Act of 1753; Reflections on the Marriage Act; with Some Hints for a New Law: Humbly Offered to the Consideration of Parliament* (London: G. Woodfall, 1764); and *Reflections on the Repeal of the Marriage-Act, Now Under Consideration of Parliament* (London: J. Fletcher & Co., 1765).

41. Burke, "Speech," 432.

42. Ibid., 434; see also "On the Bill to Explain and Amend the Marriage Act," in *The Speeches of the Right Honourable Richard Brinsley Sheridan*, 3 vols. (London: Henry G. Bohn, 1842), 1:16–17.

43. Although Fox initially brought in a bill to repeal the Act, he later introduced provisions that sought to amend the law by lowering the ages at which children could marry without obtaining their parents' assent. On the Lords' defeat of the bill, see Outhwaite, *Clandestine Marriage*, 115–16.

44. *Letters on Love, Marriage, and Adultery; Addressed to the Right Honourable the Earl of Exeter* (London: J. Ridgway, 1789), 34.

45. Ibid., 75.

46. "Coachmakers Hall," *Daily Advertiser*, February 25, 1790.

47. Ibid.; see also "Westminster Forum," *Daily Advertiser*, January 20, 1790.

48. Outhwaite, *Clandestine Marriage*, 145. Parliament did not repeal the provisions in question until 1822, and even then the amended law required minors to obtain parents' consent, signified in writing and attested by witnesses' oaths (153; see also Robert Philip Tyrwhitt, *The Marriage Act, 3 Geo. IV. c. 75 . . . and an Abstract Thereof*, 2nd ed. [London: A. Strahan, 1822], 12). The Civil Marriage Act of 1836 likewise retained the requirement of parental consent even as it ended the Anglican Church's virtual monopoly over marriage (163–65).

Erin Sheley

Doubled Jeopardy: The Condemned Woman as Historical Relic

IN *LETTERS ON DEMONOLOGY AND WITCHCRAFT* (1830), SIR WALTER Scott returns to a theme that had reappeared throughout his literary oeuvre: the trial and condemnation of women for specious crimes under the aegis of improperly construed authority. In this work Scott traces the history of the belief in witchcraft from the time of the ancients until his present day, with an emphasis on the means by which supposed witches were detected and prosecuted. He dwells on the role of political ferment displaced, through formal punishment, onto the witch's body, characterizing Joan of Arc's martyrdom at the stake, for example, as "not . . . a sacrifice to a superstitious fear of witchcraft, but a cruel instance of wicked policy mingled with national jealousy and hatred."[1] In describing the seventeenth-century English "witchfinder" Matthew Hopkins, he asserts that such a "monster . . . could only have existed during the confusion of civil dissension."[2] And of the execution of the Scottish noblewoman Janet Douglas, Lady Glammis, he notes "one of the earliest real cases of importance founded upon witchcraft was, like those of the Duchess of Gloucester and others in the sister country, mingled with an accusation of a political nature, which, rather than the sorcery, brought the culprits to their fate."[3] Periodically Scott enters the text himself through reference to his own physical access to legal history, noting where, in the records he surveys to reconstruct the trials of several Scottish peasant women, "[t]he margin of the court-book again bears the melancholy and brief record, '*Convicta et combusta*' [convicted and burned]."[4] This essay will explore how, like these archival remains of executed witches, Scott's fictional condemned women serve as relics through which a history of evolving British legal identity becomes present and legible, and the manner in which the sentimentalized body of the punished woman became a touchstone around which eighteenth-century penal discourse became organized.

Walter Scott was, of course, a lawyer, and a number of critics have examined his literary use of the law to convey cultural and political change, particularly in the *Waverly* novels. Wolfram Schmidgen, arguing that, in *Waverly* (1814), Baron Bradwardine's loss and subsequent restoration to his estate Tully-Veolan represents the incorporation of Scotland into Great Britain, points to the stronger title to real property enjoyed by Scottish lords as opposed to their English counterparts (whose rights were formally limited by a fiction of derivation from those of the Crown) and the extent to which this property-centered legal tradition took on a Scottish nationalist significance.[5] Further, Schmidgen argues convincingly that Scott explicitly recognizes a relationship between property and the legitimacy of the common law that derives from the ultimate unknowability of the origins of the latter: for Scott (as for Blackstone, as I will discuss in greater detail below) "the epistemological inaccessibility of the common law's origin ensures its indivisibility from local custom and hence its legitimacy and national significance."[6] Likewise, Daniel Cottom has identified the role of the rule of law in the *Waverly* novels as, in lieu of violence, the distinguishing characteristic of the modern world.[7] And Joan Garden Cooper has shown how *Waverly* may be read as a criticism of the imposition of English treason law on Scotland, with particular attention to Scott's relationship with Baron David Hume, his law professor at the University of Edinburgh, whose *Commentaries of The Law of Scotland Respecting Crimes* is noteworthy for distinguishing the English treason law as harsher than that of Scotland.[8] This body of scholarship has made a compelling case that Scott the novelist incorporated the concerns of Scott the lawyer into both the structure and substance of his romances. While this work has largely focused on how Scott uses the law to highlight concerns over national identity and English sovereignty, I will argue that his treatment of gender aestheticizes a particular concept of and reaction to the condemned woman in the context of the common law tradition generally. To demonstrate the narrative concerns galvanizing the evolution of seventeenth- and eighteenth-century penal practice, I will show how Scott establishes the characters of Constance de Beverly in *Marmion* and Rebecca of York in *Ivanhoe* as aesthetic objects necessarily fixed in time in order to contemplate legal change through a historically controlled process.

"Convicta et Combusta": Punishing Women under the Common Law

Around the time of upheaval and discontinuity in sovereignty occasioned by the English Revolution, Interregnum, and Restoration, with their accompanying revisions to English law, the great legal commentators of the seventeenth and eighteenth centuries became preoccupied with the relationship between the English common law system, temporality, and history. In one of the most influential masterworks on English law, the *Institutes of the Lawes of England* (published between 1628 and 1644), Sir Edward Coke famously describes principles of law as natural and fixed, dating back to the imagined Trojan foundations of English civilization and susceptible of being discerned through deductive legal reasoning.[9] Largely in response to Coke, Sir Matthew Hale, a Royalist jurist whose work became the basis for much Restoration-era legal reform, developed a philosophy of more active evolution of the laws, in which the action of historical experience forms a central part. In his essay "Considerations Touching the Amendment or Alteration of Lawes" Hale claims that "Antient lawes . . . are not the issues of the prudence of this or that council or senate" but rather of "time, which as it discovers day after day new inconveniences, so it doth successively apply new remedies. . . . a kind of aggregation of the discoveries results and applications of ages and events."[10] According to James Boyd White, Hale thus "conceives of the law not as a series of particular rules or decisions but as a cultural process, with its own modes and standards of transformation."[11] White says that by "time" Hale means "the community and culture over time" and that it is "Hale's word for our collective experience, the test of a rule or practice in many contexts, from many points of view."[12]

Writing a century later in his 1769 *Commentaries on the Laws of England*, Blackstone too describes legal change as a temporally inflected process, in which English essentialism and teleological progress play equally important roles. English criminal law is, he claims, "more rude and imperfect than the civil," though intrinsically superior to that of the other European powers.[13] He stresses the danger posed by the weight of history: where some laws "seem to want revision and amendment" it is due to "too scrupulous an adherence to some rules of the ancient common law, when the reasons have ceased upon which those rules were founded; from not repealing such of the old penal laws as are either obsolete or absurd."[14] For example, he claims that had Parliament referred the law more frequently for revision to "some of the learned judges" then "it is impossible that in the eighteenth century it could ever have been made a capital crime 'as it was for many years' to break down . . . the mound of a fishpond . . . or to cut down a cherry-tree in an orchard."[15] In other words, laws could change but the possibility for absolute correctness remained; so long as the proper authorities were consulted, certain inappropriate outcomes would be "impossible." Though the *Commentaries* is ostensibly a treatise on the state of English law as it actually was, Blackstone incorporates the mechanism for change—and, quite frequently, the calls for specific changes—into his task of compilation and description. Indeed, the treatise ends with a chapter entitled "The Rise, Progress, and Gradual Improvements, of the Laws of England," which highlights how the articulation of new legal norms can occur at a great historical remove from their realization in fact.[16] For example, he states that it was from the reign of Edward I—"from the exact *observation* of *Magna Charta*, rather than from its *making* or *renewal* [under Edward's grandfather and father] . . . that the liberty of Englishmen began again to rear its head."[17] This interrelated coexistence between archaic practice and evolved norm reveals the potentially schizophrenic cultural effects of common law evolution, which will remain important to the rest of my argument. Ian Ward has discussed how Scott's awareness of Enlightenment principles of progress coupled with his antiquarian conservatism created a similar schizophrenia: "[i]n a sense the core belief in the Enlightenment was like a rock constantly battered by reactionary doubt . . . Like so many literary and intellectual figures at the turn of the century,

Scott developed an almost pathological dread of civil unrest."[18] For these reasons, I will assert, the trials of Constance and Rebecca dramatize the implicit need for legal change over time, while simultaneously rendering their subjects fixed in their victimization.

The end of the eighteenth century saw a significant legal turning point respecting criminal punishment generally and the punishment of female criminals specifically. Karl Shoemaker has characterized this moment as a shift in thinking about the role of physical pain in criminal punishment. In contrast to a medieval view of physical suffering as a largely internal mediation between the human soul and the divine good of salvation, the Enlightenment era brought a reconception of pain as a necessary evil to be imposed by external authorities to achieve utilitarian ends.[19] In other words, this shift constituted the abandonment of "transcendent aims" in punishment.[20] (In Foucault's famously pessimistic formulation, of course, the decrease in state-authorized violence to the body is accompanied by an increase in authoritative violence to the mind.)[21] Whether or not we accept a Foucaultian reading of this historical moment, however, one thing remains clear: "punishment" as a subject for cultural scrutiny is accompanied by its history in a legal tradition characterized, at least in aspiration, by discursive continuity. In other words, the punished body in a given historical moment is of necessity partially defined by its relationship to past bodies punished by the same legal tradition used to justify all of them.

This problem, which I will refer to as one of historical simultaneity, is particularly demonstrable in the late eighteenth-century abolition of burning at the stake as a punishment for women convicted of treason. A brief look at the history of this debate will show, first, how the endurance of the historical burned female body as an object in the cultural imagination complicated the discourse about the contemporary penal practice and, second, how the historical demands of the medieval concept of chivalry served contradictory purposes in structuring the legal relationship between the state and the condemned woman.

Until the reforms of the late eighteenth century, the punishment at common law for high treason—meaning rebellion or acts of violence against the sovereign itself—was, for a man, to be hanged, disemboweled, and quartered, while for a woman it was to be burned alive. In contrast to high treason, petty treason consisted of murders committed as rebellion against non-sovereign forms of authority: a wife killing her husband, a servant killing his master or mistress, or a clergyman killing his prelate. Unlike the equally brutal punishments for high treason, in these cases the distinction between the genders mattered in terms of suffering: a woman convicted of petty treason was still burned, while a man only hanged. Furthermore, until the Treason Act of 1351 elevated it to high treason, the counterfeiting of silver or gold coins (insofar as it was a usurpation of the sovereign privilege to coin money) was considered petty treason at common law. Even after the 1351 Act, however, the punishments for "coining" were not changed, meaning that while a male counterfeiter would be hanged, a female could, as an outraged 1788 editorial in the *Sunday Times* put it, be "roasted . . . alive, for putting a pennyworth of quicksilver on a half-penny worth of brass."[22] The distinction was enough to register for Defoe's cutpurse Moll Flanders, who blithely commits numerous capital offenses—sometimes apparently motivated by no more than sheer enjoyment—but for whom the prospect of coining occasions the first moment at which the text depicts true terror of the law:

> [H]ad I been taken, [the punishment] had been certain death, and that at a stake—I say, to be burnt to death at a stake; so that though I was to appearance but a beggar, and they promised mountains of gold and silver to me to engage, yet it would not do. It is true, if I had been really a beggar, or had been desperate as when I began, I might perhaps have closed with it; for what care they to die that can't tell how to live? But at present this was not my condition, at least I was for no such terrible risks as those; besides, the very thoughts of being burnt at a stake struck terror into my very soul, chilled my blood, and gave me the vapours to such a degree, as I could not think of it without trembling.[23]

Eighteenth-century legal commentators have described this distinction between sexes as, paradoxically, part of a kind of chivalric tradition. In his *Commentaries* Blackstone notes that "in treasons of every kind the punishment of women was the same, and different from that of men" because "as the decency due to the sex forbade the exposing and publicly mangling their bodies, their sentence (which is to the full as terrible to sensation as the other) was to be drawn to the gallows and there to be burned alive."[24] The anonymous 1777 treatise *The Laws Respecting Women as They Regard Their Natural Rights* puts an even finer point on it: "the public exhibition of their bodies, and dismembering them, in the same manner as is practiced to the men, would be a violation of that natural decency and delicacy inherent, and at all times to be cherished in the sex."[25] By contrast, in 1797 Scott's professor David Hume, explicating the English law of treason, which was imported into Scotland for the purposes of construing the 1708 Treason Act in the wake of the Old Pretender's assertion of his claim to the English throne, alludes to the paradox inherent in this practice. To avoid the "shocking indecencies" of drawing and quartering, Hume writes, a woman convicted of treason must be "burned alive" despite the fact that such indecencies "have been generally dispensed with by the royal mercy, even in the case of men" and further describes it as a "strange distinction" that a woman coiner "has judgment to be burned alive" where a man would only hang.[26]

Historian Simon Devereaux has pointed out that this justification for the punishment sits in strange tension with the rhetoric of eighteenth-century reformers, whose arguments against burning turned in large part on precisely the same notions of feminine delicacy. As a 1788 editorial in *The Times* put it, for example, "The very savages in the wildest parts of the world, pay respect to their females, while Great Britain selects their tender bodies as the only objects for excruciating torture." Devereaux, arguing in favor of attention to more practical circumstances surrounding the abolishment of burning in addition to the accepted master narrative of changing cultural ideals, notes "the issue seems not to have been so clear-cut amongst many contemporaries who regarded the actual practice of burning women already to be a sufficiently chivalrous concession to female delicacy."[27]

In any case, one year after the coiner Christian Murphy was the last woman to be burned for treason, the punishment was abolished by the Treason Act of 1790.[28] Less interesting for our purposes than the relative importance of chivalric rhetoric as opposed to pragmatic concerns in the specific abolishment of burning is the role of chivalry surrounding the female body as an organizing rhetorical structure for understanding the common law in the first place. In *The Laws Respecting Women* the punishment is justified in a Coke-style formulation of fixed principles deduced by reason: because feminine delicacy has "at all times" been cherished, the immolation of the female body is the "natural" penal consequence. The history of chivalry plays an equally important role for reformers: as suggested by the *Times* column, which establishes Great Britain as the presumed end of a legal teleology starting with the "savages," increased care for the tenderness of women is a feature of the potentially evolving common law tradition imagined by Hale and Blackstone.

Furthermore, the protest over burning in the 1780s turned on an outdated image of the burned woman. As noted in *The Laws Respecting Women*, "the humanity of the English nation has authorized by a tacit consent, an almost general mitigation of such part of their judgments as favors of torture and cruelty . . . there being very few instances (and those accidental . . .) of any person being emboweled or burnt, till previously deprived of sensation by strangling."[29] Indeed from the 1690s onward it was the norm for executioners to hang the prisoner at the stake before lighting the fire. In 1726 Catherine Hayes became the last woman on record as having been literally burned alive, for murdering her husband, and that due to the accidental burning of the executioner's rope before he could pull it taut.[30] Despite this fairly significant fact, Devereaux notes, the elite cries for reform published in the 1780s frequently discuss the punishment as though the outdated model of live burning were still in effect: the *Times* reference to "roasting alive" being an example.[31] This schizophrenic quality to the debate was augmented by the fact that these condemnations of live burning were published in the same papers alongside accurate descriptions of the executions.[32] Furthermore, the fixation on the suffering of the burning woman is likewise apparent in the popular broadsheet publications circulated amongst the lower classes on the occasions of these executions, and written from the perspectives of the condemned. In *The Last Farewell to the World of Phoebe Harris*, the author describes her burning as "a terrible death to die" and in *The True and Remarkable Life and Adventures of Catherine Heyland*, the death is described quite explicitly as an example of the transcendent physical suffering associated, as described above, with a much earlier penal culture:

I Catherine Heyland, doom'd to death,
Must in the flames resign my breath,
O Lord receive my soul on high,
When to the stake I'm brought to die.

O Lord, my soul with fright doth shrink,
I dread this cup which I must drink,
O Jesus Christ I pray look down,
Prepare for me a heavenly crown.[33]

This quick survey of examples selected by Devereaux to demonstrate the lack of unified cultural sentiment against the burning of the "delicate" sex shows likewise how the image of the burning woman has the effect of unifying and reifying a whole legal history into one bifurcated image. In the historical simultaneity of the living with the already-dead burning woman we find a history of transcendent punishment embedded within the post-Enlightenment practice of the "necessary evil," and a historically specific role for chivalry, unifying the present with the past even as it changes the latter.

Before moving on to Constance and Rebecca, it should be noted that the doubled role of chivalry in constructing the female body in its relationship to state violence had rhetorical significance beyond the debate over modes of capital punishment. In describing the threats to national well-being posed by the disruption of history through revolution, Scott's fellow Tory Edmund Burke famously dwells on the violated and punished body of Marie Antoinette. In *Reflections on the Revolution in France* he describes her arrest in 1789 not only as a rape of an individual woman, but as an act of violence to the people of the state whose royal line was thus interrupted:

> A band of cruel ruffians and assassins . . . rushed into the chamber of the queen, and pierced with an hundred strokes of bayonets and poniards the bed, from whence this persecuted woman had but just time to fly almost naked . . . The king . . . and his queen, and their infant children (who once would have been the pride and hope of a great and generous people) were then forced to abandon the sanctuary of the most splendid palace in the world, which they left swimming in blood. . . .[34]

And with respect to her execution in 1793 he lamented:

> It is now sixteen or seventeen years since I saw the Queen of France, then the Dauphiness, at Versailles; and surely never lighted on this orb, which she hardly seemed to touch, a more delightful vision. . . . But the age of chivalry is gone; . . . The unbought grace of life, the cheap defense of nations, the nurse of manly sentiment and heroic enterprise is gone.[35]

For Burke, the historically sound foundations to statehood were shattered by revolution, and this political disintegration is accompanied by a corresponding destruction of the chivalric tradition necessary to protect the female body. Yet in this disintegration, the feminine body itself became a terror with political significance. In *Reflections* Burke goes on to describe the Parisian women in the mob during the arrest of the royal family as "the furies of hell, in the abused shape of the vilest of women" who "according to their insolent fancies" sometimes "mix and take their seats amongst men."[36] Scott's condemned women represent the same outrages to chivalry as Burke's Marie Antoinette but remain safely constrained, avoiding the horrors of the other extreme.

An Old Tale, Often Told: the Entombment of Constance de Beverly

In the 1808 epic poem *Marmion*, Scott narrates the adventures of the brutal English nobleman Marmion in connection with the Battle of Flodden Field (in which, historically, King James IV of Scotland died fighting the armies of King Henry VIII). In the letter introducing the first canto of the poem, Scott approaches his subject in the same mode of historical examination he used in his account of the court records of the Scottish witch trials. He immediately locates his poetic voice as a mediator of masculine heroic tradition through the physical artifacts of the present; unlike the perpetual turn of the seasons through which summer brings "new life," historical England remains in a perpetual winter state due to the physical entombment of its heroes represented by Nelson's "shrine" and Pitt's "hallowed tomb."[37] Scott suggests that his poetic act is to serve as a mediator between relic and history through the possibility that a "powerful call" could "bid arise / the buried warlike and the wise" (15).

The poem revolves around two highly gendered criminal trials: Ralph de Wilton's trial by combat and subsequent banishment for treason, and Constance's perfunctory trial and condemnation by the commission of clergy for breaking her vows as a nun (in order to aid Marmion in his false accusation of the former). Both trials suffer from procedural failures flowing from what Scott portrays as antiquated Catholic religious practice. When Marmion arrives at Heron's castle, he is lauded for his defeat of de Wilton, whose crest Heron's courtiers declare he "wears with worthy pride" and demonstrate the falsely assumed equivalence between strength of arms and justice of cause when they state that de Wilton was "conquered in the right" (25). Likewise they underscore the condemnatory function of this martial encounter in noting that Marmion tied de Wilton's shield "on the gibbet-tree, reversed"; though de Wilton is not sentenced to death, he is symbolically hanged like a petty criminal. Marmion's subsequent allusion to the actually guilty pretender Perkin Warbeck, "that Flemish counterfeit, / Who on the gibbet paid the cheat," re-characterizes Warbeck's treason as an act of counterfeiting much like his own act of forging de Wilton's letter, for which crime the "gibbet" punished the wrong party (28).

Likewise, though Scott describes Constance's trial as a council "of life and death," as though both were theoretically possible outcomes, it is clear at once that the proceeding is as procedurally unjust as de Wilton's and that her punishment is a foregone conclusion. No one so much as questions the prisoners before the (symbolically blind) abbot rises "To speak the Chapter's doom / On those the wall was to enclose" (59). Only Constance's continued attempts to speak prompt the proceeding to take on any testimonial function, but when she has concluded, the blindness and false religiosity of her judges is reiterated: "with stupid eyes, the men of fate / Gazed on the light inspired form" and the abbot once again "rais[es] his sightless balls to heaven" before passing the death sentence (63). Scott renders the connection between these two failed trials explicit through the character of the abbess, who both presides over Constance's trial and, in passing on Constance's papers to the disguised de Wilton, demonstrates a failure to comprehend the injustice of de Wilton's trial as well: even upon realizing that he had been falsely accused, she wonders if "some form was unobserved" or "in prayer or faith he swerved," because it was otherwise impossible to account for the fact that the "blessed ordeal" failed (141).

Nonetheless, the failure of the archaic church as the dispenser of penal justice has dramatically divergent effects according to gender, which Scott aestheticizes accordingly. As in his introductory letter, where he claims chivalric tales allow him the poetic efficacy to defeat the workings of Time and to transcend the static space of the Gothic cemetery, the chivalric nature of the trial by combat fails to suppress or objectify Ralph de Wilton. Not only is his punishment of banishment unsuccessful, but he subverts the exact religious authority that condemned him by adopting the guise of a pilgrim to range through the country from which he is legally excluded. Furthermore, Marmion himself is never punished for his crimes against de Wilton but permitted to die in exalted style in battle, "a gallant knight, / With sword in hand, for England's right" (187). Even the mishap by which his remains were mistaken for those of a peasant, who was consequently buried in his tomb, has the effect of freeing Marmion himself from the fixity of the relic with which the introductory letter opens.

By contrast, Scott depicts the clerical punishment of a woman as transfiguring her into a historical object and fixing her suspended in space and time. Scott takes care to spatially locate Constance's trial "in a secret aisle beneath" the fireside at Lindisfare Abbey, where the other nuns are enjoying a rare evening of society (54). Her entombment has been symbolically effected even before her punishment, as she is already "numbered with the dead" by the Church for breaking her vows (57). Constance's depiction throughout the scene—anticipated by the stasis implicit in her very name—is one of aestheticized stillness. The narrator lauds her for the "matchless constancy" of her "composed look" and "steady eye" and invites us to contemplate her as an artistic object open to the gaze: "a form of wax . . . wrought to the very life . . . So still she was, so pale, so fair" (57). The impressiveness of her stillness is thrown into relief against the ravings of her male coconspirator, who "shamed not loud to moan and howl, / His body on the floor to dash, / And crouch, like hound beneath the lash" while she "Waited her doom without a tear" (57–58). Immediately before her sentence is passed the narrator praises "Such high resolve and constancy" embodied in a "form so soft and fair" (59).

The image of Constance entombed retains a spectral presence throughout the rest of the text, particularly at moments where poetry and storytelling threaten to undermine the primary martial aims of Marmion. Before her death Constance herself notes that she has become an archetype for the use of minstrels, noting that hers was "an old tale, and often told . . . Of maiden true betrayed for gold" (60). When Fitz-Eustace subsequently sings precisely such a ballad of a maiden betrayed, Marmion has the uncanny experience of seeming to hear "a death-peal rung / Such as in nunneries they toll / For some departing sister's soul" (79). In a moment of dramatic irony, the narrator states that Marmion mistakenly "deemed her well, / And safe secured in distant cell," drawing the parallel between Constance's entombment and the quasi-entombment of the cloistered nun generally (80). While Marmion never "augured of the doom / Which on the living closed the tomb," he does eventually come to the realization that, having enjoyed the comparative freedom of living as his lover:

> Her convent's peaceful solitude
> Is now a prison harsh and rude;
> And, pent within the narrow cell,
> How will her spirit chafe and swell! (81)

The ironic use of the word "spirit" and the intended metaphor "prison" underscore that the literally entombed Constance has come to stand in for the feminine object of punitive religious authority, even its routine exercise of suppressing living nuns.

The disturbance to Marmion's thoughts caused by these images of Constance resurface after yet another piece of minstrelsy: the innkeeper's tale of the Elfin knight. This story prompts Marmion to ride off from his camp seeking battle with the enchanted foe "for the right / To ask one question at the sprite" (89). The vagueness of the "one question"—presumably the fate of Constance—locates her, this time, as the object of a chivalric quest. The quest itself, in which Marmion is bested by the disguised de Wilton, is a reversal of the trial by combat in which Marmion had triumphed. Unlike Constance's punishment, which has been sublimated and aestheticized as a static quest object, Marmion's "punishment" in this altercation returns him to the active role of chivalric hero, which Fitz-Eustace observes, based upon his knowledge of the romances "Of Caxton, or de Worde" (99). Like Constance, Scott's later heroine Rebecca of York occupies the position of knightly quest object but, as we shall see, Scott renders her relationship to the evolution of English legal tradition even more explicit.

Honor or Justice: the Trial of Rebecca of York

The legal context of *Ivanhoe* (1820) is inherent to the structure of the novel's plot: the antagonist Prince John is best known historically for being forced to sign the *Magna Carta,* the document from which all of the common law "rights of Englishmen" so celebrated by conservatives like Scott and Burke theoretically flow. Scott therefore opens his chivalric romance with the plight of the inferior gentry "who, by the law and spirit of the English constitution, were entitled to hold themselves independent of feudal tyranny," and associates it with the illegitimacy of the Norman ruling class, which had imposed French onto "the courts of law," where "the pleadings and judgments were delivered" in that language, and made it "the language of honour, of chivalry, and even of justice."[38] (Scott hastens to note, of course, that the current English language is the superior product of historical evolution, "in which the speech of the victors and the vanquished have been so happily blended together" and "been so richly improved" by other importations [5].) Scott avoids impugning the actual monarch, King Richard, with this political state of affairs by focusing on his official absence and John's corresponding illegitimacy, and Richard's anonymous physical presence, as the ambiguous Black Knight whose alliance with the Saxons allows him to occupy a liminal space between oppressor and oppressed; his deprivation of his own title, this structure suggests, aligns him narratively with his tyrannized subjects: all were in some sense or another deprived of rights to which they were entitled at law.

Furthermore, two aspects of Scott's contemporary legal landscape manifest throughout the text and particularly in the confinement and trial of the Jewish heroine Rebecca for witchcraft. Amy Witherbee has written of Scott's concern over the suspension of the English writ of *habeas corpus* in 1817 and 1818, as a reaction to the French Revolution, and the resulting trials for sedition, which took place in both England and Scotland. The writ was originally passed by Parliament in reaction to the persecution and extralegal detention of religious dissidents by the Stuart crown: the writ—translated as "produce the body"—may be invoked by any subject seeking to have his arrest adjudicated in a court of law.[39] Witherbee has discussed the role of the Great Writ in Scott's *Old Mortality*, set during the period in which it was originally passed, but Scott's allusions in *Ivanhoe* to the impending *Magna Carta* underscore the debate between English liberty as a historical tradition and the arbitrary exercise of power asserted by contemporary critics of the suspension.[40] For example, of the rapacious Norman nobles who unjustly hold Rowena and Rebecca captive he writes, "It is grievous to think that those valiant barons; to whose stand against the crown the liberties of England were indebted for their existence should themselves be such dreadful oppressors and capable of such excesses, contrary not only to the laws of England but to those of nature and of humanity.[41]

The second relevant legal context was the ongoing agitation for the emancipation of the Jews in the United Kingdom, which would not culminate in Jewish males being permitted to serve in municipal office until the 1840s or in Parliament until the 1850s. Throughout Rebecca's captivity and subsequent trial she remarks upon her minority religious status as rendering her uniquely helpless for recourse against her persecutors. Her would-be ravisher Brian de Bois-Guilbert describes her as "in all save youth and beauty a very witch of Endor,"[42] anticipating Scott's later treatment in *Letters on Demonology and Witchcraft* of the Hebrew character of the biblical Witch of Endor as an archetype for subsequent Judeo-Christian penal conceptions of female witches:

> To illustrate the nature of the Hebrew witch and her prohibited criminal traffic, those who have written on this subject have naturally dwelt upon the interview between Saul and the Witch of Endor, the only detailed and particular account of such a transaction which is to be found in the Bible; a fact, by the way, which proves that the crime of witchcraft (capitally punished as it was when discovered) was not frequent among the chosen people, who enjoyed such peculiar manifestations of the Almighty's presence.[43]

Against the legal backdrop of Scott's day, then, Rebecca's portrayal as a beautiful, would-be martyr to the superstitions of the thirteenth century, prior to the purported protections of the *Magna Carta*, carries the doubled signification of contemporary oppression with those protections in doubt or misunderstood. We first intimate Rebecca's state of temporal suspension through the character of Urfried, the Saxon "hag" whose tower chamber Rebecca comes to occupy when she is imprisoned in Torquilstone Castle by the Normans. Her options in the scene in which she meets Urfried are either, through failure to resist the illegitimacy of her Norman captors as Urfried did, becoming a victim of their sexual predations until old age renders her unsuitable for that role, or killing herself. When Rebecca enters the turret Urfried is "murmuring to herself a Saxon rhyme, as if to beat time to the revolving dance which her spindle was performing upon the floor," the act of spinning itself a symbol of the endless passage of time (244). According to Rebecca's guard, Urfried must "leave this chamber to a fairer guest" because, like

an old warhorse, she has had her "paces in . . . time, but now a broken amble is the best of them" (245). If Urfried's wasted and entrapped femininity is the remainder of Saxon subordination to the Normans, Scott aestheticizes Rebecca's willingness to seek another sort of timelessness: when prepared to throw herself from the tower rather than bow to Bois-Guilbert's advances she looks—like Constance de Beverly during her trial—particularly beautiful:

> [H]er high and firm resolve, which corresponded so well with the expressive beauty of her countenance, gave her the looks, air and manner of a dignity that seemed more than mortal. Her glance quailed not, her cheek blanched not, for the fear of a fate so instant and so horrible; on the contrary, the thought that she had her fate at her command and could escape at will from infamy to death, gave a yet deeper colour of carnation to her complexion, and a yet more brilliant fire to her eye. (253)

Bois-Guilbert's exchange with Rebecca during this scene is grounded in his own illegitimate views on legal authority. "Thou art the captive of my bow and spear, subject to my will by the laws of all nations; nor will I abate an inch of my right, or abstain from taking by violence what thou refusest to entreaty or necessity" (251). When she responds by threatening to disclaim him as a heretic, he responds that "loud must be thy voice of complaint if it is heard beyond the iron walls of this castle," implying that the legal process normally commenced with a "complaint" has become trumped by the lawless exercise of physical force (251). Again like Constance, Rebecca's imprisonment within traditionally Gothic confines reifies and aestheticizes the absence of rule of law. That Scott's strategy here is consciously gendered becomes clear in the comparison of Rebecca's plight to that of Athelstane, whose "resurrection" after being entombed alive by greedy monks Scott depicts as almost entirely humorous, and unrelated to the legal problems that trouble the rest of the text.

Furthermore, Bois-Guilbert's attempts on Rebecca's body reflect the historical evolution of social contract theory, one of the basic traditions of the liberal legal order. Bois-Guilbert attempts to entice her with his view of his own power as a Knight Templar who loses "his social rights, his power of free agency, but he becomes a member and a limb of a mighty body, before which thrones already tremble" (255). This language echoes Thomas Hobbes's conception of legitimate government in *Leviathan* (1651), in which subjects surrender their individual wills to an all-powerful sovereign in exchange for protection against one another. (The language of limb and body seems an explicit reference to the famous frontispiece of *Leviathan*, etched by Adam Bosse with Hobbes's input, which features a crowned giant whose body is made up of hundreds of tiny individuals.)

After Bois-Guilbert states that a Templar "can possess neither lands nor goods, and lives, moves and breathes but at the will and pleasure of another," Rebecca declares that wielding power is "an evil recompense . . . for the surrender of the rights which are dearest to humanity" (254). Here she appears to anticipate the iteration of contract theory associated with John Locke, who in his *Second Treatise on Government* (1690) argued that the right to private property could be reasoned from natural law and that the protection, rather than usurpation, of private property was one of the most important functions of a legitimate government. Scott's association of the debate over the philosophical status of property rights across the seventeenth century with Bois-Guilbert's threats to rape the captive Rebecca under color of his thirteenth-century religious order is yet another example of the feminine body serving as an object simultaneously at stake in the legal regimes of two historical moments.

From the point at which Rebecca becomes accused of witchcraft, the appropriateness of her trial by the Grand Master of the Knights Templar is framed as a debate between spiritual and secular jurisdictions. The Templar Malvoisin first objects by mentioning "the laws of England," but the Grand Master states that because "the laws of England permit and enjoin each judge to execute justice within his own jurisdiction" it cannot be the case that "that power be denied to the Grand Master of the Temple within a perceptory of his order" (405). Malvoisin subsequently notes the basic lawlessness of the spiritual authority when he observes that "trial moves rapidly on when the judge has determined the sentence beforehand" (408).

Rebecca's simultaneous identity as an individual woman and a symbol of an oppressed people becomes reemphasized through reference to her physical embodiment. Bois-Guilbert complains that "the devil, that possessed her race with obstinacy, has concentrated its full force in her single person," and Mont-Fitchet says, "Were the souls of the twelve tribes in her single body, it were better she suffered alone" (406–9). Against the backdrop of the Jewish emancipation efforts of the nineteenth century, Scott compresses an entire history of anti-Semitism within Rebecca's potentially burned body. Likewise Malvoisin claims that "the death of a Jewess will be a sin-offering sufficient to atone for all the amorous indulgences of the Knights Templar," presenting a paradoxical acknowledgment of the illegitimacy of the Knights Templar as spiritual authorities while suggesting that its remedy is through the exercise of that illegitimate authority on the person of one woman (407).

During the trial itself Rebecca's aesthetic embodiment becomes the dialectical framework through which her guilt is debated. When objecting to being commanded to unveil herself "the sweet tones of her voice, and the softness of her reply, impressed on the audience a sentiment of pity and sympathy" and "[e]ven [the Grand Master] Lucas Beaumanoir himself was affected by the mien and appearance of Rebecca" (421–26). Nonetheless, "her exceeding beauty excited a murmur of surprise, and the younger knights told each other with their eyes . . . that Bois-Guilbert's best apology was in the power of her real charms, rather than of her imaginary witchcraft" (421–22).

Scott incorporates this awareness of Rebecca's physicality into his appraisal of the evidentiary standards at work in her trial. He first notes, in a laudatory gesture toward the justice of contemporary criminal proceedings, that the evidence against her "would have been, in modern days, divided into two classes—those which were immaterial and those which were actually and physically impossible" (422). As it was, in Rebecca's proceeding, "[l]ess than one half of this weighty evidence would have been sufficient to convict any old woman, poor and ugly, even though she had not been a Jewess. United with that fatal circumstance the body of proof was too weighty for Rebecca's youth, though combined with the most exquisite beauty" (423).

The determination of Rebecca's fate ultimately becomes, like the eighteenth-century debate over the burning of women, linked to competing conceptions of chivalry. The Grand Master characterizes Rebecca's crime in attracting Bois-Guilbert as an affront to chivalry: "she hath maddened the blood, and besotted the brain, not of a churl, but of a knight; not of a secular knight, but of one devoted to the service of the Holy Temple" (415). And yet Rebecca's potential salvation lies only in the possibility of trial by combat—a chivalric, highly un-law-like convention, but the sole procedural right the Grand Master feels moved to observe. (The absurdness of the Templars' view of chivalry is particularly clear in Bois-Guilbert's observation that Rebecca's guards are, even before conviction, "designed to conduct [her] to death . . . yet would not suffer [her] to be insulted by anyone") (438). As Rebecca puts it in her critique of chivalry, "It cannot be that in merry England, the hospitable, the generous, the free, where so many are ready to peril their lives for honour, there will not be found one to fight for justice" (425). Bois-Guilbert's efforts to use chivalry in her defense, of course, immediately become reversed when he is forced to fight on the side of the Templars.

The Grand Master expresses even the legal premise for the chivalric combat in terms of Rebecca's gendered body, stating "that by lawful *essoine* of her body, as being unable to combat in her own behalf, she doth offer, by a champion instead thereof, to avouch her case" (439–40). He cautions Rebecca that her feminine weakness translates into helplessness as a legal object: "As this thin and light glove of thine is to one of our heavy steel gauntlets, so is thy cause to that of the Temple, for it is our order which thou has defied" (427). Despite Scott's clear critique of the Templars' sadistic use of illegitimate authority, he dwells, as narrator, on the aesthetic value of Rebecca's acceptance of her unjust punishment.

Like Constance, Rebecca is notable for her stillness: "moving with a slow but undismayed step toward the scene of her fate" with "such an exquisite mixture of courage and resignation in her look that . . . each eye wept that looked upon her" (500). When encountering the pile of faggots prepared for her immolation, she "look[s] fixedly on the pile as if to familiarize her mind with the object, and then slowly and naturally turn[s] away her head" (501). In her response to Bois-Guilbert's horror of the scene, Rebecca replies "my mind and senses keep touch and time . . . and tell me alike that these faggots are destined to consume my earthly body and open a painful but a brief passage to a better world" (504). In this moment Scott draws upon the transcendent conception of punishment through pain to associate Rebecca's wronged beauty with the translation into the hereafter. Rebecca remains a chivalric quest object till the end—saved by Ivanhoe and then preserved in her virginal state forever after due to her unsuitability as a wife for her hero. Richard's slightly tardy appearance to banish the Templars with their corrupt penal processes ends the novel on a note of restored legitimacy which, Scott suggests, in some way mitigates the overall unjustness of the Norman rule with which he opens the novel (509). The aversion of Rebecca's wrongful punishment and the dismantling of her prosecutors acts as a stand-in for the whole-scale revolution that would have been necessary to undo the pervasive political wrongs Scott described at the outset. Rebecca, like Constance, is a site of convenient elision—through the preservation of her body in time (both from the flames and from ravishment) Scott can both condemn past practice and endorse the history upon which his current legal order rests.

Conclusions

The early nineteenth-century cultural preoccupation with medievalism, of which Scott is such a well-known exemplar, brought with it a nostalgia for chivalric tradition and the centering of the threatened female body that accompanies it. Yet this impulse should be understood against the backdrop of eighteenth-century developments in the philosophy of punishment and tensions surrounding the role of history in sustaining English constitutional legitimacy. *Marmion* and *Ivanhoe* are but two examples of how the chivalric tradition subtends the problem of feminine punishment. Scott's romances demonstrate that the anxiety to preserve the female body serves the broader purpose of allowing common law evolution within a space of legal constraint. In these texts he works to aestheticize the same property of historical simultaneity that is apparent in broader eighteenth-century discourse about the burning of women.

Notes

This chapter is an extract from "Doubled Jeopardy: The Condemned Woman as Historical Relic," first published in 24 *Law and Literature* 211 (2014). I would like to think Dr. Tara Ghoshal Wallace of George Washington University for her mentorship and support, both in connection with this project and generally.

1. Walter Scott, *Letters on Demonology and Witchcraft* (1830) (London: Routledge, 1884), 164.
2. Scott, *Letters*, 207.
3. Scott, *Letters*, 230.
4. Scott, *Letters*, 130.
5. Wolfram Schmidgen, "Picturing Property: *Waverly* and the Common Law," *Studies in the Novel* 29:2 (1997): 191.
6. Schmidgen, *Waverly*, 200.
7. Daniel Cottom, "Violence and Law in the Waverly Novels," *Studies in Romanticism* 20:1 (1981): 65.
8. Joan Garden Cooper, "Scott's Critique of the English Treason Law in *Waverly*," *Scottish Studies Review* 4:2 (2003): 17–22.
9. Edward Coke, *Institutes of the Laws of England*, 7 vols. (London, 1794).
10. Matthew Hale, "Considerations Touching the Amendment or Alteration of Lawes," in *A Collection of Legal Tracts Relating to the Law of England*, ed. Francis Hargrave (Dublin: E. Lynch, 1787), 254.
11. James Boyd White, *Acts of Hope: Creating Authority in Literature, Law, and Politics* (Chicago: The University Chicago Press, 1994), 129.
12. Ibid., 135.
13. William Blackstone, *Commentaries on the Laws of England: Of Public Wrongs* (1765–1769) ed. Robert Malcolm Kerr (Boston: Beacon Press, 1962), 3.
14. Blackstone, *Commentaries*, 3.
15. Blackstone, *Commentaries*, 4.
16. Blackstone, *Commentaries*, 479.
17. Blackstone, *Commentaries*, 497.
18. Ian Ward, "The Jurisprudential *Heart of Midlothian*," *Scottish Literary Journal* 24:1 (1997): 25–27.

19. Karl Shoemaker, "The Problem of Pain in Punishment: Historical Perspectives," in *Pain, Death, and the Law*, ed. Austin Sarat (Ann Arbor: University of Michigan Press, 2001), 17–18.

20. Shoemaker, "Pain," 36.

21. Michel Foucault, "Discipline and Punish: The Birth of the Prison," in *The Norton Anthology of Theory and Criticism* , ed. Vincent Leitch (New York: Norton, 2001), 1636–39.

22. Simon Devereaux, "The Abolition of the Burning of Women in England Reconsidered," *Crime, History and Societies* 9:2 (2005): 73.

23. Daniel Defoe, *Moll Flanders*, ed. David Blewett (New York: Penguin, 2012), 203.

24. Blackstone, *Commentaries*, 88–89.

25. *The Laws Respecting Women as They Regard Their Natural Rights*, ed. Joseph Johnson (London: Johnson, 1777), 344.

26. Baron David Hume, *Commentaries of the Law of Scotland Respecting the Description and Punishment of Crimes* (Edinburgh, 1797–1800), 1. Hume notes here that this punishment at common law was rendered moot by statute after the abolishment of burning in the Treason Act of 1790.

27. Devereaux, "Abolition," 4.

28. Devereaux, "Abolition," 6.

29. Johnson, "Laws Respecting Women," 344.

30. "Catherine Hayes," *Oxford Dictionary of National Biography* (Oxford: Oxford University Press, 2004), http://www.oxforddnb.com/view/article/12753.

31. Devereaux, "Abolition," 7.

32. Devereaux, "Abolition," 7.

33. Devereaux, "Abolition," 8.

34. Edmund Burke, *Reflections on the Revolution in France*, ed. L. G. Mitchell (Oxford: Oxford University Press, 1993), 71.

35. Burke, *Reflections*, 75.

36. Burke, *Reflections*, 76.

37. Walter Scott, *Marmion*, ed. Mary Willard (Stockbridge, MA: Hard Press, 2006), 11. Subsequent references will be given parenthetically within the text.

38. Walter Scott, *Ivanhoe* (New York: Modern Library, 2001), 5. Subsequent references will be given parenthetically within the text.

39. Amy Witherbee, "*Habeas Corpus*: British Imaginings of Power in Walter Scott's *Old Mortality*," *New Literary History* 39:2 (2008): 355.

40. Witherbee, "Habeas Corpus," 363–64.

41. Witherbee, "Habeas Corpus," 242.

42. Witherbee, "Habeas Corpus," 249.

43. Scott, *Letters*, 53–54.

Peter de Bolla

The Madness of Sovereignty: George III and the Known Unknown of Torture

THROUGHOUT THE AUTUMN OF 1788 THE KING OF ENGLAND, George III, was widely believed to be losing his mind. The sovereign was suffering from a "malady" that had no agreed-upon cause or prognosis.[1] While some said that the king had definitively lost his senses, others opined that he was suffering from the effects of a fever that began in his legs—caused by getting very wet on his horse—which had subsequently traveled to his brain. As days drifted into weeks, the nation itself became feverish with speculation. Matters were far from helped by the fact that no one in or close to the court, most especially his physicians, would venture a secure estimation of how long this malady might last. Politically this was a calamity. Parliament was effectively suspended and the governance of the country at a standstill. The newspapers and coffee houses of the capital were abuzz with opinion, rumor, and gossip.[2] Was the sovereign terminally insane or merely suffering from a fever that temporarily incapacitated his ratiocinative powers? As autumn turned to winter and the malady demonstrated no sign of improvement, the king's First Lord of the Treasury, Pitt the younger, came under enormous pressure from the opposition benches in Parliament—most notably and volubly from Charles James Fox—to agree to the appointment of the Prince of Wales as effective sovereign.[3] Such a move, Pitt well knew, would result in his losing office as the Foxite Whigs swept a new broom through the administration.[4] This story, the story of "mad King George" familiar to modern audiences by dint of a hugely popular stage play by Alan Bennett and subsequently successful film starring Nigel Hawthorne, suggests that from the moment his "malady" became public knowledge it prompted a crisis at the heart of the British empire and its sovereign family. Put simply, it was proposed that the still reigning—but mad—sovereign be deposed by an act of Parliament that would install as regent his first son, the Prince of Wales, whom George certainly distrusted and may even have strongly disliked. Such an act, as many argued, was without precedent and would arrogate to the two houses of parliament the power to appoint the sovereign of the state. In one swift move elective monarchy would be installed at the heart of the British constitution. All the efforts of the wise men who had, in 1688, constructed a beautiful system of government that preserved the mechanism of hereditary sovereignty would have been in vain. Their careful triangulation of legislative institutions—the sovereign, Lords, and Commons—would be undone as the two houses of Parliament assumed primacy. What has come to be known as the Regency Crisis of 1788–1789 was not, then, merely a battle between rival factions in court and Parliament, as it is commonly assumed. It was a crisis in how government was conceived that has at its center a very human, even sentimental predicament.

It is not an exaggeration to call this hiatus in government a "crisis." There was no precedent for a sitting monarch losing his senses. Every legislative act required the king's seal. Parliament itself could not be summoned without the king so doing.[5] The delicate balance between the three estates of government that had been established in 1688 required all three branches to operate. Indeed, without the sovereign the entire edifice was in danger of collapse. For some—mainly those who advocated reform of the political system and supported for the most part the Foxite Whigs[6]—the only solution was to appoint a successor to George III but, as all who informed themselves of the debates in Parliament and the country at large knew, the king was not dead and the crown was still very much upon his head. For others the appointment of a person charged with the responsibility—no matter how curtailed his powers might be—of carrying out the office of the sovereign while the king continued to be upon the throne was nothing less than treason.

Neither party, however, dissented from the view that no branch of government had within it the power to depose the monarch, nor was it proposed that anyone except the monarch had the right to summon Parliament. So they faced a major problem: since the king was indisposed for an unknowable length of time, the country was, effectively, rudderless. Without government. This was indeed a crisis.

It is true to say that the political scheming around the "king's malady" was intense, but if we neglect the human story at the center of the crisis we fail to notice a far more disturbing and potentially explosive consequence of its detail. Since eighteenth-century law deemed that those insane had no legal rights, the description of the king's malady, his temporary or permanent mental condition, was of the utmost importance.[7] Moreover, as shall be seen, the "treatment" of the monarch effectively condoned torture, thereby presenting a significant difficulty in the conceptualization of legitimate government.

The story that needs to be told, then, concerns the ways and means found for avoiding the complete disintegration of the complex forces
that held in tension person and rights, citizen and state, and sovereign and subject. Since the rights of persons rested on—in fact were unintelligible without—the sanctity of the person *primum inter pares*, the king, it is not immediately apparent how the legal framework that upheld the constitution and citizens' participation within it could remain intact. If the personhood of the sovereign no longer guaranteed the personhood of all other persons, the entire fabric of the polity and its legitimating legal provisions would have to be redrawn. This would entail separating out what had heretofore been taken axiomatically to be "whole and entire," namely the conjoint natural person of the king in his physical body and the political person, his function as sovereign in the constitutional triangulation of powers. The story that has not been told, then, is how the subjects and citizens of the first modern constitutional monarchy reconceptualized the body and person of the sovereign, itself, of course, a reconceptualization of the body politic.

The Legal Subject

Anglophone eighteenth-century legal practice owed everything to William Blackstone's *Commentaries on the Laws of England*, the digest of precedent and statute that Britain's foremost jurisprude began to publish in

1765.[8] Reprinted in countless editions, the *Commentaries* not only formed the basis for legal thinking in Britain for over a century, it also formed the backbone of the American colonists' practice of law and was bolted on to the Indian subcontinent's indigenous legal traditions. It would not be an exaggeration to say that for over a century, throughout the British empire, Blackstone was the authority for any legal matter. The *Commentaries* provided the platform upon which eighteenth-century systems of government and legality were built; they made sense of what it was to be a subject in and of the law in what was widely claimed and believed to be the most refined social, legal, and political system ever devised, a system that proudly announced and lived by its complete immersion in the ideology of the freeborn Englishman.[9] To be a subject in the British world of the eighteenth century was to be bathed in liberty.[10] It is, therefore, far from happenstance that the first volume of the *Commentaries* is overwhelmingly devoted to the rights of persons. And the third to seventh chapters of that first volume set out the rights of the person who guarantees the liberty of all others, the king.

The king, in fact, occupied a position that under the *ancien regime* would have been taken to indicate the subservience of all others, the subjects who give up part of their person in order to serve the sovereign. Blackstone, however, and the seventeenth-century jurists and political philosophers who brokered the settlement of 1688 ingeniously drove a wedge into the core of the feudal constellation by dispersing the centralizing and centrifugal power of divine right. The trick was to derive the legitimacy of the sovereign from the consent of the people whom he or she was to govern. Thus, although the only person in the state who has his own personhood merely by dint of being a subject was the sovereign. The king *is*. And the king is the *only person* who is on account of himself. Moreover, without the king no other person *is* in the sense that he or she has rights as a person. As Blackstone writes: "The executive power of the English nation being vested in a single person, by the general consent of the people, the evidence of which general consent is long and immemorial usage."[11] Typically the authority for this view is said to be "long and immemorial usage," a strategy that Blackstone and his contemporaries found extremely useful in their meld of positive law and precedent that formed the edifice of the English common law. But it is not its authority that we need to attend to here; rather it is the structural position occupied by this single person in a system that made visible, even guaranteed, the liberty of the freeborn Englishman. It is far from inconsequential, then, that one understands both who that person is and how such a person comes to occupy such a position. Blackstone continues:

> [I]t becomes necessary to the freedom and peace of the state, that a rule should be laid down, uniform, universal, and permanent; in order to mark out with precision, *who* is that single person, to whom are committed (in subservience to the law of the land) the care and protection of the community; and to whom, in return, the duty and allegiance of every individual are due. (I:183)

It is of the "highest importance," according to Blackstone, that the rule governing this be both "clear and indisputable": the singular person who provides the immobile center of this sophisticated system of balances that gives definition to each person's rights, dues, and obligations occupies a throne and wears a crown by dint of inheritance. And there are four features of this scheme that are each equally nonnegotiable: "First, that the crown is hereditary; secondly, that it is hereditary in a manner peculiar to itself; thirdly, that this inheritance is subject to limitation by parliament; lastly, that when it is so limited, it is hereditary in the new proprietor" (I:184).

Thus, by this "peculiar" scheme the person *primum inter pares* cannot be merely selected by any other person or group of persons—no institution has authority to elect or appoint the sovereign—yet at the same time, under certain conditions, the institution of Parliament may limit a hereditary line, even alter it. In this way the office of the king, the throne or crown that symbolically stands as the emblem of that office, is not identical to the *person* occupying it. Consequently,

> however the crown may be limited or transferred, it still retains it's descendible quality, and becomes hereditary in the wearer of it: and hence in our law the king is said never to die, in his political capacity; though, in common with other men, he is subject to mortality in his natural: because immediately upon the natural death of Henry, William or Edward, the king survives in his successor; and the right of the crown vests, *eo instanti*, upon his heir; (I:189)

This doctrine was stretched or tested to the limit in the case examined below in which George III was in danger of being pronounced dead in his political capacity while remaining alive in his natural. Such an eversion of the principle clearly had substantial consequences for the agency that presumed power to decide the life and death of the symbolic person of the crown. But it also was in danger of failing to respect the sanctity of the king's body. For according to Blackstone, without that *any* infringement of a person's rights became incoherent. This is because in effect any offense brought to the law is an offence against the body of the king. In order to understand this we need to take into account "that special pre-eminence" belonging to the king, a preeminence he holds "over and above all other persons." On account of this "the prerogative is that law in case of the king, which is law in no case of the subject" (I:232). In order to guarantee our freedom as subjects, then, we need a "preeminent" subject who is himself subject to a unique law, applicable only to him. In effect the king is both guarantor of the law and, at the same time, outside it. So it transpires that "by law the person of the king is sacred . . . for no jurisdiction upon earth has power to try him in a criminal way; much less to condemn him to punishment" (I:235). Furthermore the king "is not only incapable of *doing* wrong, but even of *thinking* wrong" (I:239). Rather like the hub of a wheel that provides stability and rigidity for all its spokes, the person of the sovereign "entire and whole" is required in order for the legal and political fabric of the state to function legitimately.

The Management of the King

In late 1788 when it became clear that George III was incapable of carrying out his official duties, the British Parliament was faced with a conundrum. As a legislature it held no authority within itself to govern or pass acts; even its assembling required the official summons of the sovereign. As far as anyone knew, the king's condition might improve very quickly or, equally, he might never recover. Matters were made even more difficult by the fact that the professional opinion of his physicians was both far from conclusive and disturbingly inconsistent. Some opined that he was suffering from a fever that had gone to his brain, while others suspected that he had become insane.[12] Perhaps one should find this uncertainty unsurprising, since the protocol which dictated that one remain silent in the presence of the monarch unless directly addressed by him made assessments of his health precarious. One must also take into account that eighteenth-century medical practice for the most part eschewed physical inspection or diagnostics. Even taking the sovereign's pulse was deemed by Sir George Baker, one of his physicians, an extraordinary step. It was hardly surprising, then, that they were at a loss as to what to do.

Difficult as it is to be certain of the facts surrounding the case, it nevertheless seems incontrovertible that the king was not himself. Lady Harcourt, for example, wrote in her diary on November 5:

> Every alarming symptom seemed increased; the bodily agitation was extreme, and the talking incessant, indeed it was too evident that his Majesty had no longer the least command over himself. His eyes, the Queen has since told me, she could compare to nothing but black currant jelly, the veins in his face were swelled, the sound of his voice was dreadful; he often spoke till he was exhausted . . . while the foam ran out of his mouth.[13]

Things deteriorated at such a speed that by Sunday, November 9, it was widely reported that he had died: "the belief was universal throughout the metropolis, that his Majesty was no more, and that the awful event was with-held from publication, till the Mayor of London was sworn into office."[14] In fact something else had transpired; the king, as Earl Stanhope noted, was no longer the king: "this was the precise moment when ceased the dominion of a Sovereign over his subjects, and when began, on the contrary, the dominion of sound minds over an unsound one." Here, he noted with great prescience "let History pause."[15]

After a little over a month the physicians determined to remove the patient to Kew. Unhappily for all concerned, the king was completely opposed to any relocation, so against his wishes that the removal of the court was organized in secret and the monarch effectively tricked into taking a journey whose termination point was an unheated and sparsely furnished residence ill equipped for the harsh winter. Once there it was resolved that the patient was to be kept in isolation, in a suite of rooms that were kept locked.

By December 1788, then, the king of Britain was effectively held prisoner by physicians who were clueless as to how to treat a "malady" they knew nothing about: it was surely a known unknown. The course of "treatment" that was instituted from this point on doubtless appears overly invasive or extreme to our modern eyes. It included bleeding through the application of leeches, cupping and purging through the ingestion of natural and proprietary emetics.[16] This was supposed to bring the king's evident delirium under some sort of control. Alas, it was signally ineffectual in so doing, so another course of action was embarked upon. On Friday, December 5, the king was first introduced to his new physician, Dr. Willis, a former clergyman and keeper of a madhouse in Lincolnshire. From now on the sovereign, who according to the law was incapable of doing wrong, was under the control of a lay practitioner of "mad doctoring" whose primary technique of treatment was a form of brainwashing. The sovereign was to be coerced into modes of behavior deemed correct by Dr. Willis and forced to learn by rote a script that this former clergyman thought to be appropriate for the ruler of the British empire.

Willis's techniques, including "giving the eye," that is, looking directly and sustainedly into the patient's eyes as a way of establishing dominion over him, were essentially directed at "correcting" the behavior of his charges.[17] One of the most extraordinary and most noted features of George III's illness was his constant speaking, indeed his inability to stop talking. Much of the time it would appear that he made little or no sense, and he was reported to have addressed inanimate objects as if they were people. At times during his most acute attacks he would become hoarse and almost unable to articulate on account of the overuse of his voice. He was also reportedly very loose in what he said, using curses or swear words and making lewd or improper comments. All of this was regarded by Willis as in need of "correction." This entailed him training his patient to say what was deemed to be "correct," and when he failed to do so, various methods of coercion were employed. Among them were constraining the patient in a cloth straitjacket, tying him down on his bed, and in the later stages of "treatment" strapping him into a specially constructed restraining chair. All of these physical restraints and coercive strategies were used on a person who was physically weakened from continual purges, an exclusively vegetarian diet, and frequent bloodletting. His legs were so frequently blistered they could no longer bear the weight of his emaciated body. Matters were not improved when the patient—as happened quite frequently—used what power was left to him by refusing to eat the gruel he was offered. On more than one occasion throughout the long months at Kew he seemed to be close to death.

The details of this "management" were variously known to his close circle, his ministers, and the wider public: some unknowns were certainly known.[18] Since Willis deemed that it would "inflame" his majesty's nerves by seeing his wife, Queen Charlotte, whom he adored, the queen may or may not have been closely aware of the details of the treatment. Indeed part of Willis's strategy was to bar access to his patient, and he succeeded somewhat in doing so, making it difficult, therefore, to assess how widespread accurate knowledge of the program of treatment was. It is, however, important to take measure of its cruelty.

Facts in this matter are not easy to establish. Although bulletins on the king's condition were issued daily (and even more frequently at the height of the crisis), the political situation inflamed and corrupted the flow of information.[19] The three physicians who claimed no expertise in the "management" of the mentally ill, Drs. Richard Warren, Sir George Baker, and Anthony Addington, were extremely cautious in their reports. Having no firm view about when or indeed whether the king might recover was, of course, fuel for the opposition who were advocating the appointment of the Prince of Wales as regent. This was certainly recognized by the three doctors, and some claimed that one or more of them were in league with the opposition faction. Willis, however, was confident from the outset that his patient would recover, although he was circumspect in his prognosis as to the timing of such a return to normality.[20]

There is a source, however, that remained unpublished until 1930, which may provide a more accurate if also deeply embedded version of what actually transpired in the private apartments in which the king was confined. One should recognize that even this "eyewitness" report has its own lapses, blind spots, and proprieties, since its author, an equerry to the king at the time, was not only very attached to his sovereign but also recognized the power relations that flowed through the court. Taking all this into account, it still opens a window onto the treatment of the sovereign that cannot fail to arouse sympathy. Greville's diary entry for Saturday, December 5, for example, reads: "About 5 o'Clock in the Morning H.M^{y} became so ungovernable that recourse was had to the strait Waistcoat: His legs were tied, & He was secured down across his Breast, & in this melancholy situation He was, when I came to make My Morning Enquiries—"[21] And then, preserving the dignity of his sovereign, he notes:

> However persuaded I had been of the necessity of obtaining positive submission from H. M^{y} under his Afflicting Malady, as the best means whereby his recovery might be ultimately expected, I have not been prepared for those harsher processes, which have followed— (127)

It seems very clear that the king was indeed delirious and abusive to his captor Willis and his "attendants," the men he brought from his madhouse in Lincolnshire to help in the physical "management" of the patient. But such violence was almost certainly exacerbated if not prompted by the cruelty of his treatment. Even so, there were moments of lucidity and touching calm. Greville notes of Tuesday, December 3:

> About 7 o'Clock it was proposed that He should go to bed. He objected & resisted much but was bound down in bed in a strait Waistcoat. His spirits were at this time very extraordinary. He was not violent, Neither did his Situation, and his restraint seem to press uncomfortably on Him, and now as He lay stretch'd out on his Bed, He sang. (131)

By late January the routine of coercion and reprieve was well established. If the king desisted from continuous verbal production and learned the lines fed to him by his captor, Willis, he was allowed to walk outside, even see members of his family. If he fell into "wrong" speech or was physically unruly, the restraining devices would be employed. On January 24 this included for the first time a specially constructed chair, as Greville notes:

> The King did not remain long under coercion—The Chair in which He had now been confined was a new one made on purpose. It is a common chair placed upon a floor of its own, which prevents a Person from moving it, nor can it be thrown down as a common Chair might be. When it was

> first brought into the Room to be made use of, the Poor King is said to have eyed it with some degree of Awe. (187)

A more extreme account of the harsh treatment of the sovereign might also give one pause for thought. Countess Harcourt, a member of the court, put it in the following manner:

> The unhappy patient . . . was no longer treated as a human being. His body was immediately encased in a machine which left it no liberty of motion. He was sometimes chained to a staple. He was frequently beaten and starved, and at best he was kept in subjection by menacing and violent language, The history of the King's illness showed that the most exalted station did not wholly exempt the sufferer from this stupid and inhuman usage.[22]

These eyewitness accounts provide enough evidence to suggest that whatever status was accorded to the monarch throughout his illness, it certainly did not map onto the "person" as defined by Blackstone's *Commentaries*. So what had happened to the king's own person? This was a matter of considerable public speculation.

The King Is Absent from Himself

Once the gravity of the situation became apparent to Parliament, three committees were established, one by the Lords and two by the Commons, whose business was to interrogate all the physicians attending the king in order to ascertain the likely outcome of the malady. Although they disagreed about much, the physicians were nevertheless of one mind that His Majesty was indeed incapable of "coming to Parliament, or attending to public business."[23] And so the following four months were spent debating a Regency Bill.[24] These debates were followed intensely by the public, and many pamphlets and newspaper columns contributed to the feverish speculation.[25]

Although reading through the record of the parliamentary sessions can sometimes provoke the impression that the "mother of all parliaments" tends to attract and nurture bellicose and self-important grandstanding, it is worth noting that the issue they were debating and the problem they faced had the utmost importance and consequence for the longevity of a mixed legislative system of government. The settlement of

1688 had ingeniously constructed a three-wheeled cart that could only function if all three wheels were touching the ground.[26] It is instructive, therefore, to follow the discussion closely.

Given that no one imagined that a miraculous and imminent recovery was likely, the first thing to be decided was if the two houses, the Lords and Commons, had legitimate power to appoint someone else who could carry out the functions of the sovereign. Many on the opposition benches already knew the answer: the regent was, naturally, the person who should step into the shoes of the king.[27] But what did it mean to "step into his shoes"? Would the regent have the same powers as the king, able to appoint individuals to the upper house as well as provide the seal which legitimated acts of government? Would this person have power over the king who was, as many remarked, hardly enamored of his first son? How long was this interregnum to last, and who should decide if and when the king's senses had returned, thereby allowing him to resume his duties as sovereign?[28] Danger signals blasted all around these questions as they exposed the delicate fabric of the constitution that had been woven over a century before.

On Friday, January 16, for example, Pitt rose in the house to remind his fellow parliamentarians—not for the last time—that "above all things . . . they were *not* placing a King on Throne." And to reinforce the point, he asked them to remember that "the Throne was full."[29] There was little dissent from this view, but it hardly solved the problem they faced: the person of the "king" was unique according to the legal and political practices that had worked so well in preserving the liberty of Englishmen for over a century. Those who were proposing the installation of the prince regent as quasi sovereign, that is, with all the powers attached to that office, had to negotiate that problem, and they did so by arguing that the crown and the king were two separate agents.[30] But as Lord North explained to the house, the bill before them:

> contradicted that wise maxim of our Constitution, *that the King never dies*; the King, in his individual and natural capacity, it was true, suffered a demise, but the political capacity of the Crown was both by Law and the Constitution always held to be whole and entire; (209)

The crucial point here is the integrity of the Crown: it is always "whole and entire." Those like Pitt who were proposing to extract some of the functions of the Crown, essentially sanctioning some powers but not others, "had contrived to produce that evil, which the Constitution had so wisely and so cautiously guarded against, and had devised the means of the political death of the Crown" (209). Continuing in the same vein, he noted that

> That House had resolved, that it was their Right and Duty to provide the means of supplying the defect in the personal exercise of the Royal Authority. What could that mean, more than they were to provide for the interval of his Majesty's illness, by not suffering any advantage to be taken to despoil the Crown of its just and constitutional Rights? It was their duty to take care that when his Majesty should be capable of reassuming the Royal functions, he should find them in as good a state as he left them in; undiminished, whole, and entire. (210)

The proposals in front of the house for a regency with limited powers were clearly disruptive to this principle. Indeed, as North pointed out, they would establish a completely different basis for understanding the king's *person* "because the object of the Resolutions was to appoint a person to the regal office, and separate from that office the Royal Authority" (210). Such arguments could be marshaled for party political gain on either side of the house: those in favor of a regency could use this to argue for no restrictions at all on the regent's capacity to act as the sovereign, and those hoping and wishing to stay in power could use it to argue against a regency proper. But however one cut the cloth, the problem remained that the legitimating principle at the heart of the constitution was the unique personhood of the sovereign. As the speaker of the house, Mr. Grenville, noted:

> We have already declared, that we acknowledge no right existing in any person, however exalted his rank may be, to act in this instance on the King's behalf, except under the authority of Parliament. And if it be true, that no act which is substantially and really of a legislative nature can be performed, even in such a case as the present, by the Lords and Commons alone, it is impossible that we can cure this defect by appointing some person, who deriving his authority from us, shall exercise the Royal functions in the place of the Sovereign; (233)

They were, in effect, snookered: if they took it upon themselves to appoint the *Crown*, the principle of hereditary right went out the window.

Moreover, by appointing someone to effectively *stand in for* the sovereign they arrogated to themselves the source of legitimate government, since the regent would have no "authority to give such assent except what he derives from our proceedings" (233). The constitutional point was easy to grasp: the authority to govern derived from the interlocking mechanism that held the Crown, Lords, and Commons in tension with each other. If Parliament by an act of will were to distribute the functions of the Crown around a number of offices or persons, if in effect it "were in the constant habit of regulating and directing the exercise of the prerogatives of the Crown, those prerogatives would in fact become the prerogatives, not of the Crown, but of Parliament itself" (245).

At the heart of the problem lay the nature of personhood and what it was to be the person of the sovereign. The difficulty was admirably set out by Colonel Fullerton in his contribution to the debate on Friday, January 16, 1789. He understood the chancellor to have contended that "all the powers and authorities belonging to the Crown, attached as it were to the person of the Sovereign" remained "entire in the King, although he was incapacitated from the personal exercise of them." Not only this, it was also claimed that "the political capacity of the King continued perfect, and could neither suffer diminution nor defect" (253). This was all well and good if one also accepted that while such "powers and authorities of executive Government, remained entire in the person of the King," it did not prevent those powers from being "exercised *in trust* for him" (253). But if it meant something else, if

> by the contemplation of law, and the political capacity of the King remaining entire when his faculties were not entire, was meant, that the powers and authorities of executive government might remain dormant, unemployed, unproductive for the public service, as long as the King was incapacitated from the personal exercise of them; if that was the meaning of the expression, they were doctrines [that] deserved to be treated as *treason* against the State. (253)

What lay behind this was a theory of the subject *primum inter pares*: the monarch who guaranteed the legitimacy of government and the unique legality of the citizen. And that subject was both a person and a symbol whose "great and godlike attributes" were not a "mere appendage, attached to the person of the Royal Individual; to sleep when he sleeps, and only to wake when his faculties cease to lie dormant!" (254). The problem, then, was built in to the settlement of 1688 which conceived of the sovereign as "whole and entire." Now, however, faced with a sovereign who had lost his wits, there was no way out unless they could disarticulate the king's person from the crown.

These debates were closely followed in the country at large, and a good number of citizens joined in the discussion.[31] It fell to one John de Lolme to push the envelope of rationality, arguing that in fact

> The King is *absent*; and no person can say where he is to be found. He is absent; and no man can tell when he will come back. Nay, it is not known where he will come back. Nay more, in case he does come back, it is not known whether he will be able to make himself acknowledged to be the *same person*.[32]

Thus the real dilemma facing his subjects is the possibility of a changed person, or of a counterfeit person returning in the guise of the king: this is the "difficulty at some future time in ascertaining the King's real *return*, and the true *identity* of his person" (8).[33]

Such an extreme view was not taken seriously, but it beautifully focuses the issue: what was the nature of the king's person? By putting this question firmly in the forefront of their deliberations, Pitt and others sought to head off the opposition's advocacy of a split person by playing the sentimental card. As Pitt more than once reminded the house, they were not only bound to "the care of the Royal Person of his Majesty"—this, of course, could be interpreted as care for his office as well as his physical person—but also to the "preservation of his dignity which ought to be inseparable from him during his present indisposition."[34] But it was the speaker of the house, Grenville, who deployed this strategy in the most effective manner. He argued that it was "self evident on every ground of public duty and of private sentiment, in a case where even private sentiment should not be disregarded" (250) that the care of the king's person ought to be entrusted to the queen. Moreover, it would be "inconsistent with the sentiments which we all entertain towards our Sovereign" (250) to diminish the size of the royal household, as some had proposed. This was because the king's virtues were the inspiration for the "sentiments . . . so deeply rooted in the hearts of all his subjects" (250). The sentimental card, then, was played in order to keep "whole and entire" the person of the king in spite of the fact that he was (temporarily, as it turned out) at that moment *not himself*. And it was this sleight of hand that enabled his loyal subjects to turn a collective blind eye to the fact that for months their sovereign was held captive and exposed to depravations that were effectively torture: there are known unknowns, but we also know there are some things that we do not know, as a more recent apologist for crimes against humanity put it.

Notes

1. The publication of Ida Macalpine and Richard Hunter, *George III and the Mad-Business* (Harmondsworth: Allen Lane, 1969), prompted a significant revision in modern attempts to understand the royal malady. This book made the case for the cause of George III's illness to be porphyria. Since then, arguments both for and against this diagnosis have come and gone. See John C. Rohl, Martin Warren, and David Hunt, *Purple Secret: Genes, "Madness" and the Royal Houses of Europe* (London: Bantam Press, 1998). Whether or not the thesis is correct, all subsequent accounts of the royal malady are in debt to Macalpine and Hunter's study.

2. The intensity of speculation and interest around the king's illness is demonstrated by the fact that digests of parliamentary debate, collections of pamphlets and newspaper opinions, and even poems were put into hardcover. See, for example, *Thoughts on the Present Crisis. Humbly Addressed to Both Houses of Parliament. By a Well-Meaning Briton* (London: T. Hookham and J. Bew, 1788); D. O'Bryen, *The Prospect Before Us. Being a Series of Papers upon the Great Question Which Now Agitates the Public Mind. To Which Is Added a New Postscript* (London: J. Almon, 1788); *The Debate on the Subject of a Regency in the House of Commons on Tuesday December 16th, 1788* (London: John Stockdale, 1788); *A Dialogue on the Regency* (London: J. Debutt, 1789); *The Regency; A Poem* (London: J. Walter, 1789); Philip Withers, *History of the Royal Malady, with a Variety of Entertaining Anecdotes* (London: n.p., 1789).

3. One of Pitt's strategies was to engage Parliament in lengthy and complex debates around the issue of the right of anyone, the Prince of Wales included, to act as sovereign while the king was very much still alive. Such a strategy was effective in allowing time to pass and for the possibility of the king's recovery to increase. This was indeed successful. See Saul David, *Prince of Pleasure: The Prince of Wales and the Making of the Regency* (London: Little, Brown and Company, 1998), 112–13.

4. Sheridan exposed Pitt's motives in his proposing a Regency Bill, which curtailed the power of the regent as "governed by party considerations, and by the impulse of his own personal ambitions." See *The History and Proceedings of the Lords and Commons of Great Britain, in Parliament Containing the Speeches on the Proposed Regency Bill, from November 20 1788 to March 10 1789* (London: J. Stockdale, 1789), 224.

5. Parliament had been prorogued until November 23 and was required to meet on that day because no one but the king could prorogue it further. This effective checkmate is well described by W. Grenville in a letter to the Marquis of Buckingham on November 8, 1788, where he notes that "Parliament cannot proceed to business without the session being opened by the King, or by some Commission authorized by him. No regent can be appointed or authorized to exercise acts of royal authority but by Act of Parliament; nor can any such Act be valid and binding in law without the King's consent." See *The Court and Cabinets of George III from Original Family Documents by the Duke of Buckingham and Chandos*, 4 vols. (London: Hurst and Blackett, 1853), I:439.

6. This faction did not always see eye to eye. Sheridan and Fox, for example, disagreed over tactics. On this, see Stanley Ayling, *Fox: The Life of Charles James Fox* (London: John Murray, 1991), 163.

7. On this see K. Jones, *Lunacy, Law and Conscience 1744–1845: The Social History of the Care of the Insane* (London: Routledge & Paul, 1955).

8. By this date, as Blackstone's most recent and accomplished biographer Wilfred Prest observes, the course of lectures that were the basis for the *Commentaries* had become "an established Oxford institution with a national, indeed international, reputation." See Wilfred Prest, *William Blackstone: Law and Letters in the Eighteenth Century* (Oxford: Oxford University Press, 2008), 215.

9. One among many iterations of this view has it: "That a constitution of which we so justly boast, allowed by the general consent of all enlightened men, to be superior to any scheme of policy that the wisdom of man has planned. . . ." See *Reflections on the Case of a Regency. By a Gentleman of Lincoln's Inn* (London: J. Ridgway, 1789), 5.

10. This did not mean, of course, that every person alive qualified as such. Far from it, as women and indentured servants knew only too well. The best recent discussion of these issues is Robin Blackburn, *The American Crucible: Slavery, Emancipation and Human Rights* (London: Verso, 2011).

11. Sir William Blackstone, *Commentaries on the Laws of England*, facsimile of first edition, 4 vols. (Chicago: The University of Chicago Press, 1979), I:183. Subsequent references in text.

12. As W. Grenville noted, whichever way things turned out, they were in trouble. Writing on November 7, 1788, he observes: "It appears that Warren, Heberden and Sir G. Barker, who are the three physicians who attend him, profess themselves unable to decide whether the disorder is or is not of such a nature as may soon produce a crisis which may lead either to health or death. The other alternative is one to which one cannot look without horror—that is a continuance of the present derangement of his faculties, without any other effect upon his health." See *The Court and Cabinets of George III from Original Family Documents by the Duke of Buckingham and Chandos*, 4 vols. (London: Hurst and Blackett, 1853), I:433.

13. *Harcourt Papers*, ed. E. W. Harcourt, 14 vols. (Oxford: J. Parker & Co, 1880), 4:21–2.

14. L. Dutens, *An History of the Late Important Period; from the Beginning of His Majesty's Illness . . . to the Period of His Majesty's Re-appearance in the House of Lords* (London: J. Walter, 1789), 4–5.

15. Earl Stanhope, *Life of the Right Honourable William Pitt*, 3rd ed., 4 vols. (London: John Murray, 1867), I:391.

16. The felicitously named mad doctor William Battie noted that the standard treatment at Bethlem hospital, the oldest institution in the country for treating illnesses of the mind, included "bleeding, blisters, caustics, rough cathartics, the gums and foetid antihysterics, opium, mineral waters, cold bathing, and vomits." See William Battie, *A Treatise on Madness* (London: Whiston and White, 1758), 93–94. For a good account of the treatment of madness in the eighteenth century, see Jonathan Andrews and Andrew Scull, *Undertaker of the Mind: John Monro and Mad-Doctoring in Eighteenth-Century England* (Berkeley: University of California Press, 2001).

17. Robert Greville, one of the king's equerries, noted in dismay in his diary that Willis described his method a "breaking in" of his patients like "horses in a menage." See *The Diaries of Colonel the Hon. Robert Fulke Greville*, ed. F. M. Bladon (London: John Lane The Bodley Head, 1930), 186.

18. The depositions made by the physicians to the parliamentary committees, both Lords and Commons, were published. It is, of course, possible that the wider public was poorly equipped to decipher the language used by the medics, but the style or tenor of the management of the illness must have been perspicuous. In a digest of these parliamentary reports organized so as to make

the testimony of Dr. Willis appear the least robust, Dr. Warren's deposition of December 13, 1788, states that the king had been allowed a very brief audience with the queen. It continues by observing that "His majesty was soon afterwards in a great state of irritation, and the STRICT COERCION was, I believe, FOR THE FIRST TIME, actually applied that Night—the blisters were put on that Night likewise." See *Important Facts Relative to the King; Faithfully Collected from the Examination of the Royal Physicians and Clearly Arranged under General Heads* (London: Ridgeway, 1789), 43.

19. From the outset those close to the government were highly sensitized to the precarious position of the administration. Writing from Whitehall on November 5, 1788, W. Grenville alerted the Marquis of Buckingham to the prospect of a lengthy royal illness and noted that this was likely to destabilize the government: "You may naturally conceive the exaltation, not wearing even the appearance of disguise, which there is in one party, and the depression of those who belong in the other." See *The Court and Cabinets of George III from Original Family Documents by the Duke of Buckingham and Chandos*, 4 vols. (London: Hurst and Blackett, 1853), I:432.

20. The problems faced by those concerned about the health of their monarch are described by William Grenville in a letter to the Marquis of Buckingham: "You can . . . hardly conceive the difficulty which we have, even at this small distance [from Whitehall], to procure such information as can be in any degree depended on. All the private accounts are so strongly tinctured by the wishes of those who send them, that no reliance can be placed upon them; and the private letters of the physicians are frequently inconsistent with each other, and even with the public account which they send to St James's. In general, that account has been uniformly found to be the least favourable; and seems as it was drawn for the purposes of discouraging the hopes which their own letters and conversation excite." *Memoirs of the Court and Cabinets of George III*, ed. Duke of Buckingham and Chandos, 4 vols. (London: Hurst and Blackett, 1853–55) II: 3–4.

21. *The Diaries of Colonel the Hon. Robert Fulke Greville*, ed. F. M. Bladon (London: John Lane The Bodley Head, 1930), 127.

22. Quoted in J. H. Jesse, *Memoirs of the Life and Reign of George III*, 3 vols. (London: Tinsley Brothers, 1867) III:257.

23. *Report from the Committee Appointed to Examine the Physicians Who Have Attended His Majesty during His Illness; Touching the Present State of His Majesty's Health. Ordered to Be Printed by the Hon. House of Commons, 13 January, 1789* (London: J. Walter, 1789), 3.

24. For a good account of the debates see John W. Derry, *The Regency Crisis and the Whigs 1788–9* (Cambridge: Cambridge University Press, 1963), especially chapter 2.

25. For a good account of Pitt's handling of the political situation see John Ehrman, *The Younger Pitt*, 3 vols. (London: Constable, 1969) I:644–66.

26. As Sir James MacKintosh noted eloquently: "There is not a principle more distinctly established by our constitution, or more essential to the existence of it, than this, 'that each of the three estates has its inherent rights, independent of each other, and which can neither be altered nor confounded.' This division of power, these privileges so accurately distinguished, and so nicely balanced by the wisdom of our forefathers, form the very essence of our constitution. . . ." See Sir James MacKintosh, *Arguments Concerning the Constitutional Right of Parliament to Appoint a Regency* (London: J. Debrett, 1788), 7.

27. In fact, by November 8 the prince had already begun to act as if he had been appointed regent. See Saul David, *Prince of Pleasure: The Prince of Wales and the Making of the Regency* (London: Little, Brown and Company, 1998), 101.

28. As Edmund Burke pointed out at length, this gave enormous power to Dr. Willis; moreover, it lacked credibility, since it was impossible to prove "whether a person who had been insane was perfectly recovered or not." See *The History and Proceedings of the Lords and Commons of Great Britain, in Parliament Containing the Speeches on the Proposed Regency Bill, from November 20 1788 to March 10 1789* (London: J. Stockdale, 1789), 376.

29. *The History and Proceedings of the Lords and Commons of Great Britain, in Parliament Containing the Speeches on the Proposed Regency Bill, from November 20 1788 to March 10 1789* (London: J. Stockdale, 1789), 199.

30. Mr. Powys put to the house that there was already a statute for this, which indicated that "during the present indisposition of his Majesty" the regent should be installed "in his stead" and to "exercise and administer . . . the regal power. . . ." See *The History and Proceedings of the Lords and Commons of Great Britain, in Parliament Containing the Speeches on the Proposed Regency Bill, from November 20 1788 to March 10 1789* (London: J. Stockdale, 1789), 208.

31. See, for example, William Cunninghame, *A Short View of the Present Great Question* (London: J. Debrett, 1788); Capel Lofft, *Three Letters on the Question of a Regency* (London: Stockdale and Richardson, 1788).

32. John Lewis De Lolme, *Observations upon the Late National Embarrassment, and the Proceedings in Parliament Relative to the Same* (London: J. Debrett, 1789), 7.

33. This tract was countered by another that sought to puncture its arguments. See *An Answer to Mr De Lolme's Observations on the Late National Embarrassment. By Neptune* (London: J. Stockdale, 1789).

34. *The History and Proceedings of the Lords and Commons of Great Britain, in Parliament Containing the Speeches on the Proposed Regency Bill, from November 20 1788 to March 10 1789* (London: J. Stockdale, 1789), 263.

Ian Ward

The Great Dramatist: Macaulay and the English Constitution

IT MAY BE APOCRYPHAL, BUT IT IS SAID THAT ONLY ONE BOOK outsold Macaulay's *History of England* in Victorian England: the Bible.[1] And yet, a century and a half later, the *History*, in the words of its author's most recent biographer, remains relatively "neglected."[2] The purpose of this essay is to revisit Macaulay's *History* and to do so as an exercise in critical constitutional jurisprudence. The *History* was written in the grand tradition of Whig epic history. There are at least two jurisprudentially significant consequences of this. The first is a reverence for the constitutional settlement of 1688–1690. Indeed, so concerned was Macaulay with this particular event and this particular settlement, that the vast five-volume *History* barely ventured beyond its immediate ambit; 1,400 closely printed pages cover just sixteen years. The second consequence is methodological. Macaulay did not seek to analyze the constitution, at least not in the manner of later Victorian constitutionalists such as Dicey. Instead he sought to stimulate the mid-Victorian imagination. Writing in the considerable shadow of Burke's *Reflections on the Revolution in France*, a text that he both admired and feared, Macaulay wrote just as much to the emotions of his readers as to their intellects. While they should appreciate the historical rationality of the English constitution, so too should they be inspired to love and admire what

Bagehot would later and famously term its "dignified" aspects. Macaulay made no attempt to hide this political and methodological prejudice; for he was not, finally, writing about England in 1688, or at least he was not only writing about England in 1688. He was also writing about England in 1848, an England in which talk of Jacobinism was once again current, and in which thousands of men and women had taken to attending Chartist gatherings to talk about revolution.

The Genesis of Macaulay's "History"

The first two volumes of Macaulay's *History of England* were published in 1848. Books three and four appeared in 1855. The remaining volume was published posthumously in 1861. The dates matter, particularly the first; dates certainly mattered to Macaulay. 1848 is significant for the very obvious reason that it provides an immediate context, not least in terms of critical and popular reception. It was a year, as Macaulay put it, when the "world" was "convulsed by the agonies of great nations."[3] But other dates matter too. 1832 matters, and so does 1790, for reasons we will shortly consider. Perhaps most obviously, however, 1688 matters. Macaulay shared the mid-Victorian fascination with the seventeenth century, a fascination that his writings, of course, did much to sustain. The entire *History* moves around the events of 1688, as in their different ways had the successive histories of Hume, Burke, and Hallam, which predated and in many ways presaged Macaulay's. The focus of the eighteenth- and nineteenth-century historian was concentrated, if not quite exclusively then very nearly, on trying to make sense of what happened in 1642–1649 and 1688–1690. Before we focus more closely on the constitutional jurisprudence written into the *History* we need to contemplate the significance of these particular historical moments in the conception and composition of Macaulay's great epic.

The more anxious Victorian, of which there were many, including Macaulay, perceived 1848 to be a "year of revolutions." Despite a series of Chartist gatherings in London and other provincial cities, there was in truth little prospect of revolution in England. But this did not lessen the sense of impending doom. "All is quiet in appearance," a wary Macaulay observed, "But yet, I feel, I fear."[4] He was not alone. Carlyle pondered the "condition" of England. Matthew Arnold contemplated the "long, withdrawing roar" of comforting faith, and wondered if the English were still quite so "chosen" a people. Ruskin gazed out of his study at Coniston and wondered why so few of his compatriots seemed to appreciate art anymore. In large part, if not quite exclusively, these were the kind of men, counted not in the tens or even hundreds but in the tens of thousands, for whom Macaulay wrote. And his purpose was every bit as large as his sales figures would prove to be. He wanted to settle the nation, again.

The "declaration" of "purpose" with which the *History* opened was intended to "excite" above all a sense of "thankfulness" among its readers.[5] Among the many things which his *History* would show was "how, under that settlement" of 1688–1690, "the authority of law and the security of property were found to be compatible with a liberty of discussion and of individual action never before known." It was from this particular moment and this particular settlement that the progressive "prosperity" of England "sprang."[6] The English in short had already had a revolution, a "glorious" one in 1688, for which reason they did not need another. They certainly did not need the kind of revolution narrated by Edmund Burke in his *Reflections on the Revolution in France*, published in 1790; "the most horrible event recorded in history," Macaulay reminded readers of the *Edinburgh Review* just as the 1832 Reform Act was staggering its way through Parliament.[7] The mid-Victorian gentleman, particularly the kind of gentleman who read the *Review*, was expected to know his Burke.

The significance of 1832, of course, lay in the passage of this very Act. Macaulay had spoken loudly in its support, not because he favored democracy, but because he dreaded it: "the restless and turbid hopes of those who have everything to gain, the dimly-hinted forebodings of those who have everything to lose."[8] The purpose of the Act was "to soothe the public mind," to "avert civil discord, and to uphold the authority of the law," for the "healing of great distempers"; in short, to "reform that we may preserve."[9] Here visceral anxieties could be rationalized in terms of classical Whig constitutional history. The "great" Reform Act complemented the "glorious" revolution of 1688. It "brought Parliament into harmony with the nation" in much the same way as the 1688 Revolution had "brought the Crown into harmony with the Parliament."[10] There was "in the whole history of England, no prouder circumstance" than the passage of the Act, reflecting as it did, not just the security of a constitutional settlement, but also the "moderation" and "humanity" of a people.[11]

Macaulay was a Whig. His support for the 1832 Act, which was earnest and influential, confirmed as much, as did his liking for Holland House supper parties and his careful cultivation of Whig patrons. As to what kind of Whig, Macaulay liked to identify himself as a "trimmer." He was certainly keen to distance himself from any presumed affinity with the Radicals. Macaulay maintained a visceral distrust of the mob, the "human vermin," informing Parliament that if the demands of the Chartists were ever met, the "country" would undoubtedly be "lost."[12] The 1832 Act had passed precisely to preclude any further "grant" of electoral power, distracting about 250,000 of those who might otherwise have been tempted to wander along to a local Chartist meeting. But neither was Macaulay a reactionary Whig. Like Burke he recognized that "a constitution without the means of some change is without the means of its conservation."[13] But evolution was measured and gradual, in constitutional reform as in anything else. Macaulay's Whiggism was moderate, innately conservative, essentially practical, and for precisely these reasons reflective of the political opinion of the majority of his countrymen. There was nothing, in the final analysis, particularly grand about Russell's "Grand Whigs" any more than there was anything great about the "Great" Reform Act, which they passed; and Macaulay supported both on this strict if tacit understanding.

For all except these 250,000, the significance of the Act was rather more symbolic than real, though due to constituency reforms, it could have a more immediate impact on certain MPs, of whom Macaulay was indeed one. When he returned to the Commons following the 1833 election, Macaulay was no longer the client MP for Lord Lansdowne, but the elected representative of the voters of Edinburgh.[14] Of course, such a constituency could be no less capricious, as Macaulay discovered in 1847 when the Edinburgh electors, disapproving his support for the Maynooth grant, changed their minds and declined to reelect him. He had, Macaulay declared in slightly churlish tones, somehow "incurred your displeasure," notwithstanding his unarguable commitment to the "fundamental principles of the Constitution."[15] It was following his failure to secure reelection in 1847 that Macaulay turned with renewed vigor to completing the first volumes of his projected *History*, begun a decade before. He would be returned as MP for Edinburgh again in 1852, riding on the wave of the success of these volumes. But Westminster would never again be the focus of his attention; still less it might be said, the interests of his Edinburgh electors. Macaulay had a different constituency in mind.

For the previous twenty years Macaulay had written almost exclusively for the Whig *journal de combat*, the *Edinburgh Review*. But the audience and the ambition were now all the greater. "Cocksure Tom" intended to rewrite the history of England, and not just for his Whig friends and patrons, but also for the enlightenment of the entire nation.[16] It would, of course, still be a Whig history, a necessary corollary of which would be a pointed rebuttal of those "Court" histories which had seduced so many eighteenth-century Tory gentlemen, the most egregious of which was David Hume's *History of England*. While Hume had likewise made much of the "revolution" of 1688, the supposition that the settlement which ensued should be understood more as victory for the established Church than the established common law cut to the heart of Whig constitutional iconography. Macaulay had already taken issue with the Humean version in his essay on Hallam's *Constitutional History*. Hallam had rightly rejected the notion that the settlement of 1690 was a primarily religious event. But he had not gone anything like far enough in confirming its alternative political dynamics, nor indeed its deeper constitutional credentials. Macaulay's *History* would provide the necessary corrective. And in this, as the German historian Ranke attested in 1875, Macaulay's "victory" would be total.[17]

Here the political, historical, and the intellectual context come into a still more precise alignment, for Macaulay wrote in a particular and well-established political tradition, that of the grand liberal epic. And anyone who wrote in this tradition had the responsibility, not only of demolishing Hume, but also of reinvesting the lost prophet of eighteenth-century Whig political philosophy, Edmund Burke. Thomas Carlyle might have more recently published a *History of the French Revolution* in 1837, but it was Burke's account of the same events, and more particularly his comparative defense of the English constitutional settlement, which could still bring "tears" to a Whiggish eye—provided he was read properly.[18] In his 1841 essay on Hastings, Macaulay declared his visceral admiration for Burke, a "man in whom compassion for suffering, and hatred of injustice and tyranny, were as strong as in Las Casas or Clarkson."[19] Burke, Macaulay averred, should be read like Thucydides, as an artist stimulating the "imagination." Sadly, as Macaulay had already observed, the present generation of historians now "miserably neglect" the Burkean "art of narration, the art of interesting the affections and presenting pictures to the imagination."[20]

Burke was, for very obvious reasons, far more appealing to Macaulay than his great contemporary Jeremy Bentham.[21] Macaulay may not have been quite as romantic as Burke, consciously eschewing so "tempestuous" a "sensibility," but he was far too romantic to be persuaded by the march of utility, while the apparent affinity between utility and radicalism was thoroughly unsettling, as readers of his various *Edinburgh Review* essays were time and again reminded.[22] Like Burke, Macaulay had a visceral distrust of metaphysical "cant" of whatever variety.[23] The great mistake of men like Mill was to presume a generality of human nature on such deductive speculation, deploying "sleight of tongue" and "abject sophisms" in place of historical insight. It is, he argued, "utterly impossible to deduce the science of government from the principles of human nature."[24] In his essay on Mirabeau, Macaulay reiterated Burke's conclusion, that the French revolution was violent precisely because it was animated by "speculators."[25] The alternative to the "cant" of speculative "deduction" is the science of historical or philosophical "induction."[26] The great philosopher of induction was Francis Bacon.[27] "Our creed," Macaulay averred, "is, that the science of government is an experimental science, and that, like all other experimental sciences, it is generally in a state of progression."[28]

Macaulay too wanted to be accounted a "philosophical historian," one whose narratives "began in observations and ended in arts."[29] At the same time, however, his history was different again, for alongside Burke and Bacon loomed the equally considerable presence of Sir Walter Scott. Scott was the most successful writer of his generation, and Macaulay was again an avowed admirer. It was, Macaulay argued, the responsibility of the historian to "reclaim those materials which the novelist" such as Scott had "appropriated."[30] He must embrace the "affecting and picturesque," to "intersperse the details" of his history with "the charm of historical romances."[31] The "past in my mind," he would again confirm in testamentary tones, "is soon constructed into a romance."[32] "Facts" on the other hand "are the mere dross of history." It is not facts that the historian must excavate, but the "gold in the ore."[33] Varying the metaphor slightly, in his Hallam essay Macaulay averred that "History, at least in its ideal perfection, is a compound of poetry and philosophy."[34]

Macaulay determined that his history would be painted in like tones, a layered history of sweeping narrative, grand set pieces, and intimate anecdote.[35] "The perfect historian," the young Macaulay again observed in his 1828 essay, "is he in whose work the character and spirit of an age is exhibited in miniature," in pictures of "ordinary men as they appear in their ordinary business and in their ordinary pleasures."[36] In his review of Macaulay's *History*, Walter Bagehot admired precisely this ability to reveal the "nation" alongside the "court, the camp, the senate," as well as the "anecdote," which might, to other historians, have seemed too "insignificant."[37] Time again, in his essays and in his *History*, Macaulay would transport his readers to a place in the past, perhaps magnificent, perhaps intimate, where they might like Adam Smith's famed "judicious spectator" be guided, ever so gently, to reach a "judgment of events and men." "The poet," he averred, should always try to "place his readers, as nearly as possible, in the situation of the sufferers or the spectators."[38] They must be made to "mingle in the crowds of the exchange and the coffee-house."[39] No historian, as Bagehot again appraised, had even mastered the art of "spectacle" as well as Macaulay.[40]

There was, of course, a price to pay, as Macaulay had acknowledged in his 1828 "Essay on History":

> History cannot be perfectly and absolutely true . . . No picture then and no history, can present us with the whole truth: but those are the best pictures and the best histories which exhibit such parts of the truth as most nearly produce the effect of the whole.[41]

It was not an admission that would sit comfortably with later critics, still less subsequent generations of more scientifically inclined historians. But it did not, rather too obviously for some, bother Macaulay that much. He would later acknowledge a difference between the "flippant" license, which might be accorded the essayist, and the more sober responsibilities of the writer of epic history. The "natural life" of an essay, he once observed, was no more than "six weeks."[42] His *History*, in contrast, was intended to educate generations to come. And Macaulay never suggested that history should ever abandon the faculty of reason. But neither should it allow itself to be "seduced" by metaphysics or utility, and thus reduced to "dross," for which reason he "cheerfully" admitted in the preface to the *History* that his "narrative" might, when reason demanded, descend below the customary "dignity of history."[43] It would be evocative, romantic in the sense that Scott was romantic, and above all entertaining. The "talent which is required to write history thus," Macaulay had confirmed as early as 1828, "bears a considerable affinity to the talent of the great dramatist."[44] But not perhaps the great poet; at least not in Macaulay's histories, for they were never impassioned in quite the way that Burke's *Reflection* might be said to be impassioned. Macaulay, as early critics such as Bagehot observed, preferred to remain that little bit detached. He also preferred to write happy endings, as critics have also noted. Of course, any Whig history had to be happy; after all, the English were chosen, their progress assured. They just needed reminding of this from time to time.

Macaulay and the Constitution

One of the most immediately striking features of Macaulay's *History of England* is the presence of the law and of the constitution. As we have already noted, the opening lines of the *History* had sought to reassure readers in terms of political and constitutional certainty. The English were "saved," at least from further revolution, precisely because they already had a judicious "settlement."[45] In his earlier essays, Macaulay had already mined the earlier decades of the seventeenth century in order to excavate the foundations of this settlement. Like so many of his contemporaries, he was fascinated by the English civil war, thrilled by the romantic engagement of Cavalier and Roundhead, just as puzzled by the necessary ambiguities collected in the figure of Oliver Cromwell. Accordingly when Macaulay contemplated the events of 1688–1690, it was hardly surprising that he did so in jurisprudential terms. He had, of course, already written on the "revolution" of 1688, most notably in his Hallam essay, where he had concluded that it was "assuredly, a happy revolution, and a useful revolution; but it was not, what it has been called, a glorious revolution."[46] The tone might have seemed rather deflating. But Macaulay, as we shall see, put a lot of stock on what was useful, still more perhaps on what made his readers happy. The *History* is not, of course, wholly about law and constitution. But it cannot be contemplated today, just as it could not have been read a century and a half ago, without proper consideration of its irreducible constitutionality. Constitutions were "not power," but they were the "symbols of power," and no Whig history could be written otherwise than around that settled in 1690.[47]

As critics have noted, Macaulay's sweeping narrative is built around a series of often-familiar set-piece events, a mixture of parliamentary speeches, wars, conspiracies, and trials. As such the law can be found scattered about the narrative, assuming a rather more significant place in certain of these set pieces, three of which assume a particular importance in terms of constitutional history. The first is the serial abuse of judicial process instigated by Lord Chief Justice Jeffreys. Critics have long noted that Macaulay was happier narrating events than he was contemplating human complexity. Bagehot wanted to "love and hate." But Macaulay did not do love and hate, just heroic and evil, right and wrong.[48] His Jeffreys, plainly evil and plainly wrong, assumes a demeanor of melodramatic familiarity, a man of "insolence" and "angry passions," heartless and brutal, but perhaps most significantly, the arch-corrupter of the constitution.[49] It is Jeffreys who, assuming the classic guise of the king's evil counselor, advises the newly crowned James II to rule by "edict."[50] Possessed of the worse kind of legal mind, one of cunning and "sophistry," Jeffreys's propensity to judicial corruption crosses a critical constitutional boundary when he "obtained a seat in Cabinet and a peerage," for "since the judicial system of the realm had been remodelled in the thirteenth century, no Chief Justice had been a Lord in Parliament."[51] It might seem to be a narrow constitutional point, but to a historian writing in the Whig tradition of Locke any infringement of the doctrine of separate powers assumed altogether greater significance.

Jeffreys assumes an increasingly demonic theatricality when Macaulay's narrative moves forward to the failed Monmouth rebellion, and the "Bloody Assizes" over which the chief justice subsequently presided. In tones that would have resonated with any devotee of Burke, Macaulay depicted:

> The Chief Justice was all himself. His spirits rose higher and higher as the work went on. He laughed, shouted, joked, and swore in such a way that many thought him drunk from morning to night. But in him it was not easy to distinguish the madness produced by evil passions from the madness produced by brandy.[52]

The maniacal laughter recurs throughout the narrative. A little later the reader is informed that he employed a "crew of parasites" in order to extort money from the relatives of those convicted in his assizes, men who shared the same liking for "drinking and laughing'.[53] If the Exeter Assize, bedecked, as Macaulay informs his readers, in hellish red drapery, is the inferno and Chief Justice Jeffreys is Satan, these are his demons. Small wonder perhaps that those who had the misfortune to be arraigned could quite literally, it seemed, be terrified to death.[54] Alice Lisle however, whose trial had already been sanctified in Whig hagiography, was made of sterner stuff. Lady Alice, the reader is informed, fell victim to the "disgraceful" inconsistencies of the law relating to "principal and accessory," convicted and beheaded for the "noble and benevolent" crime of giving a desperate man a "morsel of bread." A "wise and good" magistrate would have punished her "tenderly."[55] Jeffreys did not, and having "strained" the law "for the purpose of destroying Alice Lisle," then moved on to enact a roaming "judicial massacre" across the rest of the southwest.[56]

A second set piece, which assumes a still larger presence in Macaulay's account of the events which lead up to the "glorious" revolution, is the arraignment of "the seven bishops" who petitioned against James's second Declaration of Indulgence in April 1688 and were subsequently prosecuted for seditious libel. Anglican clergy does not always fare that well in Macaulay's *History*. But in their defense of the principles of the established Church, the bishops are presented as defenders of the constitution, meeting the neurosis of a king "quick of temper" and screaming treason with an almost ethereal "cheerfulness"; so much so that they were "rapturously extolled by the general voice."[57] It was, as Macaulay advises, perhaps the "first and last occasion" when a common "love of freedom" seemed in "perfect harmony" with a "love of the Church."[58] Corruption of judicial process is again an animating theme. The Judges of King's Bench before whom the bishops were arraigned were the "tools" of the court.[59] The "odious" Crown prosecution tries, but fails, to pack the jury. In an account of proceedings which, as Macaulay advises, owes more to the "interest of drama" than that of cool jurisprudential reflection, the fortunes of the bishops wax and wane. But, defended by the most "eminent" legal minds of the generation, they are in the end gloriously acquitted, the forces of corruption vanquished.[60] The nation rejoices, church bells ring, stuffed popes are placed on bonfires up and down the land, and everyone goes to the tavern for a celebratory drink.

And the narrative moves on a couple of months, to the third and in purely constitutional terms most significant of Macaulay's set pieces. The coronation of William Prince of Orange may not account for quite so many pages in the *History*, but it might be said that the entire narrative pivots around this one event. At the close of the tenth chapter of his *History* Macaulay places his readers among the entranced "gazers" who "filled" the streets surrounding Whitehall on February 13, 1688. And then he takes them within, to join the assembled Peers and Commons and Yeomen of the Guard in admiring the "masterpieces of Rubens" which embellish the walls of the "magnificent" banqueting house, and watching as William and his wife, Mary Stuart, "advanced a few steps" toward the throne before being invited to listen to the clerk of the House of Lords read "in a loud voice" the Declaration of Rights. After which, and only after, Lord Halifax offers the crown. The terms are accepted, and the new King William III reaffirms his commitment to the common "law of England" as articulated in the Declaration, promising that they "should be the rules of his conduct" as would be the "welfare" of his kingdom. And, just to be sure that he will be able to fulfill these commitments, William confirms that he "should constantly recur to the advice of the Houses, and should be disposed to trust their judgment rather than his own."[61]

William, as Macaulay had previously averred, was the hero who did nothing:

> He outraged no national prejudice. He abolished no ancient form. He altered no venerable name. He saw that the existing institutions possessed the greatest capabilities of excellence, and that stronger sanctions and clearer definitions were alone required to make the practice as admirable as the theory.[62]

It is why he was a hero, a man of "phlegmatic serenity," possessed of a "singular charm" in private and a devoted family man.[63] Not every hero was of the kind who made it into Carlyle's pantheon. William was a hero in his own home, precisely the kind of hero, of course, which Prince Albert, one of Macaulay's many admirers, aspired to be. By 1848, the idea of kingship had assumed a rather different aspect. For the generation that followed the madness of George III and the excesses of George IV, there was much to be said for serenity, common sense, and sound judgment. Macaulay's William ultimately was a "trimmer," just like his creator.

He was not the only hero of the story. Macaulay's admiration for Parliament, whether it was the Parliament of 1848 or 1832, or 1688 or 1642, was pretty much unalloyed. What distinguished the Parliament of 1688 was the innate pragmatism of its members, or at least the Whig ones, who "judiciously abstained from mixing up the irritating and perplexing question of what ought to be the law and the plain question of what was the law"; an observation that would, in its scornful dismissal of metaphysical allure, have earned the common, if contrasting, approbation of both Benthamite and Burkean—though less so Carlyle, who disparaged Macaulay's mystical fetish for Parliaments of whatever age or hue.

As William and Mary slowly depart the chamber accompanied by "heralds and pursuivants," a "shout of joy" is heard outside, "kettle drums struck up, the trumpets pealed," and the Garter King of Arms invites every Englishman and woman to pray for the new king and queen. A moment for quiet reflection arrives. "Thus was consummated," Macaulay concludes with ironic simplicity, "the English revolution." And:

> When we compare it with those revolutions which have, during the last sixty years, overthrown so many ancient governments, we cannot but be struck by its peculiar character.[64]

The reach of sixty years is just far enough, inviting readers to compare and contrast the sober events at Whitehall in February 1688 with those that Burke so graphically depicted in his 1790 account of the storming of Versailles. Such "calamities our Revolution averted." It was a "strictly defensive revolution," one which as Burke had striven to emphasize, "had prescription and legitimacy on its side," its purpose extending only to the "vindication of ancient rights."[65] Where Burke had relished the chance to terrify his readers with accounts of screeching Jacobins declaiming abstract rights to "equality," Macaulay invited his to contemplate groups of sober parliamentarians in the weeks and months that followed the coronation pouring over ancient rolls of legal "parchment." The invocation of the sublime might be missing, but the resonance is evident still. In his *Reflections* Burke famously depicted an "ancient" constitution, its veracity attested by the "collected reason of ages" and embedded for generations in an English state of "mind."[66] Macaulay appraised the "main principles of our government" in similar terms:

> They were not, indeed, formally and exactly set forth in a single written instrument; but they were to be found scattered over our ancient and noble statutes; and, what was of far greater moment, they had been engraven on the hearts of Englishmen during four hundred years.[67]

The coronation of William III, on the conditions laid down by Parliament, ensures that Macaulay's *History* will have a happy ending, one that will be confirmed, with the admitted benefit of hindsight, in 1832. There may be a need for "change," and Macaulay took a further moment to suggest a more particular necessity in regard to the established Church and the need to "deprive" the Crown of its attendant "mysterious attributes."[68] But a "realm of which these," by which he meant the common law principles of liberty now enshrined in the Declaration, "were the fundamental laws stood in no need of a new constitution"[69] in 1688 or, the implication very obviously ran, in 1848. "Now, if ever," Macaulay concluded, it must be apparent to "all honest and reflecting minds" that the "highest eulogy which can be pronounced on the revolution of 1688" is "that it was our last revolution."[70] "And if it be asked what has made" England "different" from other less fortunate nations:

> It is because we had a preserving revolution in the seventeenth century that we have not had a destroying revolution in the nineteenth. It is because we had freedom in the midst of servitude that we have order in the midst of anarchy. For the authority of law, for the security of property, for the peace of our streets, for the happiness of our homes, our gratitude is due, under Him who raises and pulls down nations at his pleasure, to the Long Parliament, to the Convention, and to William of Orange.[71]

Reading Macaulay

The centrality of the constitution in Macaulay's *History* seems perhaps rather odd today. Epic histories are still written and still sell in the thousands. But few make quite such a fuss of the constitution. The reason is, in one sense, quite simple. Whig history is no longer fashionable, and because Whig history is no longer so fashionable, neither is Macaulay. The situation was, of course, rather different half a century earlier, his reputation burnished first by the hagiographic 1876 *Life and Letters* written by his nephew Sir Otto Trevelyan and then again in the various writings of great-nephew George Macaulay Trevelyan, who saw himself as the flame-carrier for that "poetic" tradition of Whig history, and whose monumental *England under Queen Anne* was written as a reverential sequel to uncle Tom's *History*.[72] While it was written as a corrective, the very fact that Sir Charles Firth published his *Commentary on Macaulay's History of England* in 1938 was suggestive that, if nothing else, Macaulay still mattered. He was, after all, not just the last historian who appreciated the "art of telling a story," but also "still *the* authority" on late seventeenth-century constitutional history.[73] But even as Firth wrote, it was becoming ever less easy to make the same assertion. Just a year later Godfrey Davis was notably less forgiving of Macaulay's "misrepresentations" of historical "fact."[74] By 1967, Ronald Weber lamented a writer who had "fallen into general oblivion."[75] There was some faint praise. Alan Taylor concluded that while Macaulay "had a very simple outlook," no historian "ever told a story better."[76] In like tones, Trevor-Roper recommended history written by an essentially "practical politician," his mind uncluttered by "abstract thought."[77] But the intellectual mood had turned against the Whig "interpretation of history," against what Herbert Butterfield famously decried as the "over-dramatisation of the historical story."[78] It was left to a dwindling band of disciples, foremost among them Sir John Plumb, to keep the flame flickering. Plumb paid tribute to a historian whose real genius lay in the depth of "his own sympathy with his age," suggesting that "his success must partly lie in the fact that the men and women who read him so eagerly, felt as he felt and believed as he believed: his truth was their truth."[79]

Robert Sullivan may be correct in concluding that what is most notable about Macaulay today is how rarely he seems to be noted.[80] But Plumb's inference remains valid. In commercial terms, the *History* was a phenomenal success. By March 1849, after just three months, the first volumes of the *History* had sold 13,000 copies.[81] When the second two volumes appeared in December 1855, the publishers Longmans had budgeted for a print run of 25,000. It was sold out within ten weeks. In March they paid £20,000 into the author's account—an enormous sum. A single-volume edition published in 1858 sold 35,000 copies. By 1876, it was estimated that 140,000 copies had been sold in the United Kingdom, and very probably in excess of 200,000 in America.[82] Macaulay assumed, in the words of William Ewart Gladstone, a "monarchy over the world of readers."[83] He certainly did the younger ones, the *History* assuming an unimpeachable authority in the later Victorian classroom. Carlyle, with typical acerbity, likened his popular idolization to that of a "molten calf."[84]

As for its critical reception, plaudits were many and loud. An admiring Prince Albert urged acceptance of the Regius Professorship of Modern History at Cambridge.[85] Lord Acton thought the *History* "wonderful."[86] Fitzjames Stephen paid tribute to "the greatest, and indeed, almost the only great advocate and expounder of Whig principles since the time of Burke."[87] At a rather different level, the proposal that a letter of thanks be written to Macaulay from assorted gentlemen of Duckinfield, near Manchester, "for having written a history which working men can understand" is perhaps more significant still.[88] There were, of course, critics. The Benthamites were predictably unimpressed. Unsurprisingly, given Macaulay's demolition of his father's *Essay on Government*, John Stuart Mill was an implacable critic, troubled most of all by the thought that the *History* will "continue popular."[89] The same fear haunted Tory critics such as Matthew Arnold who railed against "the great apostle of the Philistines."[90] John Morley doubted whether historians should seek to align themselves with "the common average sentiment."[91] Lecky sniffily dismissed a historian whose writing seemed to "influence" the "temper of modern journalism."[92] Carlyle, predictably enough, thought it "too popular," and too Whig, in contrast to Lord Russell who, equally predictably perhaps, thought it not nearly Whig enough.[93] And while he acknowledged Macaulay's *History* to be "a true and high work of art," and more particularly his "rare and marvellous" ability to present images of "ordinary life" alongside larger perceptions of historical moment, Gladstone betrayed a residual Tory sensibility in worrying, not merely that Macaulay was susceptible to "a pervading strain of exaggeration," but that the great historian did not seem sufficiently committed to "Christian dogma."[94] Intriguingly, though, perhaps detecting behind the Whig rhetoric a man of similarly pragmatic conservative sympathies, Lord Salisbury was a great admirer of Macaulay's "picturesque narrative."[95]

One of the most incisive critics, and for our purposes most intriguing, was Walter Bagehot, author of his own constitutional "history" a decade later. In the chronicle of English constitutional historians, Macaulay can be placed rather obviously between Burke and Bagehot, in what later historians have termed a Burkean "tradition." This is certainly the tradition in which Bagehot placed him in the obituary he wrote in the days following Macaulay's death in December 1859.[96] An earlier, more substantive review of the Macaulay's *History* betrayed a rather deeper ambivalence. Whilst Bagehot admitted that the *History* was a "marvellous book," he noted that Macaulay seemed to eschew a more refined Burkean "sensibility," something all the more marked given that the focus of his *History* was one of the "most passionate eras of our history."[97] The criticism has stuck.[98] It clearly played on Plumb's mind, a century later suggesting in eerily similar tones that, despite his undoubted "moral passion," Macaulay "never penetrates to the heart of human existence." Where Burke sought to terrify, Bagehot concluded, Macaulay preferred a tone of "pleasant geniality" and "easy cheerfulness."[99] The reason, he averred, was that despite his singular and, at least amongs historians, "vivid fancy," Macaulay was ultimately a Roundhead not a "Cavalier," a Baconian rather than a Burkean.[100] Like Scott, but unlike Burke, Bagehot supposed, he wrote to "charm" rather than to impassion.[101] Moreover, "still the man of '32,'" Macaulay was trapped by his own inability to look beyond the constitutional settlement he had set in historical aspic.[102]

Not, of course, that this affected sales figures, as Bagehot acknowledged. Macaulay knew his readers. If Bagehot was indeed the "greatest Victorian," as G. M. Young later averred, then Macaulay was perhaps the quintessential one.[103] He did not relish "perplexities" and neither did his readers; so they got none.[104] What they wanted was calm reassurance, the comfort of black and white.[105] Accordingly, having witnessed the massacre of Glencoe followed swiftly by the allied victory at La Hogue, they could reflect on the events of chapter eighteen grateful that, unlike the perfidious French and the primitive Highlanders, they had an "ancient constitution" which was forever, and forever cautiously, "adapting itself, by a natural, a gradual, a peaceful development, to the wants of modern society." For which reason then, and by implication as now:

> There was a sense of relief everywhere, from the Royal Exchange to the most secluded hamlets among the mountains of Wales and the fens of Lincolnshire. The ploughmen, the shepherds, the miners of the Northumbrian coalpits, the artisans who toiled at the looms of Norwich and the anvils of Birmingham, felt the change, without understanding it; and the cheerful bustle in every seaport and every market town indicated, not obscurely, the commencement of a happy age.[106]

Macaulay, as Bagehot appreciated, gave his readers what they wanted, the ability to "pass a day of easy thought, of pleasant emotion" in the company of a good, if very long, book.[107] Above all he gave them certainty, the reassurance of a happy ending.[108] The English were still chosen, their constitution the envy of the world, and it was all thanks to the events of 1688–1690, and 1832; and, of course, to men like Macaulay who ensured that the latter was passed and the former remembered.

Notes

1. Edward Adams, *Liberal Epic: The Victorian Practice of History from Gibbon to Churchill* (Charlottesville: University of Virginia Press, 2011), 158.

2. Robert Sullivan, *Macaulay: The Tragedy of Power* (Cambridge, MA: Harvard University Press, 2009), 1. A similar lament can be found in David Knowles's 1960 lecture on Macaulay. See David Knowles, *Lord Macaulay 1800–1859* (Cambridge: Cambridge University Press, 1960), 4.

3. In Joseph Hamburger, *Macaulay and the Whig Tradition* (Chicago: The University of Chicago Press, 1976), 33.

4. Macaulay was prone to such anxieties, reading into every little riot the portents of bloody insurrection. See Hamburger, *Macaulay*, 47, 115–16, 123.

5. Lord Macaulay, *The History of England* (London: Penguin, 1986), 52 [hereafter *HE*]. "The opening paragraphs must have been exciting and satisfying," George Levine observes, 'they certainly constitute one of the most elaborate and exhilarating fanfares in our literature. See his *The Boundaries of Fiction: Carlyle, Macaulay, Newman* (Princeton: Princeton University Press, 1968), at 122.

6. *HE*, 51.

7. "Essay on Mirabeau," *Edinburgh Review*, July 1832, 560 [hereafter *ER*].

8. "Essay on Hallam," *ER*, September 1828, 168.

9. *ER*, September 1828, 169.

10. A perspective he reiterated in his 1839 address to the electors of Edinburgh: "To the Whigs of the seventeenth century we owe it that we have a House of Commons. To the Whigs of the nineteenth century we owe it that the House of Commons has been purified." See here Charles Firth, *A Commentary on Macaulay's "History of England"* (London: Macmillan, 1938), 260, and also Owen Dudley Edwards, *Macaulay* (London: Weidenfeld and Nicolson, 1988), 21–22.

11. *ER*, July 1832, 563.

12. See Sullivan, *Macaulay*, 236–38.

13. Edmund Burke, *Reflections on the Revolution in France* (London: Penguin, 1986), 106.

14. Macaulay had sat as MP for Calne, a constituency controlled by Lansdowne. In truth, Lansdowne was a conspicuously undemanding patron, with whom Macaulay remained on generally good terms. See Sullivan, *Macaulay*, 79–80.

15. Macaulay's public letter to the electors of Edinburgh is quoted in Edwards, *Macaulay*, 44.

16. The epithet "cocksure" appears to have been first bestowed on Macaulay by Lord Melbourne. See Firth, *Commentary*, 54. Contemporaries attested to an evident pomposity in Macaulay's public demeanor; something that may have hidden a deeper lack of self-confidence.

17. In Ranke's *History of England*, 6:29, quoted in Firth, *Commentary*, 15.

18. Burke famously admitted that he wrote his *Reflections* with the express purpose of bringing his readers to "tears." See *Reflections*, 175.

19. "Essay on Hastings," *ER*, October 1841, 232. For commentaries on Macaulay's admiration for Burke, see Hamburger, *Macaulay*, 154–55, 181–88, and Sullivan, *Macaulay*, 301–2.

20. See his essays on "History," *ER*, May 1828, 331, 336–39, 361, and also on "Hallam," *ER*, September 1828, 96.

21. Even if, as Macaulay admitted in his "Mirabeau" essay, Bentham was otherwise a "truly great man," the "father of jurisprudence," the "man who found jurisprudence a gibberish, and left it a science." *ER*, July 1832, 553.

22. "Essay on Hastings," *ER*, October 1841, 232–43.

23. *ER*, July 1832, 559.

24. *ER*, March 1829, 185.

25. "Essay on Mirabeau," *ER*, July 1832, 572–73.

26. The "method of Induction," he further explained in his essay on Mill's *Essay on Government*, is "by observing the present state of the world" while also "assiduously studying the history of past ages." *ER*, March 1829, 187–89.

27. Macaulay had to balance his admiration for Bacon's philosophy with countervailing distaste for both the man and the politics. For commentaries on the Bacon essay, see Hamburger, *Macaulay*, 58–62, and Sullivan, *Macaulay*, 153–80.

28. "Essay on Mackintosh," *ER*, July 1835, 281–82.

29. *ER*, July 1837, 80.

30. "Essay on Hallam," *ER*, September 1828, 97.

31. *ER*, May 1828, 331, 365.

32. The assertion was made in private correspondence. See Levine, *Fiction*, 100.

33. *ER*, May 1828, 340.

34. *ER*, September 1828, 96.

35. History, as Macaulay presaged in his 1828 "Essay on History," with both a "foreground" and a "background," and unmatched in Thucydides. *ER*, May 1828, 338–39.

36. "Essay on History," *ER*, May 1828, 364.

37. Walter Bagehot, "Mr Macaulay," in Norman St. John-Stevas, *The Collected Works of Walter Bagehot: The Literary Essays*, (London: The Economist, 1965), 414. Bagehot was in fact quoting from Macaulay's "Essay on History," *ER*, May 1828, 364.

38. *ER*, September 1828, 97.

39. *ER*, May 1828, 364.

40. "Mr Macaulay," 424.

41. *ER*, May 1828, 338.

42. In Edwards, *Macaulay*, 90, 93.

43. *HE*, 53. The allusion to the seductions of reason can be found in his earlier "Essay on History." *ER*, May 1828, 359.

44. *ER*, May 1828, 351.

45. *HE*, 51.

46. *ER*, September 1828, 159.

47. *ER*, October 1829, 110.

48. See Bagehot, "Mr Macaulay," 427.

49. *HE*, 74–77 and also 117–21. Firth suspected that Macaulay's Jeffreys might have owed rather too much to the influence of contemporary "satirists and caricaturists." See his *Commentary*, 46.

50. HE, 77.

51. HE, 77.

52. HE, 123.

53. HE, 126.

54. HE, 128.

55. HE, 118–19.

56. HE, 120–22. Hanging, according to Macaulay, a further 292 in Dorset, and 233 in Somerset, in addition to which he sentenced a further 841 to transportation. Subsequent research has cast considerable doubt on the acuity of Macaulay's figures. See Firth, *Commentary*, 286–87.

57. HE, 206–7, 212–13, 219.

58. HE, 237.

59. HE, 211.

60. HE, 224–27.

61. HE, 287.

62. "Essay on William III," *Times Literary Supplement*, May 1, 1969, 469–70.

63. HE, 174.

64. HE, 288.

65. HE, 290, 292.

66. Burke, *Reflections*, 116–17, 132–33.

67. HE, 290.

68. HE, 291.

69. HE, 290.

70. HE 294.

71. HE, 295.

72. See Jack Plumb, *Men and Places* (London: Cresset Press, 1963), 225, quoting from Trevelyan's 1926 inaugural lecture as Regius Professor of Modern History at Cambridge: "The appeal of history to us all is in the last analysis poetic."

73. Firth, *Commentary*, 1–2. The italics are in the original.

74. Godfrey Davies, "The Treatment of Constitutional History in Macaulay's *History of England*," *Huntington Library Quarterly* 2 (1939): 180–83, 197–204.

75. Richard Weber, "Singer and Seer: Macaulay on the Historian as Poet," *Papers on Language and Literature* 3 (1967), 210.

76. Alan Taylor, *Essays in English History* (London: Penguin, 1976), 57. The same conclusion is reached by Knowles in his *Macaulay*, at 30.

77. Hugh Trevor-Roper, *Historical Essays* (London: Macmillan, 1957), 252–53. Trevor-Roper also provided the introduction to the 1986 Penguin edition of the *History*.

78. Herbert Butterfield, *The Whig Interpretation of History* (London: Bell and Sons, 1931), 34, 39, 93–94. Butterfield acknowledged the responsibility of the historian to keep "sympathy alive and all our humanity awake," but concluded that Whig historian-dramatists too readily sacrificed their analytical skills to the temptations of "prejudice and passion."

79. Plumb, *Men*, 251. The same conclusion is reached by David Knowles in his *Macaulay*, at 21–22.

80. Sullivan, *Macaulay*, 1.

81. It seems that even Macaulay was taken aback by his success, in his journal entry for January 17 recording, "Of such a run I had never dreamed."

82. Many of the American sales being of pirated copies. See Sullivan, *Macaulay*, 315–16.

83. Quoted in Hamburger, *Macaulay*, 163.

84. In Sullivan, *Macaulay*, 368.

85. Macaulay declined, fearing that professorial responsibilities might prove distracting.

86. Quoted in Firth, *Commentary*, 3.

87. James Fitzjames Stephen, "Lord Macaulay," *The Saturday Review*, January 7, 1860, 9.

88. Quoted in Plumb, *Men*, 250.

89. Quoted in Sullivan, *Macaulay*, 319.

90. Matthew Arnold, *Essays in Criticism* (Chicago: The Chicago University Press, 1968), 181.

91. John Morley, *Critical Miscellanies* (London: Macmillan, 1886), 1:267.

92. Firth, *Commentary*, 33, 81–85.

93. Sullivan, *Macaulay*, 319.

94. In a review of Trevelyan's *Life and Letters* published in *The Quarterly Review*, July 1876, at 14–15, 21, 31, 49.

95. See Sullivan, *Macaulay*, 475.

96. The obituary closes with a long extract from Burke which, Bagehot suggests, confirms their intellectual allegiance regardless of methodological differences. See his "Lord Macaulay," in St. John-Stevas, *Works*, 429–31.

97. "Mr Macaulay," 397, 401, 405.

98. See Sullivan, *Macaulay*, 409–10, noting how prescient as well as intuitive Bagehot's review has proved to be.

99. "Mr Macaulay," 411.

100. "Mr Macaulay," 400, 402, 408–10, 413. For a comment on the idea that the Baconian consumed the Burkean in Macaulay's writing, see Plumb, *Men*, 259. For a more recent attribution of Macaulay as a Victorian Roundhead, see Blair Worden, *Roundhead Reputations: The English Civil Wars and the Passions of Posterity* (London: Penguin, 2002), 228.

101. "Mr Macaulay," 415, 417.

102. "Mr Macaulay," 410, 428.

103. For a neat articulation of this supposition, see Levine, *Fiction*, 79–81, concluding "No man, it seems, was more in harmony with himself or with his times" and again at 120 making the obvi-

ous collateral suggestion that his *History* might accordingly be regarded as the "quintessential Victorian work."

104. "Mr Macaulay," 411, 425.

105. "Mr Macaulay," 411. For a similar conclusion, see Plumb, *Men*, 264–65.

106. *HE*, 486.

107. Carlyle reached the same conclusion. The *History* was "pleasant, easy reading." In Robert Mowat, *The Victorian Age* (London: Senate Press, 1995), 63.

108. As Plumb concludes, praising Macaulay's sensitivity to the fact, the "men and women of his time loved to hear certainties, confidence was a part of the air they breathed." See his *Men*, 257.

Timeline of Selected Legal Publications, Legislation, and Events, 1688–1848

1688	The Glorious Revolution
1689	English Bill of Rights
	John Locke, *Two Treatises of Government*
1700	*Baron and Feme: A Treatise of the Common Law Concerning Husbands and Wives*
1704	Thomas Wood, *New Institute of the Imperial or Civil Law*
1707	Act of Union: Great Britain
1709	Charles Leslie, *The Constitution, Laws, and Government of England Vindicated*
1710	Benjamin Hoadly, *The Original and Institution of Civil Government*
1713	Sir Matthew Hale, *A History and Analysis of the Common Law of England*
1718	Transportation Act
1720	Thomas Wood, *An Institute of the Laws of England*
1723	Black Act
1732	*A Treatise of Feme Couverts: Or, the Lady's Law, Containing All the Laws and Statutes Relating to Women*
1735	Anonymous, *The Hardships of the English Laws, In Relation to Wives*
1736	Sir Matthew Hale, *The History of the Pleas of the Crown*
1737	Henry Ballow, *A Treatise of Equity*
1740	David Hume, *A Treatise of Human Nature*

	George Turnbull, *A Discourse upon the Nature and Origine of Moral and Civil Laws*
1748	Charles-Louis de Secondat, Baron de Montesquieu, *De l'esprit des lois (The Spirit of the Laws)*
1753	Lord Hardwicke's Marriage Act
1754	John Erskine, *Principles of the Law of Scotland*
1758	Henry Home, Lord Kames, *Historical Law-Tracts*
1760	Henry Home, Lord Kames, *Principles of Equity*
	George Wallace, *A System of the Principles of the Law of Scotland*
1762–1764	Adam Smith's "Lectures on Jurisprudence," University of Glasgow
1765–1769	William Blackstone, *Commentaries on the Laws of England*
1772	*Somerset* Case
1773	John Erskine, *An Institute of the Law of Scotland*
1774	Granville Sharp, *A Declaration of the People's Natural Right to a Share in the Legislature*
1776	Continental Congress issues the Declaration of Independence
	Jeremy Bentham, *Fragment on Government*
1777	*The Laws Respecting Women as They Regard Their Natural Rights, or Their Connections and Conduct*
1778	Catholic Relief Act
1779	Penitentiary Act
1780	Gordon Riots
1782	Relief of the Poor Act
1787	Adoption of the American Constitution
1787–1788	Alexander Hamilton, James Madison, John Jay, the *Federalist Papers*
1788–1789	Regency Crisis
1789	French Revolution begins
	Déclaration des droits de l'homme et du citoyen
	Jeremy Bentham, *An Introduction to the Principles of Morals and Legislation*
1790	Edmund Burke, *Reflections on the Revolution in France*
	Mary Wollstonecraft, *A Vindication of the Rights of Men*
1791	Thomas Paine, *Rights of Man*
1792	Mary Wollstonecraft, *A Vindication of the Rights of Woman*
1797	David Hume, *Commentaries on the Law of Scotland*
1799–1800	Trade Unions outlawed

1801	Act of Union: United Kingdom
1803	John Millar, *Historical View of English Government*
1807	Abolition of Slave Trade
1813	Edmond Gibson Atherley, *A Practical Treatise on the Law of Marriage and Other Family Settlements*
1814	Hugh Henry Brackenridge, *Law Miscellanies*
1815	Corn Laws
1820	R. S. Donnison Roper, *A Treatise on the Law of Property Arising from the Relation between Husband and Wife*
1825	Benjamin Disraeli, *Lawyers and Legislators*
1827	Henry Hallam, *Constitutional History of England*
1828	Repeal of the Test and Corporations Acts
1829	Catholic Emancipation Act
	Metropolitan Police Act
1830	Walter Scott, *Letters on Demonology and Witchcraft*
1831	John Stuart Mill, *The Spirit of the Age*
1832	Great Reform Act
	John Austin, *The Province of Jurisprudence Determined*
1833	Factory Act
	Abolition of Slavery Act
1834	Poor Law Amendment Act
1835	Municipal Corporations Act
	Benjamin Disraeli, *The Vindication of the English Constitution*
1836	Marriage Act
1839	Custody of Infants Act
1842	Railway Regulation Act
	Mines Act
1844	Railway Regulation Act (expanded Act of 1842)
1846	Repeal of the Corn Laws
1847	Factory Act (expanded Act of 1833)
	Poor Law Amendment Act
1848	Thomas Babington Macaulay, *History of England* (Vol. 1 and 2)
	Marx and Engels, *The Communist Manifesto*
	John Stuart Mill, *The Principles of Political Economy*
	Public Health Act

Bibliography

Primary Sources

157

"An Act for the Better Preventing of Clandestine Marriages." In *The Statutes at Large*, edited by Danby Pickering. 42 vols. Cambridge: Joseph Bentham, 1766.

Addison, Joseph. *The Spectator*. Edited by Donald F. Bond. 5 vols. Oxford: Oxford University Press, 1965.

Amos, Andrew. *Ruins of Time: Exemplified in Sir Matthew Hale's History of the Pleas of the Crown*. London: V. and R. Stevens and G. S. Norton, 1856.

An Answer to Mr De Lolme's Observations on the Late National Embarrassment. By Neptune. London: J. Stockdale, 1789.

Arnold, Matthew. *Essays in Criticism*. Edited by Sister Thomas Marion Hoctor. Chicago: The Chicago University Press, 1968.

Bagehot, Walter. *The Collected Works of Walter Bagehot: The Literary Essays*. Edited by Norman St. John-Stevas. London: The Economist, 1965.

Battie, William. *A Treatise on Madness*. London: J. Whiston and B. White, 1758.

Bentham, Jeremy. *A Fragment on Government; Being an Examination of What Is Delivered, on the Subject of Government in General in the Introduction to Sir William Blackstone's Commentaries*. London: T. Payne and E. Brooke, 1776.

Blackstone, Sir William. *Commentaries on the Laws of England*. 4 vols. Oxford: Clarendon Press, 1765–1769.

——. *Commentaries on the Laws of England*, facsimile of first edition, 4 vols. (Chicago: The University of Chicago Press, 1979), I:183.

The Book of Common Prayer, and Administration of the Sacraments. Oxford: W. Jackson and A. Hamilton, 1781.

Boswell, James. *Boswell: The Ominous Years, 1774–1776*. Edited by Charles Ryskamp and Frederick A. Pottle. New York: McGraw Hill, 1963.

——. *Boswell in Search of a Wife*. Edited by Frank Brady and Frederick A. Pottle. New York: McGraw-Hill Book Company, 1956.

——. *Boswell's Life of Johnson: Together with Journal of a Tour to the Hebrides and Johnson's Diary of a Journey into North Wales*. 6 vols. Edited by G. B. Hill. Revised and enlarged, L. F. Powell. Oxford: Clarendon Press, 1934–50.

——. *London Journal, 1762–63*. Edited by Gordon Turnbull. New York: Penguin, 2010.

Brackenridge, Hugh Henry. *Law Miscellanies*. Philadelphia: P. Byrne, 1814.

Buckingham and Chandos, Richard Plantagenet Temple-Nugent-Brydges-Chandos-Grenville, Duke of. *Memoirs of the Court and Cabinets of George III*. 4 vols. London: Hurst and Blackett, 1853–55.

Burke, Edmund. *Reflections on the Revolution in France*. Edited by Conor Cruise O'Brien. New York: Penguin, 1986.

——. *Reflections on the Revolution in France*, ed. L. G. Mitchell (Oxford: Oxford University Press, 1993), 71.

——. "Speech on the Second Reading of a Bill for the Repeal of the Marriage Act." In *The Works of Edmund Burke*. 9 vols. Boston: C. C. Little & J. Brown, 1839.

——. *Three Letters Addressed to a Member of the Present Parliament on the Proposals for Peace with the Regicide Directory of France*. In *The Works of Edmund Burke*. 9 vols. Boston: Charles C. Little and James Brown, 1839.

Burney, Frances. *Frances Burney: Journals and Letters*. Edited by Peter Sabor and Lars E. Troide. New York: Penguin, 2001.

——. *The Journals and Letters of Fanny Burney (Madame D'Arblay). Vol. 1, 1791–1792*. Edited by Joyce Hemlow with Curtis D. Cecil and Althea Douglas. Oxford: Clarendon Press, 1972.

——. *The Wanderer; or, Female Difficulties*. Edited by Margaret Anne Doody, Robert L. Mack, and Peter Sabor. New York: Oxford University Press, 2001.

Coke, Edward. *Institutes of the Laws of England*, 7 vols. (London, 1794).

The Correspondence of James Boswell with David Garrick, Edmund Burke, and Edmond Malone. Edited by Peter S. Baker, Thomas W. Copeland, George M. Kahrl, Rachel McClellan, and James M. Osborn. London: W. Heinemann, 1986.

The Court and Cabinets of George III from Original Family Documents by the Duke of Buckingham and Chandos. 4 vols. London: Hurst and Blackett, 1853.

Cunninghame, William. *A Short View of the Present Great Question*. London: J. Debrett, 1788.

De Lolme, John Lewis. *Observations upon the Late National Embarrassment, and the Proceedings in Parliament Relative to the Same*. London: J. Debrett, 1789. "Debate in the Commons on the Clandestine Marriage Bill." In *The Parliamentary History of England*. 36 vols. London: T. C. Hansard, 1813. Reprint, New York: AMS Press, 1966.

"Debate in the Lords on the Clandestine Marriage Bill." In *The Parliamentary History of England*. 36 vols. London: T. C. Hansard, 1813. Reprint, New York: AMS Press, 1966.

The Debate on the Subject of a Regency in the House of Commons on Tuesday December 16th, 1788. London: John Stockdale, 1788.

Defoe, Daniel. *Moll Flanders*. Edited by David Blewett. New York: Penguin, 2012.

A Dialogue on the Regency. London: J. Debutt, 1789.

Du Ponceau, Peter S. *A Dissertation on the Nature and Extent of the Jurisdiction of the Courts of the United States*. Philadelphia: Abraham Small, 1824.

Dutens, Louis. *An History of the Late Important Period; from the Beginning of His Majesty's Illness . . . to the Period of His Majesty's Re-appearance in the House of Lords*. London: J. Walter, 1789.

Fitzjames Stephen, James. "Lord Macaulay." *The Saturday Review*. January 7, 1860.

Gally, Henry. *Some Considerations upon Clandestine Marriages*. 2nd ed. London: J. Hughes, 1750.

Greville, Hon. Robert Fulke. *The Diaries of Colonel the Hon. Robert Fulke Greville*. Edited by F. M. Bladon. London: John Lane The Bodley Head, 1930.

Hale, Sir Matthew. "Considerations Touching the Amendment or Alteration of Lawes." In *A Collection of Legal Tracts Relative to the Law of England*, edited by Francis Hargrave. Dublin: E. Lynch, 1787.

———. "Reflections by the Lrd. Cheife Justice Hale on Mr. Hobbes His Dialogue of the Lawe." In *A History of English Law* by Sir William Holdsworth, 5th vol. London: Methuen & Co., 1945.

Harcourt, Edward William, ed. *Harcourt Papers*. 14 vols. Oxford: J. Parker & Co, 1880.

The History and Proceedings of the Lords and Commons of Great Britain, in Parliament Containing the Speeches on the Proposed Regency Bill, from November 20 1788 to March 10 1789. London: J. Stockdale, 1789.

Hume, David. *Commentaries on the Law of Scotland Respecting the Description and Punishment of Crimes: Volume I*. Edinburgh: John Bell and John Bradfute, 1797–1800.

———. *A Treatise of Human Nature*. Edited by Ernest Campbell Mossner. New York: Penguin Classics, 1984.

Important Facts Relative to the King; Faithfully Collected from the Examination of the Royal Physicians and Clearly Arranged under General Heads. London: J. Ridgeway, 1789.

Jesse, J. H. *Memoirs of the Life and Reign of George III*. 3 vols. London: Tinsley Brothers, 1867.

Johnson, Samuel. *A Dictionary of the English Language*. 2 vols. London: W. Strahan, 1755.

Kames, Henry Home, Lord. *Historical Law-Tracts*. 2 vols. Edinburgh: A. Kincaid, 1758.

The Laws Respecting Women as They Regard Their Natural Rights. London: J. Johnson, 1777.

Letters on Love, Marriage, and Adultery; Addressed to the Right Honourable the Earl of Exeter. London: J. Ridgway, 1789.

Locke, John. *Two Treatises of Government*. Edited by Peter Laslett. Cambridge: Cambridge University Press, 1988.

Lofft, Capel. *Three Letters on the Question of Regency*. London: J. Stockdale and J. Richardson, 1788.

Macaulay, Thomas Babington, Lord. "Essay on Bacon." *Edinburgh Review*, July 1837: 1–104.

———. "Essay on Hallam." *Edinburgh Review*, September 1828: 96–169.

———. "Essay on History." *Edinburgh Review*, May 1828: 331–67.

———. "Essay on Mackintosh." *Edinburgh Review*, July 1835: 265–322.

———. "Essay on Mill." *Edinburgh Review*, March 1829: 159–89.

———. "Essay on Mirabeau." *Edinburgh Review*, July 1832: 552–76.

———. "Essay on William III." *Times Literary Supplement*, May 1969: 469–70.

———. *The History of England*. London: Penguin, 1986.

MacKintosh, Sir James. *Arguments Concerning the Constitutional Right of Parliament to Appoint a Regency*. London: J. Debrett, 1788.

More, Hannah. *Village Politics*. In *The Impact of the French Revolution: Texts from Britain in the 1790s*, edited by Iain Hampsher-Monk. Cambridge: Cambridge University Press, 2005.

Morley, John. *Critical Miscellanies*. 3 vols. London: Macmillan, 1886.

O'Bryen, D. *The Prospect Before Us. Being a Series of Papers upon the Great Question Which Now Agitates the Public Mind. To Which Is Added a New Postscript*. London: J. Almon, 1788.

The Poetical Works of Hannah More. London: Scott, Webster & Geary, 1836.

Pufendorf, Samuel. *Two Books of the Elements of Universal Jurisprudence*. Edited by Thomas Behme. Indianapolis, IN: Liberty Fund, 2009.

Reflections on the Case of a Regency. By a Gentleman of Lincoln's Inn. London: J. Ridgway, 1789.

Reflections on the Marriage Act; with Some Hints for a New Law: Humbly Offered to the Consideration of Parliament. London: G. Woodfall, 1764.

Reflections on the Repeal of the Marriage-Act, Now under Consideration of Parliament. London: J. Fletcher & Co., 1765.

The Regency; A Poem. London: J. Walter, 1789.

Report from the Committee Appointed to Examine the Physicians Who Have Attended His Majesty during His Illness; Touching the Present State of His Majesty's Health. Ordered to Be Printed by the Hon. House of Commons, 13 January, 1789. London: J. Walter, 1789.

Scott, Sir Walter. *Ivanhoe: A Romance*. New York: Modern Library, 2001.

———. *Letters on Demonology and Witchcraft*. London: George Routledge and Sons, 1884.

———. *Marmion*. Edited by Mary R. Willard. Chicago: Hard Press, 2006.

Sheridan, Richard Brinsley. "On the Bill to Explain and Amend the Marriage Act." In *The Speeches of the Right Honourable Richard Brinsley Sheridan*. 3 vols. London: Henry G. Bohn, 1842.

Smith, Adam. *Lectures on Jurisprudence*. Edited by R. L. Meek, D. D. Raphael, and P. G. Stein. Indianapolis, IN: Liberty Fund, 1982.

——. *Lectures on Rhetoric and Belles Lettres*. Edited by J. C. Bryce. Indianapolis, IN: Liberty Fund, 1985.

——. *The Theory of Moral Sentiments*. Edited by D. D. Raphael and A. L. Macfie. Indianapolis, IN: Liberty Fund, 1982.

Smollett, Tobias. *The Expedition of Humphry Clinker*. Edited by Lewis M. Knapp. Oxford: Oxford University Press, 1966.

Stanhope, Philip Henry Stanhope, Earl of. *Life of the Right Honourable William Pitt*, 3rd ed. 4 vols. London: John Murray, 1867.

Stebbing, Henry. *A Dissertation on the Power of States to Deny Civil Protection to the Marriages of Minors Made with the Consent of their Parents or Guardians*. London: C. Davis, 1755. Reprinted in *The Marriage Act of 1753: Four Tracts*. New York: Garland, 1984.

——. *An Enquiry into the Force and Operation of the Annulling Clauses in a Late Act for the Better Preventing of Clandestine Marriages, with Respect to Conscience*. London: M. Cooper, 1754. Reprinted in *The Marriage Act of 1753: Four Tracts*. New York: Garland, 1984.

Stewart, Dugald. "Account of the Life and Writings of Adam Smith, L.L.D." In *Essays on Philosophical Subjects*, edited by W. P. D. Wightman, J. C. Bryce, and I. S. Ross. Oxford: Clarendon Press, 1980.

Thoughts on the Present Crisis. Humbly Addressed to Both Houses of Parliament. By a Well-Meaning Briton. London: T. Hookham and J. Bew, 1788.

Tyrwhitt, Robert Philip. *The Marriage Act, 3 Geo. IV. c. 75 . . . and an Abstract Thereof*. 2nd ed. London: A. Strahan, 1822.

The Windham Papers. Edited by Lewis Melville. 2 vols. Boston: Small, Maynard, 1913.

Withers, Philip. *History of the Royal Malady, with a Variety of Entertaining Anecdotes*. London: n.p., 1789.

Wollstonecraft, Mary. *An Historical and Moral View of the French Revolution*. In *The Works of Mary Wollstonecraft*, edited by Janet Todd and Marilyn Butler. 7 vols. New York: New York University Press, 1989.

——. *A Vindication of the Rights of Men*. In *A Vindication of the Rights of Men with A Vindication of the Rights of Woman and Hints*, edited by Sylvana Tomaselli. Cambridge: Cambridge University Press, 1995.

Secondary Sources

Abbott, H. Porter. *The Cambridge Introduction to Narrative*. Cambridge: Cambridge University Press, 2002.

Adams, Edward. *Liberal Epic: The Victorian Practice of History from Gibbon to Churchill*. Charlottesville: University of Virginia Press, 2011.

Amsterdam, Anthony G. and Jerome S. Bruner. *Minding the Law*. Cambridge: Harvard University Press, 2000.

Anderson, Emily Hodgson. *Eighteenth-Century Authorship and the Play of Fiction: Novels and Theater, Haywood to Austen*. New York: Routledge, 2009.

Andrew, Donna T., comp. *London Debating Societies, 1776–1799*. London: London Record Society, 1994.

Andrews, Jonathan and Andrew Scull. *Undertaker of the Mind: John Monro and Mad-Doctoring in Eighteenth-Century England*. Berkeley: University of California Press, 2001.

Ayling, Stanley. *Fox: The Life of Charles James Fox*. London: John Murray, 1991.

Bandes, Susan A. "Empathy, Narrative, and Victim Impact Statements." *University of Chicago Law Review* 63 (1996): 361–412.

Bandes, Susan A. and Jeremy A. Blumenthal. "Emotion and the Law." *Annual Review of Law and Social Science* 8 (2012): 161–81.

Barker-Benfield, Graham J. *The Culture of Sensibility: Sex and Society in Eighteenth-Century Britain*. Chicago: The University of Chicago Press, 1992.

Beebee, Thomas O. "Doing Clarissa's Will: Samuel Richardson's Legal Genres." *International Journal of Law and Semiotics* 2:5 (1989): 159–82.

Beesemyer, Irene Basey. "'The Vision of Enchantment's Past': Walter Scott Rescripts the Revolution in *Marmion*." *Scottish Studies* 1:1 (2000): 63–77.

Bender, John. *Imagining the Penitentiary: Fiction and the Architecture of Mind in Eighteenth-Century England.* Chicago: The University of Chicago Press, 1987.

Benedict, Barbara. *Framing Feeling: Sentiment and Style in English Prose Fiction, 1745–1800.* New York: AMS Press, 1994.

Black's Law Dictionary: Standard Ninth Edition. Edited by Bryan Garner. St. Paul, MN: West Publishing, 2009.

Blackburn, Robin. *The American Crucible: Slavery, Emancipation and Human Rights*. London: Verso, 2011.

Blumenthal, Jeremy A. "Law and the Emotions: The Problems of Affective Forecasting." *Indiana Law Journal* 80 (2005): 155–238.

Boorstin, Daniel J. *The Mysterious Science of the Law: An Essay on Blackstone's Commentaries*. Chicago: The University of Chicago Press, 1996.

Boyer, Allen D. "Justice Fielding, the Novel, and the Law." *Yale Journal of Law and the Humanities* 4:1.8 (1992): 187–207.

——. *Sir Edward Coke and the Elizabethan Age*. Stanford, CA: Stanford University Press, 2011.

Brady, Frank. Introduction to *Boswell in Search of a Wife*. Edited by Frank Brady and Frederick Pottle. New York: McGraw-Hill, 1956.

Brissenden, Robert. *Virtue in Distress: Studies in the Novel of Sentiment from Richardson to Sade*. New York: Barnes & Noble, 1974.

Brooks, Peter and Paul Gewirtz. *Law's Stories: Narrative and Rhetoric in the Law*. New Haven, CT: Yale University Press, 1996.

Brown, Vivienne. *Adam Smith's Discourse: Canonicity, Commerce, and Conscience*. New York: Routledge, 1994.

Bruner, Jerome S. *Making Stories: Law, Literature, Life*. Cambridge, MA: Harvard University Press, 2003.

Burgess, Miranda J. *British Fiction and the Production of Social Order, 1740–1830*. Cambridge: Cambridge University Press, 2000.

Butterfield, Herbert. *The Whig Interpretation of History*. London: Bell and Sons, 1931.

"Catherine Hayes," *Oxford Dictionary of National Biography* (Oxford: Oxford University Press, 2004), http://www.oxforddnb.com/view/article/12753.

"City Debates," *Daily Advertiser*, February 13, 1790.

"City Debates," *Daily Advertiser*, September 11, 1790.

"City Debates," *Daily Advertiser*, November 9, 1791.

Chitnis, Anand C. *The Scottish Enlightenment: A Social History*. Lanham, MD: Rowman and Littlefield, 1976.

Clifford, James L., ed. *Twentieth-Century Interpretations of Boswell's "Life of Johnson."* Englewood Cliff, NJ: Prentice-Hall, 1970.

Clingham, Greg. *New Light on Boswell: Critical and Historical Essays on the Occasion of the Bicentenary of the "Life of Johnson."* Cambridge: Cambridge University Press, 1991.

"Coachmakers Hall," *Daily Advertiser*, February 25, 1790.

Cooper, Joan Garden. "Scott's Critique of the English Treason Law in *Waverly*." *Scottish Studies Review* 4:2 (2003): 17–36.

Cottom, Daniel. "Violence and Law in the Waverly Novels." *Studies in Romanticism* 20:1 (1981): 65–84.

Cover, Robert. "Nomos and Narrative." *Narrative, Violence, and the Law*. Edited by Martha Minow, Michael Ryan, and Austin Sarat. Ann Arbor: University of Michigan Press, 1992.

——. "Violence and the Word." *Narrative, Violence, and the Law*. Edited by Martha Minow, Michael Ryan, and Austin Sarat. Ann Arbor: University of Michigan Press, 1992.

Crump, Justine. "'Turning the World Upside Down': Madness, Moral Management, and Frances Burney's *The Wanderer*." *Eighteenth-Century Fiction* 10 (1998): 325–40.

Curley, Thomas M. "Editor's Introduction." In Sir Robert Chambers, *A Course of Lectures on the English Law*, edited by Thomas M. Curley. Madison: University of Wisconsin Press, 1986.

Cutting, Rose Marie. "Defiant Women: The Growth of Feminism in Fanny Burney's Novels." *Studies in English Literature, 1500–1900* 17 (1977): 519–30.

David, Saul. *Prince of Pleasure: The Prince of Wales and the Making of the Regency*. London: Little, Brown and Company, 1998.

Davies, Godfrey. "The Treatment of Constitutional History in Macaulay's 'History of England.'" *Huntington Library Quarterly* 2 (1939): 180–204.

De Man, Paul. *Allegories of Reading: Figural Language in Rousseau, Nietzsche, Rilke, and Proust*. New Haven, CT: Yale University Press, 1979.

De Sousa, Ronald. *The Rationality of Emotion*. Cambridge, MA: MIT Press, 1987.

Deigh, John. "Emotion and the Authority of Law." In *The Passions of Law*, edited by Susan Bandes. New York: New York University Press, 1999.

Derrida, Jacques. *Of Grammatology*. Translated by Gayatri Chakravorty Spivak. Baltimore, MD: Johns Hopkins University Press, 1998.

Derry, John W. *The Regency Crisis and the Whigs, 1788–9*. Cambridge: Cambridge University Press, 1963.

Desan, Suzanne. *The Family on Trial in Revolutionary France*. Berkeley: University of California Press, 2004.

Devereaux, Simon. "The Abolition of the Burning of Women in England Reconsidered." *Crime, History and Societies* 9:2 (2005): 73–98.

Doody, Margaret Anne. *Frances Burney: The Life in the Works*. New Brunswick, NJ: Rutgers University Press, 1988.

Edwards, Owen Dudley. *Macaulay*. London: Weidenfeld and Nicolson, 1988.

Ehrman, John. *The Younger Pitt*, 3 vols. London: Constable, 1969.

Emsley, Clyde. *British Society and the French Wars, 1793–1815*. London: Rowman and Littlefield, 1979.

Epstein, Julia. *The Iron Pen: Frances Burney and the Politics of Women's Writing*. Madison: University of Wisconsin Press, 1989.

Evensky, Jerry. *Adam Smith's Moral Philosophy*. Cambridge: Cambridge University Press, 2005.

Firth, Charles. *A Commentary on Macaulay's History of England*. London: Macmillan, 1938.

Foucault, Michel. "Discipline and Punish: *The Birth of the Prison*," in *The Norton Anthology of Theory and Criticism*, ed. Vincent Leitch (New York: Norton, 2001), 1636–39.

Fraser, Russell. "Boswell the Retailer of Phrases." *Sewanee Review* 114:4 (Fall 2003).

Ganz, Melissa J. "*Moll Flanders* and English Marriage Law." *Eighteenth-Century Fiction* 17:2 (2005): 157–82.

Griswold, Jr., Charles. *Adam Smith and the Virtues of Enlightenment*. Cambridge: Cambridge University Press, 1999.

Guillory, John. *Cultural Capital: The Problem of Literary Canon Formation*. Chicago: The University of Chicago Press, 1993.

Hagstrum, Jean H. *Sex and Sensibility: Ideal and Erotic Love from Milton to Mozart*. Chicago: The University of Chicago Press, 1980.

Hamburger, Joseph. *Macaulay and the Whig Tradition*. Chicago: The Chicago University Press, 1976.

Henderson, Amanda K. *Romanticism and the Painful Pleasures of Modern Life*. Cambridge: Cambridge University Press, 2008.

Holdsworth, Sir William. *A History of English Law*. 16 vols. London: Methuen, 1922–1952.

Horowitz, Morton J. *The Transformation of American Law, 1780–1860*. Cambridge, MA: Harvard University Press, 1977.

"How to Make All the World Happy," *Morning Chronicle*, December 5, 1796.

Hunt, Lynn. *Inventing Human Rights: A History*. New York: W. W. Norton, 2007.

Jerinic, Maria. "Challenging Englishness: Frances Burney's *The Wanderer*." In *Rebellious Hearts: British Women Writers and the French Revolution*, edited by Adriana Craciun and Kari E. Lokke. Albany: State University of New York Press, 2001.

Johnson, Claudia. *Equivocal Beings: Politics, Gender, and Sentimentality in the 1790s*. Chicago: The University of Chicago Press, 1995.

Jones, Darryl. "Radical Ambivalence: Frances Burney, Jacobinism, and the Politics of Romantic Fiction." *Women's Writing* 10 (2003): 3–25.

Jones, Kathleen. *Lunacy, Law and Conscience, 1744–1845: The Social History of the Care of the Insane*. London: Routledge & Paul, 1955.

Kahan, Dan M. and Martha C. Nussbaum. "Two Conceptions of Emotion in Criminal Law." *Columbia Law Review* 96 (1996): 269–374.

Knowles, David. *Lord Macaulay, 1800–1859*. Cambridge: Cambridge University Press, 1960.

Lacey, Nicola. "Contingency, Coherence and Conceptualism: Reflections on the Encounter between 'Critique' and 'the Philosophy of the Criminal Law.'" In *Philosophy and the Criminal Law: Principle and Critique*, edited by Antony Duff. Cambridge: Cambridge University Press, 1998.

——. "In Search of the Responsible Subject: History, Philosophy and Social Sciences in Criminal Law Theory." *Modern Law Review* 64 (2001): 350–71.

Levine, George. *The Boundaries of Fiction: Carlyle, Macaulay, Newman*. Princeton, NJ: Princeton University Press, 1968.

Lieberman, David. "Adam Smith on Justice, Rights, and Law." In *The Cambridge Companion to Adam Smith*, edited by Knud Haakonssen. Cambridge: Cambridge University Press, 2006, 225–30.

——. "Blackstone's Science of Legislation." *Journal of British Studies* 27 (1988): 117–49.

——. *The Province of Legislation Determined: Legal Theory in Eighteenth-Century Britain*. Cambridge: Cambridge University Press, 1989.

"London Forum," *Daily Advertiser*, February 12, 1794.

Lustig, Irma. "Boswell, Alexander, Lord Auchineck (1707–1782)." In *Oxford Dictionary of National Biography*. Oxford: Oxford University Press, 2004. Online edition, May 2005.

Lynch, Deidre. "Domesticating Fictions and Nationalizing Women: Edmund Burke, Property, and the Reproduction of Englishness." In *Romanticism, Race, and Imperial Culture, 1780–1834*, edited by Alan Richardson and Sonia Hofkosh. Bloomington: Indiana University Press, 1996.

Macalpine, Ida and Richard Hunter. *George III and the Mad-Business*. Harmondsworth: Allen Lane, 1969.

Maroney, Terry A. "Law and Emotion: A Proposed Taxonomy of an Emerging Field," *Law and Human Behavior* 30 (2006): 119–42.

Mauger, Matthew. "'Observe how parts with parts unite / In one harmonious rule of right': William Blackstone's Verses on the Laws of England." *Law and Humanities* 6 (2012): 179–96.

Meehan, Michael. "An Anatomy of Australian Law or 'The Human Element in Legal Argument.'" In *The Happy Couple: Law and Literature*, J. Neville Turner and Pamela Williams, eds. Sydney: Federation Press, 1994.

Milne, Hugh M. Introduction to *The Legal Papers of James Boswell. Vol. I*. Edinburgh: The Stair Society, 2013.

Modéer, Kjell Å. "Living Ruins of the Law: On Legal Change and Legal History in Late Modernity." *Scandinavian Studies in Law* 53 (2008): 219–30.

Monk, Leland. "The Novel as Prison: Scott's *The Heart of Midlothian*." *Novel* 27 (1994): 287–302.

Mowat, Robert. *The Victorian Age*. London: Senate Press, 1995.

Mullan, John. *Sentiment and Sociability: The Language of Feeling in the Eighteenth Century*. Oxford: Oxford University Press, 1988.

Nussbaum, Martha C. *Political Emotions: Why Love Matters for Justice*. Cambridge, MA: Harvard University Press, 2013.

—— and Alison L. LaCroix, eds. *Subversion and Sympathy: Gender, Law and the British Novel*. New York: Oxford University Press, 2013.

O'Connell, Lisa. "Marriage Acts: Stages in the Transformation of Modern Nuptial Culture." *differences* 11 (1999): 68–111.

Outhwaite, R. B. *Clandestine Marriage in England, 1500–1850*. London: The Hambledon Press, 1995.

The Oxford Handbook of Adam Smith. Edited by Christopher J. Berry, Maria Pia Paganelli, and Craig Smith. London: Oxford University Press, 2013.

Parker, Kunal M. *Common Law, History, and Democracy in America, 1790–1900: Legal Thought before Modernism*. Cambridge: Cambridge University Press, 2011.

Perkins, Pam. "Private Men and Public Women: Social Criticism in Fanny Burney's *The Wanderer*." *Essays in Literature* 23 (1996): 69–83.

Phillipson, Nicholas. *Adam Smith: An Enlightened Life*. New Haven, CT: Yale University Press, 2010.

Plumb, Sir John H. *Men and Places*. London: Cresset Press, 1963.

Pocock, J. G. A. *Virtue, Commerce, and History*. Cambridge: Cambridge University Press, 1985.

Polloczek, Dieter. *Literature and Legal Discourse: Equity and Ethics from Sterne to Conrad*. Cambridge: Cambridge University Press, 1999.

Posner, Richard. *Law and Literature: A Misunderstood Relation*. 3rd ed. Cambridge: Harvard University Press, 2009.

Potkay, Adam. *The Passion for Happiness: Samuel Johnson and David Hume*. Ithaca, NY: Cornell University Press, 2000.

Pottle, Frederick. *James Boswell: The Earlier Years, 1740–1769*. New York: McGraw-Hill, 1966.

Prest, Wilfrid. "Blackstone as Architect: Constructing the *Commentaries*." *Yale Journal of Law and the Humanities* 15 (2003): 103–33.

——. *William Blackstone: Law and Letters in the Eighteenth Century*. Oxford: Oxford University Press, 2008.

Probert, Rebecca. *Marriage Law and Practice in the Long Eighteenth Century: A Reassessment*. Cambridge: Cambridge University Press, 2009.

Rogers, Katharine M. *Frances Burney: The World of 'Female Difficulties.'* New York: Harvester Wheatsheaf, 1990.

Rohl, John. C., Martin Warren, and David Hunt. *Purple Secret: Genes, "Madness" and the Royal Houses of Europe*. London: Bantam Press, 1998.

Rose, Carol M. "Canons of Property Talk, or, Blackstone's Anxiety." *Yale Law Journal* 108 (1999): 601–32.

Rothschild, Emma. *Economic Sentiments: Adam Smith, Condorcet, and the Enlightenment*. Cambridge, MA: Harvard University Press, 2001.

Sarat, Austin, Matthew Anderson, and Catherine O. Frank. *Law and the Humanities: An Introduction*. Cambridge: Cambridge University Press, 2010.

Scanlan, J. T. "Law." In *Samuel Johnson's Legal Context*. Edited by Jack Lynch. Cambridge: Cambridge University Press, 2012.

Schmidgen, Wolfram. *Eighteenth-Century Fiction and the Law of Property*. Cambridge: Cambridge University Press, 2002.

——. "Picturing Property: *Waverly* and the Common Law." *Studies in the Novel* 29:2 (1997): 191–213.

Scott, Geoffrey. "The Making of the *Life of Johnson* as Shown in Boswell's First Notes." In *Twentieth-Century Interpretations of Boswell's "Life of Johnson": A Collection of Critical Essays*, edited by James L. Clifford. Englewood Cliffs, NJ: Prentice-Hall, 1970.

Sherman, Steven J. and Joseph L. Hoffman. "The Psychology and Law of Voluntary Manslaughter: What Can Psychology Teach Us about the 'Heat of Passion' Defense?" *Journal of Behavioral Decision Making* 20 (2007): 499–519.

Shevlin, Eleanor F. "'Imaginary Productions' and 'Minute Contrivances': Law, Fiction, and Property in Eighteenth-Century England." *Studies in Eighteenth Century Culture* 28 (1999): 131–54.

Shoemaker, Karl. "The Problem of Pain in Punishment: Historical Perspectives." In *Pain, Death, and the Law*, edited by Austin Sarat. Ann Arbor: University of Michigan Press, 2001.

Simmons, Clare A. "Medievalism and the Romantic Poet-Editor in Scott's *Marmion*." *Poetica* 39 (1993): 93–109.

Simon, Fabrizio. "Adam Smith and the Law." In *The Oxford Handbook of Adam Smith*, edited by Christopher J. Berry, Maria Pia Paganelli, and Craig Smith. London: Oxford University Press, 2013.

Stern, Simon. "Blackstone's Criminal Law: Common-Law Harmonization and Statutory Reform." In *Foundational Texts in Criminal Law*, edited by Markus D. Dubber. Oxford: Oxford University Press, 2014.

Stone, Lawrence. *Road to Divorce: A History of the Making and Breaking of Marriage in England, 1530–1987*. New York: Oxford University Press, 1995.

Straub, Kristina. *Divided Fictions: Fanny Burney and Feminine Strategy*. Lexington: University of Kentucky Press, 1987.

Sullivan, Robert. *Macaulay: The Tragedy of Power*. Cambridge, MA: Harvard University Press, 2009.

Taylor, Alan J. P. *Essays in English History*. London: Penguin, 1976.

Thompson, James. *Models of Value: Eighteenth-Century Political Economy and the Novel*. Durham, NC: Duke University Press, 1996.

Todd, Janet. *Mary Wollstonecraft: A Revolutionary Life*. London: Weidenfeld and Nicholson, 2000.

——. *Sensibility: An Introduction*. London: Methuen, 1986.

Traer, James F. *Marriage and the Family in Eighteenth-Century France*. Ithaca, NY: Cornell University Press, 1980.

Trevor-Roper, Hugh. *Historical Essays*. London: Macmillan, 1957.

Van Sant, Ann Jessie. *Eighteenth-Century Sensibility and the Novel: The Senses in Social Context*. Cambridge: Cambridge University Press, 1993.

Vance, John A., ed. *Boswell's "Life of Johnson": New Questions, New Answers*. Athens: University of Georgia Press, 1985.

Vogel, Ursula. "The Fear of Public Disorder: Marriage between Revolution and Reaction." In *Shifting the Boundaries: Transformation of the Languages of Public and Private in the Eighteenth Century*, edited by Dario Castiglione and Lesley Sharpe. Exeter: University of Exeter Press, 1995.

Wagner, Ann K. "Sexual Assault in the Shadow of the Law: Character and Proof in Samuel Richardson's *Clarissa*." *Law and Literature* 25:2 (2013): 311–26.

Walker, David M. *A Legal History of Scotland. Vol. V. The Eighteenth Century*. Edinburgh: T. & T. Clark, 1998.

Wallace, Tara Ghoshal. "Rewriting Radicalism: Wollstonecraft in Burney's *The Wanderer*." *Eighteenth-Century Fiction* 24 (2012): 487–508.Ward, Ian. "The Jurisprudential *Heart of Midlothian*." *Scottish Literary Journal* 24:1 (1997): 25–39.

——. *Law and Literature: Possibilities and Perspectives*. Cambridge: Cambridge University Press, 1995.

Weber, Richard. "Singer and Seer: Macaulay on the Historian as Poet." *Papers on Language and Literature* 3 (1967).

"Westminster Forum," *Daily Advertiser*, January 20, 1790.

White, James Boyd. *Acts of Hope: Creating Authority in Literature, Law, and Politics*. Chicago: The University of Chicago Press, 1994.

——. *Heracles' Bow: Essays on the Rhetoric and Poetics of the Law*. Madison: University of Wisconsin Press, 1985.

——. *The Legal Imagination: Studies in the Nature of Legal Thought and Expression*. Boston: Little Brown, 1973.

Whitehead, A. N. *The Aims of Education*. New York: The Free Press, 1927.

Wiener, Jonathan B. "What Begat Property?" *History of Political Economy* 43 (2011): 353–60.

Witherbee, Amy. "*Habeas Corpus*: British Imaginings of Power in Walter Scott's *Old Mortality*." *New Literary History* 39:2 (2008): 355–67.

Worden, Blair. *Roundhead Reputations: The English Civil Wars and the Passions of Posterity*. London: Penguin, 2002.

Zonitch, Barbara. *Familiar Violence: Gender and Social Upheaval in the Novels of Frances Burney*. Newark: University of Delaware Press, 1997.

Cases Cited

Butler v. Duncomb, (1718), 1 P.W. 448; 24 Eng. Rep. 466.
Noy v. Ellis, (1676) 2 Chan. Cas. 220; 22 Eng. Rep. 918.
Walton v. Tryon, (1753) Dick. 244; 21 Eng. Rep. 262.

Index

Contributors

Peter de Bolla is professor of cultural history and aesthetics at the University of Cambridge, where he also directs the Concept Lab. He is the author of nine books, including *The Architecture of Concepts: The Historical Formation of Human Rights* (Fordham University Press, 2013); *Art Matters* (Harvard University Press, 2001); and *The Discourse of the Sublime* (Blackwell, 1989). He is on the board of management of the Re:Enlightenment Project and a Fellow of King's College, Cambridge.

Melissa J. Ganz is assistant professor of English at Marquette University. Her essays on the relation of literature, law, and ethics have appeared in journals such as *Eighteenth-Century Fiction*; *The Eighteenth-Century: Theory and Interpretation*; and *ELH*. She is currently completing a book entitled *Public Vows: Fictions of Marriage in the English Enlightenment*, which examines the role of novels in debates about the legal regulation of the nuptial tie.

Nancy E. Johnson is associate professor of English and chair of the English Department at the State University of New York at New Paltz. She is the author of *The English Jacobin Novel on Rights, Property and the Law: Critiquing the Contract* (Palgrave, 2004) and articles on law and literature in the 1790s. She is currently editing *The Court Journals and Letters of Frances Burney, Vol. VI* (Clarendon Press, forthcoming 2016).

J. T. SCANLAN is associate professor of English at Providence College. Scanlan writes for both popular and scholarly publications. He has written a range of essays on various aspects of the eighteenth century, including essays on Samuel Johnson and the law in *Samuel Johnson after 300 Years* (Cambridge University Press, 2009) and *Samuel Johnson in Context* (Cambridge University Press, 2012). He is currently writing a book on legal issues, tentatively titled *A Spirit of Contradiction: Law and Literature in Eighteenth-Century London*. He is a former president of the Northeast American Society for Eighteenth-Century Studies. He is also coeditor of *The Age of Johnson: A Scholarly Annual*. At Providence College, he teaches eighteenth-century literature and serves as the prelaw advisor.

ERIN SHELEY is assistant professor of law at the University of Calgary. She holds a PhD in English from the George Washington University and a JD from Harvard Law School. Her legal scholarship focuses on how narrative affects the individual and cultural experience of criminal harm and has appeared in a number of journals including the *Indiana Law Journal* and the *BYU Law Review*. Her literary scholarship includes articles on the relationship between adultery and sovereignty in the eighteenth- and nineteenth-century cultural imagination; juvenile punishment in the nineteenth-century fairy tale; Gothic landscapes in the work of Byron; and classical mythology in the poetry of John Keats. She is currently completing her dissertation *Criminality and the Common Law Imagination*.

SIMON STERN is associate professor of law and English at the University of Toronto. His recent publications include articles and book chapters on criminal procedure and narrative perspective, the history of copyright, obscenity law and nineteenth-century fiction, and legal fictions. He is editing the second volume of Blackstone's *Commentaries* for a variorum edition to be published by Oxford University Press in 2015.

IAN WARD is professor of law at Newcastle University, United Kingdom. He is the author of a number of books and essays in the areas of law and literature, legal history and constitutional law. His most recent publications include *Law and the Brontës* (Palgrave, 2012) and *Sex, Crime and Literature in Victorian England* (Hart, 2014). His current research is focused on the "writing" of English constitutional law during the nineteenth century.

www.ingramcontent.com/pod-product-compliance
Lightning Source LLC
LaVergne TN
LVHW052325200926
848481LV00002B/672
* 9 7 8 1 6 1 1 4 8 6 7 7 3 *